A Bilateral Bicentennial

John Adams—engraving by Reinier Vinkeles, 1782

A BILATERAL BICENTENNIAL

A History of Dutch-American

Relations, 1782-1982

EDITED BY

J. W. Schulte Nordholt and Robert P. Swierenga

OCTAGON BOOKS

A division of Farrar, Straus and Giroux

AND

MEULENHOFF AMSTERDAM

Copyright © 1982 Meulenhoff International bv Amsterdam
All rights reserved
Printed in the United States of America
Published simultaneously in Canada
by McGraw-Hill Ryerson Ltd., Toronto
Designed by Constance Fogler

First printing, 1982

Library of Congress Cataloging in Publication Data
Main entry under title: A Bilateral bicentennial.
1. United States—Foreign relations—Netherlands
—Addresses, essays, lectures.   2. Netherlands—
Foreign relations—United States—Addresses,
essays, lectures.   I. Schulte Nordholt, J. W.
II. Swierenga, Robert P.
E183.8.N4B54 1982   327.730492   82-8096
ISBN 0-374-96120-4   AACR2

Contents

Part Three: Bilateral Perception

Introduction

The life of the historian these days seems to be determined by commemorations. Almost every year some city or treaty or declaration has been around for exactly so many centuries; captains and kings, though departed, celebrate their birthdays with pomp and circumstance. A new set of servants is ready to oblige them, to hold conferences, read papers, write books—in short, to observe the holy occasion with due respect. All this is fine and good; it brings people together, it advances knowledge, it revives the past. The one condition is that the servants remain independent, free to say whatever they want to say. The historian needs his own way to celebrate.

That is why in this introduction we shall resist the temptation to express our gratitude for the fact that we are celebrating two hundred years of friendship between the Netherlands and the United States. All we want to say is that it is precisely this friendship, this interdependence of liberty of our Western world, that makes our independence as historians possible. We should never forget that fact.

What it means to us here and now is that we can argue and discuss in full freedom what the relations between the two nations have meant in their historical perspective. Thanks to the wise decision of the Dutch government, an opportunity has been provided for historical reflection in this bicentennial year. Thanks to the Dutch Ministry of Education and Science, that reflection has been well organized in a symposium, held in Amsterdam, June 1–4, 1982. Thanks to the Dutch Historical Association and the Netherlands American Studies Association, who sponsored the symposium, there was an audience willing to listen to and participate in the discussions. Thanks to the Dutch publishing firms of Meulenhoff and Nyhoff and the American firm of Farrar, Straus and Giroux (and its division Octagon Books), the Acta of the symposium could be printed in this book and illustrated with so many attractive pictures.

Thanks are due to many people but most of all to the speakers who so gracefully accepted our invitation to share their knowledge with us and enlighten our understanding of what is really a rather complicated relation. As will be seen from the contents of the book, we divided the subject into three parts, corresponding to the three days of the symposium. The first day dealt with the diplomatic and

economic relations of the two countries; the second was devoted to
Dutch immigration to and settlement in the United States; and the
third day focused on the perception that the two nations had and
perhaps still have of each other. Of course, much more could be said;
we could have gone on for seven days instead of three. But we hope
that we have at least covered some of the most essential aspects of our
bilateral bicentennial and stimulated further research and discussion.

JULY 1982   *J. W. Schulte Nordholt and*
                                        Robert P. Swierenga

Part One

·⟨⟩·

DIPLOMATIC
AND ECONOMIC
RELATIONS

Two Americans in
Two Dutch Republics

The Adamses, Father and Son

· ᙋᙏᙅᙏᙅᙒ ·

R. R. PALMER

O N April 19, 1782, the States General formally received John Adams as minister plenipotentiary from the United States. A reception by the Stadtholder, William V, soon followed, and a treaty between these two "powers of the earth," to use a phrase from the American Declaration of Independence, was signed the following October. It is not a treaty of military alliance, such as the United States signed with France in 1778. It is what diplomats call a treaty of amity and commerce. It is a long document, in twenty-nine articles. All the articles but one pertain to trade, merchant shipping, guarantees to seamen, and such matters. But the first article states that "there shall be a stable, inviolable and universal peace and sincere friendship between their High Mightinesses the States General of the United Provinces and the United States of America." Time has rendered many of the commercial provisions obsolete, and their High Mightinesses long ago disappeared, but the friendship remains; it has indeed been one of the least troubled of any between two peoples, and we hope and expect that it will continue to be so.

Except for France, the Dutch government was the first in the world to recognize the United States. Last year, on a brief visit to Morocco, I learned that this honor is claimed for the Sultan of Morocco, but a little research has assured me that the priority of the Dutch treaty cannot be successfully challenged, for one article of the Dutch-American agreement provided for Dutch assistance to the Americans in negotiations with Morocco and the Barbary states, and the American treaty with Morocco was signed in 1787.

It is still a question whether the Dutch were a little slow in not extending recognition until six years after the Declaration of Independence. Why did they wait until after the battle of Yorktown and

[3]

the surrender of Cornwallis' army? Was it simply Dutch prudence? The Amsterdam merchants had given surreptitious aid to the American insurgents throughout the war, passing a stream of munitions and other goods through the Dutch island of St. Eustatius in the West Indies. But the point is that this aid was surreptitious and illegal, for the Stadtholder and the highest authorities in the Netherlands favored the British. A further cause of delay was that the French tried to prevent or postpone Dutch recognition of the United States, in the belief that the Dutch wealth and merchant marine were more useful in the war against England if the Dutch government remained neutral. And another cause, as John Adams so painfully learned, was the slow and cumbersome operation of the various provinces, towns, assemblies, admiralties, councils, boards, and committees of which the United Provinces were composed.

The fact is that it took a small Dutch revolution, or quasi revolution, or the beginning of what is called the Patriot Movement in the Netherlands, to bring about the recognition of the United States. And this brings me to my real purpose, which is not to dwell on diplomacy and treaties, but to speak in general of the revolutionary era in Europe and America at the end of the eighteenth century, drawing somewhat distantly on a book I wrote twenty years ago. More particularly, I should like to venture some ideas about two Americans in two Dutch republics. The two Americans are John Adams and his son John Quincy Adams. They later became the second and the sixth Presidents of the United States. The two Dutch republics are the old United Provinces at the time of the abortive Patriot Movement in the 1780's and the Batavian Republic that emerged in 1795 in the course of the war between Revolutionary France and the conservative powers of Europe. John Adams was American minister to the United Provinces from 1780 to 1788, though mostly absent in London after 1782. John Quincy Adams was American minister to the Batavian Republic from 1794 to 1797. They were strikingly different in their attitude toward the Dutch scene. My main purpose is to examine these differences and the reasons for them.

Both the United Provinces and the United States were small countries in terms of population at the end of the eighteenth century, each having hardly more people, if we exclude the American slaves, than one of the larger French provinces. Both nevertheless played an important part in the revolutionary movement that swept over the area of Western civilization at that time. In this movement the French Revolution was unquestionably by far the largest and most decisive component. On the vicissitudes of France everything else depended. The French Revolution was preceded by the American Revolution, in which the French monarchy effectively intervened, by the Dutch

Patriot Movement, which the French monarchy favored, though ineffectively, and by revolution in Belgium, or what was then called the Austrian Netherlands, by which time the French monarchy was impotent and collapsing. The French Revolution was followed, after the French armies proved victorious in the war that began in 1792, by the incorporation of Belgium and the German Rhineland into the French Republic and by the setting up of nominally independent republics on the French Revolutionary model elsewhere—the Batavian in 1795, followed by the Cisalpine, Ligurian, Roman, and Neapolitan republics in Italy and the Helvetic in Switzerland. It is not enough to see these annexations and dependent republics as mere consequences of French conquest, for in each case the French worked with local persons who had long been dissatisfied with their respective old regimes. To round out the picture, it may be noted that revolutionary attempts were made in Poland in 1794 and in Ireland in 1798, but that they were quickly suppressed, in part because the French could not or did not support them. In general, what we see in the last quarter of the eighteenth century is what some have called the Atlantic revolution, some the democratic revolution, and some the bourgeois revolution, but these terms are not mutually exclusive, and may even denote the same thing.[1]

There is not sufficient space here to explore in detail the issues in this transnational upheaval or to analyze the resemblances and the differences between various countries. Instead, I shall quote at some length from a figure well known in Dutch history, Gijsbert Karel van Hogendorp. In the 1780's he was the young scion of an important Rotterdam family; a quarter century later he became the main author of the constitution by which the House of Orange was restored as a constitutional monarchy. He was an acute observer. "Two great parties are forming in all nations," he wrote at Rotterdam in 1791. "For one, there is a right of government to be exercised by one or several persons over the mass of the people, of divine origin and to be supported by the church, which is protected by it. These principles are expressed by the formula: Church and State." Note that van Hogendorp makes no distinction here between the established Protestant churches and Roman Catholicism, or between absolute monarchies, aristocracies of birth, and self-perpetuating oligarchies; all are forms of an old regime. "To this," he goes on, "is opposed the new system, which admits no right of government except that arising from the free consent of those who submit to it, and which maintains that all persons who take part in government are accountable for their actions. These principles go under the formula: Sovereignty of the People, or Democracy."[2]

When John Adams arrived at The Hague in 1780 this proto-

Thomas Jefferson, 1789, by Jean-Antoine Houdon

democratic disturbance was barely beginning in the United Provinces. The Dutch Patriots, as they called themselves, were a miscellaneous grouping, including a few of the governing families, many substantial Amsterdam merchants who had been trading illicitly with the Americans, and some leisured gentlemen and impatient youth who had caught the new ideas of the European Enlightenment. They objected to the semi-royal pretensions of William V and the House of Orange and to the persistent Anglophilism of the Orange establishment even at a time when Britain was assailing the Dutch commerce and colonies. The Patriots were therefore pro-American and pro-French. Adams found his warmest reception and made his best Dutch friends among them. He was delighted at the signs of incipient revolution, praised the Patriots lavishly, plunged into the agitation by helping to organize a wave of petitions—in short, took sides in the affairs of a foreign country in a way that in later years he would consider shocking. He got what he wanted: recognition of the United States and then a loan of five million guilders, after which he left for Paris to take part in the negotiation of a peace treaty with England. He soon became the first American minister to the former mother country, on which his opinions remained highly ambiguous. As for the Patriots, their movement went on to new heights, only to be crushed in 1787 by the diplomatic skills of England and intervention by the Prussian army. Several thousands of the Patriots fled to France, where they were welcomed and financially assisted by the monarchy of Louis XVI while awaiting their chance to return and complete their republican revolution.

John Adams, at first on the ground in Holland, then in Paris and London, remained sympathetic to the Dutch Patriots but was disappointed at the confusion of their objectives, their weakness, and their lack of success. He tried to inform himself by industrious reading on Dutch history and affairs, but the complexities of the Dutch political system continued to baffle him. The United Provinces were in fact an assemblage of local elements that had originated in the medieval Holy Roman Empire, then combined in the Union of Utrecht in the sixteenth century to carry on the revolt against Spain, with elaborate provisions to guard against any central authority by confirming the liberties of provinces, towns, burgomasters, estate assemblies, and the Dutch Reformed Church. The result was indecision, procrastination, and everlasting absorption in vested rights. In London, Adams wrote a large book on the comparative anatomy of republics, to support his belief that the best government must be a mixture of monarchy, aristocracy, and democracy. He found it hard to classify the United Provinces in his system. The trouble with the Dutch was that they did not have the right mixture. In discussing "democratical republics" he noted in

passing "certain remnants of democratical powers' in Overijssel and
Friesland. Mainly he classified this strange country under "aristo-
cratical republics." The Hollanders, he said, were preserved from
tyranny—that is, from an excess of the monarchical principle—"partly
by the stadholder, partly by the people in mobs, but more especially
by the number of independent cities and sovereignties associated together, and the great number of persons concerned in the government
and composing the sovereignty, four or five thousand, and finally, by
the unanimity that is required in all transactions." In his feelings he
continued to side with the Patriots, and in his theory to believe that
what the Dutch needed was more of the democratic principle. When
the Patriots were suppressed he thought that their weakness had been,
apart from relying too much on France, to be "too inattentive to the
common people of their own country."[3]

At this very time, in 1787, back in the United States, certain
Americans were attempting to devise a new federal constitution in
which a central government should have more authority. The Dutch
example was often cited in their arguments. Some Americans, clinging
to the original Articles of Confederation, praised the Dutch for their
careful preservation of all manner of local liberties. Those wanting
a stronger United States, the Federalists, and especially James Madison,
took a more negative and more realistic view. Not only were the
United Provinces a mere confederation of aristocracies, said Madison,
"where the legislature consists of men who hold their offices for life,
who fill up offices and appoint their salaries themselves," but the Dutch
could not even maintain their political independence. The Prussian
military intervention presented "the awful spectacle" of invasion by
foreign armies. The Dutch system was completely unworkable. Its
worst fault was its weakness. "The important truth," said Madison,
"is that a sovereignty over sovereigns, a government over governments,
a legislation over communities as contradistinguished from individuals
. . . is subversive of the order and ends of civil polity." And Madison
also expressed the hope, writing in 1788, that the troubles then afflict-
ing the Netherlands would "issue in such a revolution as will establish
their union."[4]

Such a revolution came seven years later with the proclamation
of the Batavian Republic. It was again made possible by foreign
intervention, this time by the invading French, since the restored
government of William V had the misfortune of belonging to the
coalition with which the French Revolutionaries were at war. The
Dutch exiles of 1787 accompanied the French army as it entered
Holland. Exiles and French republicans were alike welcomed by old
Patriots and their sympathizers. William V fled to England. Their
High Mightinesses the States General faded away. A Dutch National

Convention assembled and after much difficulty produced a constitution resembling the French constitution of 1795.

The new Batavian constitution began with a declaration of the rights of man. The republic took the mystic triad of Liberty, Equality and Fraternity as its motto. As in France, an Executive Directory of five persons came into being, with a two-chamber legislature elected by individual voters. The Reformed Church was disestablished, and Roman Catholics, minority Protestants, and Jews, who together made up 40 percent of the population, for the first time were given equality of political rights. The old provinces and towns were abolished as corporate entities, replaced, as in France, by new departments and municipalities. Group representation yielded to the principles of individual citizenship. The new Dutch government also declared war on England, which thereupon occupied the Dutch colonies, notably Ceylon and the Cape of Good Hope.

The Batavian Republic was the first of the satellite republics, or sister republics as they were also called, that emerged in connection with the Wars of the French Revolution. Although many Batavians soon became disillusioned with the demands of the French, especially the financial demands, the Batavian Republic was an object of admiration for French sympathizers in other countries. For these reformers and potential revolutionaries it was more satisfactory to have their own republic, however dependent, than to remain as an occupied area or to be annexed to France like the Belgians. Along the German left bank of the Rhine, before annexation to France was decided on, a group of pro-French Germans launched a short-lived Cisrhenane movement, in the hope of founding a Cisrhenane Republic on the model of the Batavian. In Italy, in the Cisalpine and other new republics, the main features of the Batavian were repeated. The Irish revolutionary Wolfe Tone, while in Paris hoping to induce the French to invade Ireland, believed that if successful they would sponsor an Irish Republic on the Batavian model.

The Batavian Republic sought to correct the very evils and weaknesses that John Adams and James Madison had condemned in the old United Provinces. The main issue in the new republic, especially from 1795 to 1798, the very time when John Quincy Adams was stationed at The Hague, was the dispute between unitarists and federalists. "Federalism" in the Netherlands, as in France in 1793, had the opposite meaning from what the same word then meant in America. American federalists worked for a stronger national government, which was precisely what Dutch federalists tried to prevent. Dutch federalists, during the debates on the new constitution, wished to maintain the separate identity and autonomy of the old provinces and towns, which meant preserving the position of men already important

Wilhelm V and Wilhelmina on a visit to Amsterdam on May 30, 1768—
detail of an engraving of Reinier Vinkeles

under the old order. Federalists therefore were denounced as aristocrats. Persons of more democratic opinions were unitarists. In the provinces and towns they saw, rightly enough, the strongholds of the traditionally privileged and ruling elements of the population. They therefore insisted on abolishing the old provincial and town organizations, with their ancient and disparate charters and liberties, and replacing them with a uniform system of departmental and municipal administration, in which all citizens could hope to participate on a more equal basis. The struggle between unitarists and federalists was so fierce that even the French envoys, with memories of their own French Revolution, were amazed by it. The unitarists won out in the constitution of 1798. Despite subsequent modifications, the unitary principle prevailed permanently. A real transformation occurred. Where the United Provinces, modern though they were in commercial and financial matters, had been in their political and legal arrangements a bundle of medieval survivals, the Batavian Republic and the constitutional monarchy that ensued in 1814 were modern states.

It was at the height of agitation in the Netherlands, on October 31, 1794, that John Quincy Adams arrived at The Hague. Revolutionary committees in the Dutch cities were preparing to welcome the French army, which arrived a few weeks later. Dutch patriots put on tricolor cockades, planted trees of liberty, and sang the "Marseillaise" in the streets. The Adams who saw all this was a young man, only twenty-eight years old, but well qualified for a diplomatic appointment. He had been brought as a boy by his father to Europe years before, had gone to school in Paris and become fluent in French, and had even been enrolled for a few months in 1781 as a student at the University of Leyden, where he acquired some knowledge of Dutch. He was even a Harvard graduate. As the son of John Adams, he had met and spoken with many personages of international consequence. He had traveled widely. His father had trained him to make careful observations, on which he reported at length in long letters to his father, his famous mother, Abigail, and the American Secretary of State. He also kept a diary with assiduous faithfulness, day by day, for many years. There is therefore no shortage of evidence for what John Quincy Adams thought and said. He remained in the Netherlands until June 1797, except for a few months on a mission to London, during which he was married to an American girl.

The extraordinary thing is that John Quincy Adams, while in the Netherlands, showed so little perception, understanding, or sympathy for what was happening around him. Where his father had praised and fraternized with the Patriots, John Quincy held aloof. It was not that he underestimated the strength of the Dutch revolutionary movement. Half the nation, he reported to the American Secretary of State, was "panting for the success of the invaders." Patriotic clubs had sprung up everywhere. He had been invited to join one, but had declined. "I was not sent here," he wrote to his father, who had been so enamored of the Dutch Patriots fifteen years before and who was now Vice-President of the United States, "to make myself a partisan of Dutch factions." Or as he wrote to his mother: "I have therefore invariably avoided every act that could be charged with partiality to the Patriots."[5]

He was indeed under orders from the Secretary of State to remain neutral. And neutral he was on the larger issues in the struggle between England and France. As for England, he confessed to "a dislike both of the government and the national character, perhaps amounting even to a prejudice," and as for France, "the unsettled revolutionary state of that country" offset any sentiments he might otherwise entertain in its favor. For England he said he felt an aversion, and for France indifference.[6] It was from France, however, at this time, that he saw the greatest threat to the internal peace and even the territorial integrity of the United States. The French were in truth interfering in American domestic politics. Their minister in Philadelphia sponsored the emerging Jeffersonian or Democratic-Republican party. The French, believing that the United States government had turned pro-British by signing a treaty with England in 1794, and even declaring that the administration of George Washington no longer represented the American people, openly took sides in the presidential election of 1796, preferring the election of Jefferson to that of John Adams, John Quincy's own father, who did in fact become the second President and attempted to carry on the policy of neutrality which the French considered to be hostile. The French therefore stopped American shipping bound for England; an undeclared naval war with the United States actually followed. They rebuffed the American agents sent to negotiate with them. There was even talk in the French Foreign Office of supporting a movement for an independent republic west of the Alleghenies. Working with dissident Americans, it might be possible to create something like a Batavian Republic in the region between the Alleghenies and the Mississippi, a region that had been French within living memory and where the scattered Americans, as yet few in number, felt little attachment to the new government east of the mountains.

There was therefore every reason why John Quincy Adams should lack enthusiasm for a Batavian Republic which, however real its Dutch roots, did in truth represent an extension of French power and of the French Revolution. There was every reason why in his long letters to the State Department, to his parents, and to other correspondents he mainly dealt with the international situation and the dangers presented to the United States by the war in Europe. On these matters his reports were diligent and detailed. But we may still ask why he paid so little attention to internal Dutch affairs, the intense controversy between unitarists and federalists, the significance of the Dutch factions, and the nature of the Batavian revolution.

Was it that he lacked the time to inform himself, being preoccupied with more urgent problems? Or that he lacked contacts with the Dutch leaders, from whom he might have learned more of their pressing concerns? From his diary it appears that this is not the explanation. This dutiful young Puritan tells us several times how he spent his day.[7] Typically, he arose about six in the morning, then translated a few pages of Tacitus to keep up his Latin, wrote letters, breakfasted at ten, received callers or paid visits in the afternoon, often seeing Dutchmen in the Batavian government, took a three- or four-mile walk before or after dinner, and in the evening went out into society, at some hospitable house like the Danish minister's, where the company engaged in conversation (naturally in French), played cards, or indulged in parlor games such as *bouts-rimés*, an amusement which consisted of making up verses to go with a given rhyme. He found time also for lessons in Italian. When he had an evening at home he devoted it to his beloved books, occasionally reading a contemporary Dutch writer like Pieter Paulus, but more often Homer, Cicero, Ovid, Lucan, or Tasso.

John Quincy Adams can be contrasted with a young man who became his best friend at The Hague, Baron Bielfeld, who was secretary to the Prussian legation. Prussia made peace with France in 1795 and declared itself neutral, like the United States. There was no great business to transact between Prussia and the Netherlands, so that Bielfeld's position, like Adams', was mainly a listening post, and his principal duty was to make observations and submit reports to his home government, which he did, addressing them directly to King Frederick William II. The two young men saw much of each other. They took their Italian lessons together, attended the theater together, and met at evening parties. They also went on long walks to Scheveningen and other nearby places, during which they talked about the Batavian and French revolutions. Bielfeld, says Adams in his diary, "appears to be no enemy of the principles of equality." Or again, he calls him "my democratic baron." They talked about "the rights of man, the origin and foundation of human society, and the proper principles of government,' on all of which Baron Bielfeld held a more tolerant view than John Quincy Adams. Bielfeld even thought that the "smothered flame of democracy" was burning in Germany.[8]

Every week or two Bielfeld sent a long report to the King of Prussia.[9] His letters were factual, with no sign of ideological prefer-

John Quincy Adams, 1796, by John Singleton Copley
(*Courtesy of the Museum of Fine Arts, Boston.*
Gift of Mrs. Charles Francis Adams)

ences. They were full of information about internal Dutch affairs. They explained the issues between the federalists and the unitarists, distinguished between moderates and radicals in each camp, gave reasons why each party felt as strongly as it did, and offered particulars, noting for example that the people of Holland, with half the population of the Dutch territory and paying most of the taxes, objected to a federalist plan that would give the smaller provinces more than their proportionate share of power. There is almost nothing of this in the reports of John Quincy Adams. Perhaps the nearest he comes to it is in a letter to his brother in which he notes that in the Netherlands the more positive democrats favored a unitary central government while the so-called aristocrats favored sovereignty for the provinces, whereas the opposite was true in America, where democrats clamored for states' rights and denounced the centralizing Federalists as aristocrats. He said he was "amazed but not surprised" at this inversion of roles.[10] He made no effort to analyze its causes. It was enough to make a joke on the Jeffersonian democrats, by intimating that they knew nothing of Europe. And the American Secretary of State, reading Adams' messages, would certainly understand less of what was happening in the Netherlands than the King of Prussia.

The truth seems to be that Adams was not very much interested in the Batavian Republic. His attention was focused on France and the French Revolution and their impact on party controversies in the United States. On this matter he was by no means neutral. He saw both the Batavians and the American democrats as the dupes and tools of France. He complained to his mother that both the French and Batavian governments showed personal malice toward his father and toward himself for merely upholding the neutrality of the United States.[11] He was so personally involved as to be blind, indifferent, annoyed, or sardonically amused by the spectacle of revolution in Europe. "These people, French and Dutch," he wrote in his diary, "cannot on either side carry through their farce of equality, of independence or of republicanism."[12] He had no patience for a country that proclaimed the rights of man and yet arrested enemies of the revolution, or touted the freedom of the press while suppressing some of the newspapers.[13] He made no allowance for the war or for the counterrevolution by which any revolution is threatened. He could not tell the difference between moderates and extremists. It was not enough that the French wanted to defeat Great Britain and Austria; they must be bent on "revolutionizing *the whole world*."[14] The mildest French partisans of the Revolution seemed to him to be raging radicals. For example, when Benjamin Constant, the famous liberal, opened his political career with a pamphlet in 1796 calling for support of the French Directory against the resurgence of royalism, and was joined by Talleyrand and Madame de Staël in his efforts, Adams dismissed Constant's work as a piece of "depravity," and the new French government as sunk in "desperation."[15] The French Revolution of the last six years, he wrote to his father in 1795, had "contributed more to the restoration of Vandalic ignorance than whole centuries can retrieve. . . . Whether the arts, the sciences, and the civilization of Europe will not perish with it, must yet remain a problem."[16] This was written at the very moment when the French government was installing the Institut de France, the Ecole Polytechnique, and other learned bodies of a kind unknown in America. And where Adams feared that the "myrmidons of Robespierre" would burn libraries as the Moslem hordes had burned the library at Alexandria, what happened was that the myrmidons of the French Republic, when Bonaparte went to Egypt, founded the science of Egyptology.

Perhaps we should conclude that John Adams was after all a revolutionary in his younger days, whereas John Quincy Adams, as the son of a founder of the Republic, was fast becoming a founder of the American Eastern Establishment. Yet with all their differences they were alike. Both made the interests of their own country, or of an independent American republic, foremost. For John Adams in 1780, the enemy of American independence was England, and he favored the Dutch Patriots because they were anti-English. For John Quincy Adams for a few years in the 1790's, the greater danger came undoubtedly from France, and he could feel no enthusiasm for a Batavian Republic that was allied to and subordinated to that hotbed of revolution. The American democrats with their predilection for France were as obnoxious to him as the American Loyalists with their attachment to England had been to his father.

There is another resemblance also. J. W. Schulte Nordholt has published an article, which I first heard him give as a lecture at the University of Michigan some years ago, in which he showed how thoroughly the Americans of the 1780's studied the history of the Dutch republic when debating on how best to organize the United States. To simplify his message, he found that the Americans were nevertheless not really very much interested in Dutch history, in why it was what it was, or in the forces and pressures and real problems that had shaped its course, but that they used it only as a storehouse of practical examples, as was usual in the eighteenth century in Europe as well as America. In the Dutch storehouse the Americans mostly found examples of what was to be avoided. In the history of the United Provinces they saw an exhibit of weakness, confusion, party strife, foreign influence, and interminable delay. Much the same can be said of John Quincy Adams, and indeed of Americans generally, as they viewed the Batavian Republic in the setting of contemporary affairs.[17] It offered an example of what was to be avoided. The Americans did not go either to history or to a contemporary political science in a search for new knowledge or to explore the inner dynamics of faraway foreign countries. They already knew what they wanted; they had their own goals and purposes and their own stresses and strains. For those of us for whom history and social science are a profession, this is surely an inadequate basis of knowledge. But we do not judge statesmen for their qualities as historians or social scientists. We judge them for what they do, not for what they know, except as their knowledge or the lack of it may affect the consequences of their actions. The consequences of the actions of John Adams and John Quincy Adams were advantageous to the United States. They seem to have been at least harmless for the Dutch.

It is possible to conclude on a somewhat more positive note. With all due respect to both Adamses, I believe that there is more sophistication today, in America as elsewhere, in the perception of events in other countries. The Americans in the 1790's divided into two rather simple groups for and against the French Revolution, expressing either admiration or horror. These views shaped their attitude toward the Batavian Republic. We have since then seen many revolutions, Russian, Chinese, Cuban, Iranian, and nameless others, but on the whole, thanks to historians and social scientists, to journalists who are more informed and responsible than those of the eighteenth century, and to persons in government who have thought about the world, we do not divide into two simple camps with respect to such upheavals. The most extreme spokesmen for either side tend to be fewer. There is a larger middle ground, where we find those who are genuinely interested in the internal problems of other peoples, who do not seize upon them simply as examples or use them as talking points, who can see events in a long perspective, judge actions by circumstances, weigh the arguments of contending parties, distinguish moderates from extremists, acknowledge that not all revolution is purely destructive and yet know that all revolutions may run to dangerous extremes. In the present state of the world, if we have any more wisdom than our predecessors we shall surely need it.

NOTES

1 See R. R. Palmer, *The Age of the Democratic Revolution: A Political History of Europe and America, 1760–1800* (2 vols.; Princeton, N.J., 1959 and 1964); and a paper I presented in 1979 at a conference in Bamberg, Germany, soon to be published, "La Révolution Atlantique, vingt ans après." On the theme of the present paper see also Herbert H. Rowen, "The Union of Utrecht and the Articles of Confederation, the Batavian

Constitution and the American Constitution: A Double Parallel," in R. Vierhaus, ed., *Herrschaftsverträge, Wahlkapitulationen, Fundamentalgezetze* (Göttingen, 1977), pp. 281–93. I am glad to find myself in agreement with Professor Rowen's views.

2   These thoughts of van Hogendorp's, written in French, may be found in his *Brieven en Gedenkschriften* (The Hague, 1876), III, 60–61.

3   John Adams, *Defense of the Constitution of the United States* (3 vols.; London, 1794 [written in 1786–87]), I, 22, 69, and III, 355; and Charles F. Adams, ed., *The Works of John Adams* (10 vols.; Boston, 1850–56), VIII, 462. See also his letters and diary for the time spent in the Netherlands, 1780–82.

4   J. W. Schulte Nordholt, "The Example of the Dutch Republic for American Federalism," in *Federalism: History and Current Significance of a Form of Government* (The Hague, 1980), pp. 65–77; and Madison in the *Federalist* (any ed.), No. 20.

5   *Writings of John Quincy Adams* (7 vols.; New York, 1913–17). To Secretary of State, I, 338; to John Adams, I, 372; to Abigail Adams, I, 333.

6   *Writings*, I, 424. To John Adams, October 31, 1795, expressing his unwillingness to become American minister at either London or Paris.

7   *Memoirs of John Quincy Adams, Comprising Portions of His Diary from 1795 to 1848* (12 vols.; Philadelphia, 1874–77), I, 183, 187, and *passim*.

8   *Memoirs* (i.e., diary), I, 75, 79, 88, 109, 169, 179.

9   Bielfeld's reports to the King, written in French, may be found in H. T. Colenbrander, ed., *Gedenkstukken der Algemeene Geschiednis van Nederland van 1795 tot 1840* (22 vols.; The Hague, 1906–22), I, 247–356.

10 *Writings*, I, 426. There is passing reference to the unitarist-federalist issue at II, 51, and *Memoirs*, I, 185–86, but without significant comment. Since the published *Writings* and *Memoirs* are both selective, it is conceivable that Adams offered more analysis of Dutch affairs in papers hitherto unpublished, which are currently being edited by The Adams Papers at the Massachusetts Historical Society in Boston. These papers are available on microfilm at various libraries, including Yale University, where a hasty exploration suggests that the same views of the Netherlands are expressed in the unpublished as in the published material. On the "inversion" that amused John Quincy Adams, see also my contribution to *Ideas in History: Essays Presented to Louis Gottschalk*, ed. R. Herr and H. T. Parker (Durham, N.C., 1965), pp. 3–19: "The Great Inversion: America and Europe in the Eighteenth Century Revolution."

11 *Writings*, II, 254.

12 *Memoirs*, I, 96.

13 *Writings*, II, 51–53.

14 *Writings*, II, 25; Adams' italics.

15 *Writings*, II, 213.

16 *Writings*, I, 389.

17 For the Schulte Nordholt article, see note 4 above. Indexes to the writings of Washington, Hamilton, Madison, Jefferson, Monroe, and John Adams himself for the 1790's show almost nothing under "Netherlands" or "Batavian Republic."

John Adams and the Birth of

Dutch-American Friendship,

1780–82

· ꙮ ·

JAMES H. HUTSON

Since John Adams, the first American minister to the Netherlands, often called political contemporaries rope dancers, I hope you will indulge me if I go to the circus for a beginning metaphor. Historians of Dutch-American relations during the period of the American Revolution remind me of trapeze artists. The scene begins with American historians poised on their pedestals, Dutch historians on theirs. They propel themselves forward. But they do not clasp hands in midair. They pass and land on the spot the other has just vacated. To be specific and, for the moment, simplistic: American historians formerly contended that John Adams heroically won Dutch acknowledgment of their country's independence; now they claim that France contrived that event. Dutch historians formerly contended that France arranged their country's acknowledgment of American independence; now they claim that John Adams contrived that event.

From this comparative perspective, historical progress seems illusory indeed, for what the American historian regards as an advance in understanding the Dutch historian regards as a retreat and vice versa. Revision in one country is reaction in the other. Paradoxes in historiography are not unusual and in this case they seem appropriate, for John Adams found that the Dutch savored them: "every one has his prophecy, and every prophecy is a paradox," he reported to Benjamin Franklin from Amsterdam in 1780.[1] I hope that the present audience retains its ancestors' taste for paradox, because I intend to develop at some length the curious story of how Dutch and American historians have treated the period 1780–82.

First, the American historians. I think it fair to say that they have never given the Dutch role in the American Revolution the attention that it deserves. One would not expect the Netherlands to receive the scrutiny lavished by Americans on France and Great Britain—the principal foreign protagonists in their revolution. But it has not fared even as well as Spain, whose contributions to the welfare of the infant United States did not, in my opinion, match those of the Dutch, whose loans between 1782 and 1788 prevented a national bankruptcy.

Why have the Dutch been neglected? One reason is language. Although Dutch was spoken by the second-largest—certainly no less than the third-largest—number of people in the thirteen American colonies, its usage has all but disappeared in the United States. Unlike French and German, mastery of it is not necessary to obtain the Ph.D. in American universities. Since studying the Dutch role in American independence would require the acquisition of a new language, aspiring American scholars turn to other subjects. A few American historians, it is true, have employed Dutch-language sources in writing about Revolutionary diplomacy. Perhaps the greatest of American diplomatic historians, Samuel Flagg Bemis, in his *The Diplomacy of the American Revolution* (New York, 1935), cites Colenbrander, van Winter, and van Wijk, but one does not sense his usual mastery in handling these secondary works. Bemis, moreover, was interested in the Dutch role in the Revolution only insofar as it illuminated the larger question of neutral maritime rights, which were pivotal in American diplomacy through the Napoleonic period; he devoted barely two pages to John Adams' mission.[2]

Friedrich Edler, the author of the only monograph on our subject, *The Dutch Republic and the American Revolution* (Baltimore, 1911), seems to have been more at home in the Dutch language than Bemis, for he cites numerous Dutch historians and some Dutch primary material which was transcribed by Sparks, Bancroft, and others. Like Bemis, however, Edler is not primarily interested in the politics of the Dutch recognition of American independence. Rather his focus is on the relations between the Netherlands and Britain. Aside from Bemis, Edler, and, more recently, Richard B. Morris,[3] no American writer makes even a pretense of using Dutch-language sources.

Dutch historians have not supplied the deficiencies of their American colleagues, because, for the most part, they have not shown much interest in their country's efforts to establish relations with the new American state. Colenbrander, for example, mentions John Adams just twice in three volumes. Although others have been more attentive, most Dutch historians of the Patriot period have considered the American problem to be, at best, incidental and have provided little information which American writers can use; hence, the level of American analysis remains superficial.

Perhaps a Dutch Doniol is needed. Henri Doniol was a French scholar who between 1884 and 1892 published a five-volume documentary history, drawn from the archives of the French Foreign Ministry, on the role of France in the American Revolution. His *Histoire de la participation de la France à l' établissement des Etats-Unis d'Amérique* has whetted the interests of generations of American scholars. On a lesser scale the Spanish historian Utrilla has published documents illustrating his country's contributions to American independence.[4] But there is no compilation of Dutch documents which might exert a similar magnetic attraction upon prospective students.

Ignorance of Dutch seems to have discouraged Americans from seeking resources in other languages. French was the language of eighteenth-century diplomacy. It was used by Dutch diplomats, politicians, and newspapermen. France herself was a major factor in the Netherlands. But few Americans have consulted the diplomatic correspondence between the Quai d'Orsay and The Hague. How different, again, is the case of Spain, where Bemis discovered, by studying bilateral relations between France and Spain, political arrangements which had profound implications for the United States and which inspired his famous aphorism that American independence was chained to the rock of Gibraltar. Or consider Prussia, another influential power in the Netherlands. The dispatches in French of her ambassador at The Hague during the American Revolution, Thulemeyer, have been in print since 1912 and contain information about Dutch-American relations, but they have been little used by American writers.[5]

As a result of this virtual boycott of foreign languages, Americans writing on their country's relations with the Netherlands have, perforce, relied almost exclusively on the testimony of John Adams. As I hope to show presently, Adams' accounts of his own activities cannot be taken at face value. Generations of American writers have done precisely this, however, and have offered as objective fact his own self-serving celebrations of his diplomatic conduct. This process has been underway since 1805, when Adams' estranged friend, Mercy Otis Warren, relying on letters and documents which Adams himself had furnished her, described his negotiations in the Netherlands in her *History of the Rise, Progress, and Termination of the American Revolution.* Mrs. Warren's tale was one of diligence and virtue rewarded. Adams, she claimed, was "indefatigable in his efforts to cherish the attachment already felt by individual characters, toward the cause of America;" he "persevered in every prudent measure to facilitate the object of his mission"; he pleaded with the tongues of men and angels.[6] Finally, "the resolute and undaunted deportment of Mr. Adams, concurring with their [the Dutch] dispositions, and with the interests and views of the United Netherlands, at last accomplished the object of his mission," opposed, though it was, by all the powers of Europe.[7] Although there have been embellishments and modifications, this is the account that American diplomatic historians and Adams biographers have purveyed since 1805: a heroic story of Adams battling single-handedly against powers and principalities until at last, supported by the Dutch Patriots, he wrested an acknowledgment of American independence from the reluctant establishment at The Hague. That this account is simplistic puffery has not, until recently, been recognized.

In a book which I published in 1980, *John Adams and the Diplomacy of the American Revolution*, I attempted to present a more accurate picture of Adams' diplomatic mission to the Netherlands by using modern psychological concepts to explore Adams' personality and by consulting Dutch- and, especially, French-language materials. My judgment was that Adams had grossly exaggerated the importance of his own actions in producing the Dutch acknowledgment of American independence. I concluded that the prime mover in obtaining recognition was the French ambassador, Vauguyon, acting on and through the Dutch Patriot party. In the context of American historiography this conclusion was said to have "advanced" historical understanding. In academic argot, it pushed back the frontiers of knowledge—pushed them back, in the context of Dutch historiography, to the nineteenth century, to H. T. Colenbrander's celebrated *Patriottentijd* (3 vols. The Hague, 1897–99).

It was Colenbrander's thesis that Dutch political developments of the Patriot period were dictated by foreign powers. He compared Dutch politicians to clerks in mercantile firms whose headquarters were in neighboring countries. They were, to use his famous metaphor, "*marionetten*," danced on strings controlled by masters in Paris, London, and Potsdam. It followed that, as puppets of France, the Dutch Patriot party acted at the direction of the Duc de la Vauguyon and that its support for American independence was instigated by France.

Colenbrander's thesis is now in shambles. Challenged in 1921 by de Jong, the biographer of van der Capellen tot den Poll, it has crumbled under the blows inflicted after World War II by Verberne, Rogier, and, above all, Pieter Geyl.[8] Although these writers do not deny the importance of foreign influence in the Netherlands during the Patriot period, they view Dutch developments as essentially autonomous, feeding on historical trends within the country and attempting to fulfill various agenda set by the Dutch themselves. The liberation of the Dutch Patriots from foreign domination by Dutch revisionist historians has enabled the most recent—and incontestably the best-informed—Dutch historian of early Dutch-American relations, Professor J. W. Schulte Nordholt, in his *The Dutch Republic and American Independence: An Example from Afar* (1982), to portray the Dutch recognition of American independence in 1782 as the result, not of French manipulation, but of the unremitting labors of John Adams and his Dutch associates. In the context of Dutch historiography Professor Schulte Nordholt has advanced historical understanding; in the context of American historiography he has pushed the frontiers of knowledge back in the direction of Mercy Otis Warren.

The trapezes swing and Professor Schulte Nordholt and I pass each other by. What prevents us from clasping hands? One impediment is a differing understanding of the character of John Adams. Professor Schulte Nordholt, acknowledging that Adams was a tempestuous individual whose passions occasionally distorted his judgment, nevertheless regards him as a man whose insights into Dutch politics were penetrating, whose actions were appropriate, and whose mind was balanced and rational. I, on the other hand, believe that during his mission to the Netherlands Adams displayed periods of behavior that were irrational and inappropriate. I do not assert that he was mentally ill. Rather I believe that the peculiar, supercharged intellectual world in Revolutionary America in which he matured produced attitudes and behavior which resembled and, at times, mimicked the pathological.

In a series of books on the ideological origins of the American Revolution, Bernard Bailyn has argued that Americans were "propelled" into revolution by the pervasive fear of a British ministerial conspiracy to enslave them.[9] Adams was an early and ardent believer in the existence of a ministerial conspiracy: "There seems to be a direct and formal design on foot to enslave all America," he wrote in 1765.[10] The conspiracy theory gained potency from a conviction that grew in America in the 1760's that suspicion itself was a positive good. Revolutionary Americans used the term "jealousy" to mean suspicion and, unlike their twentieth-century descendants, carefully distinguished jealousy from envy, which, then as now, meant resentment of a rival's success.[11] "A perpetual jealousy respecting liberty," asserted John Dickinson in his authoritative *Letters from a Farmer in Pennsylvania* (1768), "is absolutely requisite in all free states."[12] Jealousy was extolled as a "moral" and "political" virtue from one end of the country to another.

As with the conspiracy theory, Adams was an early apostle of jealousy, commending a "jealous Watchful Spirit"[13] in 1765 and practicing what he preached throughout the conflict with Britain.

Alexander Hamilton was repelled by Adams' suspiciousness during his presidency. He possessed "a jealousy capable of discoloring every object," wrote the New Yorker, an assessment in which Mercy Otis Warren concurred a few years later when she claimed that Adams' mind was "replete with jealousy." But what Hamilton and Warren took to be a surfeit of suspicion in Adams was merely a continuation of—or, according to one observer, a moderation of—his jealousy during the Revolutionary years. Adams, wrote Theodore Sedgwick in 1788, "was formerly infinitely more democratical than at present and possessing that jealousy which always accompanies such a character was averse to repose . . . unlimited confidence" in anyone.[14]

Jealousy-suspicion flourished, indeed luxuriated, in Revolutionary America. "Jealousy was prevalent in Republicks," observed Silas Deane in December 1777, and "its greatest degree was now excited in America."[15] Fused with the fear of conspiracy, it quickened that fear to such an extent that the most innocuous political maneuvers were often interpreted as steps in a plot to persecute the innocent. The Revolutionary mentality, therefore, strikes modern scholars conversant with the literature of psychopathology as paranoiac. "The era of the American Revolution," it is asserted, "was a period of political paranoia."[16] "The insurgent whig ideology had a frenzied even paranoid cast to it," writes one scholar; another hears it sounding "a paranoiac note." A third stresses its "paranoiac obsession with a diabolical crown conspiracy."[17]

But these statements should be viewed as descriptive—as efforts to catch the flavor of the men and the times—rather than as diagnostic. American scholars do not believe that their Revolutionary forefathers were a generation of madmen. That there may have been pathological strains in some Revolutionaries is probable. One of Adams' most perceptive recent biographers has, in fact, argued that he suffered no fewer than three nervous breakdowns between 1771 and 1783.[18] But until techniques of applying psychology to history are perfected, one should reserve judgment about Adams and his contemporaries, even as he gives full weight to the intensity of the suspicions and the fears of malevolent conspiracy which infused the Revolutionary mentality and which suggest the term "paranoid" to recent observers.

The point of these observations is that from the moment Adams arrived in Europe in 1778 until the signing of the definitive peace treaty in 1783, and at no time more than during his service in the Netherlands, he was devoured by suspicions—approaching delusions—that he was the target of conspirators. Franklin was the principal plotter; the Comte de Vergennes his most assiduous confederate. In 1779, for example, Adams believed that Franklin was trying to "starve him out" of Europe to prevent him from executing a commission of whose existence the Doctor was ignorant; in 1781 Adams felt "menaced" by Franklin for attempting to deploy another commission of which he was also ignorant. Although France favored the American cause in the Netherlands, Adams convinced himself that he "was pursued into Holland by the intrigues of Vergennes and Franklin, and was embarrassed and thwarted, both in my negotiations for a loan and those of a political nature, by their friends, agents, and spies as much, at least, as I even had been in France." "The finesse and subtlety of the two ministers [Vergennes and Vauguyon]," he believed, "were exhausted to defeat me, by disgusting and discouraging me, by Neglects, Slights, Contempts, Attacks and Maneuvers." So malign were the conspirators that he imagined himself "threatened with starvation from Passy; and [had] frequently suggested to my recollection, the butcher's knife, with which the DeWitts had been cut up at the Hague."[19] Examples of these paranoid convictions could be multiplied. Their significance for this paper is that in every case in which they can be checked against the facts they were wrong.

Equally wrong were Adams' grandiose evaluations of the impact of his diplomatic activities. He actually thought it possible that his memorial to the States General of May 4, 1781, requesting acknowledgment of American independence, had produced the Dutch naval victory over the British at Dogger Bank in the North Sea in August 1781, that it had encouraged Joseph II of Austria to declare religious liberty in his dominions, and that it had ensured the success of John Laurens' special mission to France in the spring of 1781. "I shall forever believe that it contributed to second and accelerate Colonel Laurens' negotiation," he wrote. The fact was that the loan "obtained" by Laurens had been promised to Franklin by Vergennes well before the colonel arrived in France in March 1781, two months before Adams presented his memorial.[20] On another occasion, Adams asserted that his Dutch negotiation "accelerated the peace, more than the capture of Cornwallis and his whole army"; it was more decisive "than any battle or siege, by land or Sea, during the entire war"; it "produced" the British acknowledgment of American independence. The facts were just the opposite, for there is copious testimony that the British Parliament's resolution of February 27, 1782, declaring advocates of "offensive war" in America enemies of their country and authorizing the King to make peace with "the revolted colonies of North America," was a catalyst in stimulating the Dutch to acknowledge the independence of the United States.[21]

The intention in marshaling this string of farfetched anxieties and exultations is not to ridicule Adams but to demonstrate how little

Portrait of Pieter van Bleiswijk, Grand Pensionary of Holland—
engraving by Reinier Vinkeles, 1789

credibility he has as a commentator on his own activities in the Netherlands. Historians, from Mercy Otis Warren onward, who have built their accounts of Dutch-American relations on Adams' testimony have built their houses on foundations of sand.

The facts themselves militate against Adams' claims that he was a prime mover in obtaining Dutch recognition of American independence. In the first place, he did not establish the right kind of political connections in the Netherlands. Convinced that Vauguyon was persecuting him, he avoided the French ambassador and thus deprived himself of the entrée the Duc could have provided into the highest levels of Dutch political life. The Dutch friends that Adams himself made were outsiders and pariahs like van der Capellen tot den Poll, men without influence in the corridors of power. Professor Schulte Nordholt is intrigued by the friendship between Adams and van der Capellen. Both were subject to emotional turbulence which invites psychological investigation and both were deeply influenced by English Country ideology (indeed, the similarity in the impact of that ideology on American Revolutionaries and Dutch Patriots, noticed by Schulte Nordholt and Leonard Leeb, deserves much deeper exploration).[22] But neither van der Capellen, nor Luzac, nor van der Kemp—nor any of Adams' Dutch friends—remotely resembled power brokers in the Republic. This class of men, Adams admitted, avoided him "like a pestilence" or, as van der Capellen wrote on March 13, 1782, "shunned him as if he had the plague."[23] And they were the people who made the decisions in the Netherlands. Adams, moreover, was stricken with a severe illness late in 1781 which debilitated him during the very months in which the decision for American independence was made.[24] All things considered, it seems impossible to accept his claim of paternity for the Dutch acknowledgment of American independence.

Who, then, was the sire? It seems to me that France was at least the midwife. The French role in the Netherlands has been well documented, of course. We know of Vauguyon's influence, although his enemies exaggerated his powers when they called him, as Sir Joseph Yorke did, the "country's true stadholder." We know the geopolitical circumstances which gave France its influence: the French were convoying Dutch ships, had recaptured Dutch colonies from the British, had positioned a powerful army near the Dutch frontiers, and were garrisoning the East India Company's rich possessions in Ceylon and the Cape of Good Hope, making that powerful organization "more dependent on France than on Holland," as one Dutch politician conceded. We are "at the Mercy of France," lamented another.[25]

France had consistently hoped that the Dutch would recognize American independence. Toward the end of 1781 it became imperative

for French objectives that the United Provinces do so. The decisive
defeat of British arms at Yorktown produced a change of tactics in
London. The British now sought to accommodate their differences
with the Americans and the Dutch, so that they could concentrate
their military efforts against France. A crack secret service agent, Paul
Wentworth, was dispatched to The Hague in January 1782 to attempt
to negotiate a peace with the Dutch (other agents were sent in due
course to sound out American diplomats). France moved to thwart
the British strategy of detaching the Dutch from the war. The best
way to do this, the French perceived, was to promote a Dutch
recognition of American independence. Such an action, declared
Vauguyon, would "have the essential effect . . . of rendering impossible
the rapprochement of the Republic and England"; it would be "the
surest means of breaking forever the ties between the Republic and
England."[26] Consequently, in the spring of 1782 Vauguyon worked
tirelessly for Dutch recognition, repeatedly visiting the Patriots in
Amsterdam and the other cities of Holland and bringing all his powers
of persuasion and intimidation to bear. On April 19 the States General
officially acknowledged the United States as a sovereign nation and
voted Adams' admission as minister plenipotentiary. Vauguyon, reported a Dutch observer, gave "a great ministerial dinner to celebrate
the said admission, for which he had worked with zeal and much
eagerness ('*beaucoup d'empressement*')."[27]

Professor Schulte Nordholt, writing in the post-Colenbrander age,
when the approach is to acknowledge the potency of French influence
but to de-emphasize it, has presented an intriguing piece of evidence
which would seem to diminish the French role in procuring Dutch
recognition of American independence. Schulte Nordholt quotes van
der Hoop, fiscal of the Amsterdam Admiralty, who in February and
March 1782 conducted the secret negotiations with Wentworth, as
having received a letter from Vergennes disavowing French interest in
the recognition of the United States and apparently repudiating
Vauguyon's efforts to obtain it. Vergennes reputedly informed van der
Hoop that if Vauguyon "had gone too far in what he said in certain
matters, it should simply be reported to him, Vergennes, and he would
take care of it; and he also let him know that he [Vauguyon] had no
instructions to express himself about the Americans as he had done."[28]
It seems incredible that Vauguyon, in assiduously working for Dutch
recognition of American independence in February and March 1782,
could have misunderstood or violated his instructions, for he had just
returned to The Hague on February 6, 1782, after a seven-week stay
in France, where he consulted Vergennes constantly. Vergennes,
moreover, on April 27, 1782, enthusiastically congratulated Vauguyon

on his successful efforts to realize France's long-standing goal of a "coalition between the two republics." Adams' admission as minister plenipotentiary "could not be more important in the actual conjunction," wrote Vergennes, for "it is an invincible obstacle to the actual reconciliation of England and Holland."[29]

Vergennes's letter to van der Hoop seems to have been an example of the "finesse" for which eighteenth-century French diplomacy was both condemned and admired. It was France's aim to avoid incurring obligations to the Netherlands. France wanted to contrive it so that Dutch policies which served her interest would appear to be undertaken, not at her instigation, but at the Dutch's own initiative. Therefore, if the Netherlands suffered as a consequence of these policies—if Britain, indignant at her recognition of the United States, was implacable at the peace negotiations—France would be under no obligation to compensate the Dutch for losses incurred by her actions. Thus, Vergennes denied that France's policy was to encourage the Dutch to recognize the United States even as his ambassador was egging the Patriot party on. In his letter to van der Hoop, Vergennes was showing how a clever man could work both sides of the street. Whether van der Hoop actually believed the Comte's disclaimers is not clear. What is clear was Vauguyon's incessant activity to bring the Dutch and Americans together.

The third party in the recognition of American independence by the United Provinces (ignoring Britain, whose intransigence toward the Netherlands was a crucial and consistent factor in the events we have been describing) was the Dutch people themselves. I do not pretend to be an expert on Dutch politics during the Patriot period, but I would like to call attention to one problem which puzzles me. It concerns public opinion. Professor Schulte Nordholt has demonstrated convincingly that the American cause commanded wide attention in the Netherlands and that substantial numbers of Dutchmen wanted the States General to embrace the new republic for reasons running from intellectual enthusiasm to infatuated self-interest. The ardor for America was keen at Amsterdam. Yet just when it appeared to be building to a crescendo, in the fall of 1781, what Vauguyon described as a "great number" of Amsterdam magistrates assumed an anti-American posture and tried to promote a reconciliation with Great Britain.[30] What was the reason for this apparent discrepancy between public opinion and public policy? Is the explanation that the regency of Amsterdam, like those in other Dutch cities, being a self-perpetuating oligarchy, was indifferent to and even contemptuous of public opinion? Was John Adams correct when he complained that in such a polity the people had "no more share than they had in France; no more, indeed, than they had in Turkey"?[31] And if this was true, did the petition drive for American recognition in the spring of 1782, which Adams claimed to have helped instigate, have any real impact on the decision-making process?

This problem is one aspect of the conundrum of Dutch politics in the years from 1780 to 1782. I take some comfort in my own confusion when I find Professor Schulte Nordholt calling attention to the "irrational element" in the popular agitation for American recognition, when he declares that "confusion, impotence, frenzy and romanticism reigned in the Netherlands" in 1782 and concludes that the internal forces promoting the recognition of the United States may be inexplicable. "It is not easy," he observes, "to discover why the movement for recognition began so suddenly and assumed such vast proportions."[32]

The obscurity of the dynamics of Dutch politics increases the difficulty of accepting Adams' claims to a catalytic role in the affairs of the republic. Adams feared that Franklin, Vergennes, and their cronies would try to strip him of the laurels he believed he had won in the Netherlands. "I see with Smiles and Scorn," he wrote his wife on July 1, 1782, "little despicable efforts to deprive me of the Honour of any Merit in the Negotiation."[33] Adams could not have foreseen that these "little despicable efforts" would be revived two hundred years later by an American historian who would have the effrontery to represent them as progress in historical understanding. That the same historian would credit France with the major role in producing the Dutch acknowledgment of American independence would have struck Adams as traitorous. I have my fears about how such a conclusion, steering the historical current back in the direction of Colenbrander, will be received by this audience. But it is where the evidence pushes the trajectory of my own trapeze.

NOTES

1   Francis Wharton, ed., *The Revolutionary Diplomatic Correspondence of the United States* (Washington, 1889), IV, 34.

2   Bemis, pp. 167–69.

3   Richard B. Morris, *The Peacemakers* (New York, 1965).

4   *España ante la independencia de los Estados Unidos* (2 vols.; Lérida, 1925).

5   R. Fruin and H. T. Colenbrander, eds., *Dépêches van Thulemeyer, 1763–1788* (Amsterdam, 1912).

6   Warren, *History* (reprint ed.; New York, 1970), III, 164.

7   *Ibid.*, III, 169.

8 See Simon Schama, *Patriots and Liberators Revolution in the Nether-lands 1780–1813* (London, 1977), p. 659, notes 47–50.

9 Bernard Bailyn, *The Ideological Origins of the American Revolution* (Cambridge, Mass., 1967), pp. ix, 95; *The Origins of American Politics* (Cambridge, Mass., 1968), p. 11; *The Ordeal of Thomas Hutchinson* (Cambridge, Mass., 1974), p. 206.

10 Charles F. Adams, ed., *The Works of John Adams* (10 vols.; Boston, 1850–56), III, 464

11 For a discussion of the role of jealousy in America from the Revolution through the Jacksonian era, see James H. Hutson, "The Origins of the 'Paranoid Style in American Politics': Public Jealousy from the Age of Walpole to the Age of Jackson," forthcoming.

12 Dickinson, *Letters* (Dublin, 1768), p. 96.

13 Robert J. Taylor et al., eds., *The Papers of John Adams* (2 vols. to date; Cambridge, Mass., 1977), I, 136.

14 *Letter from Alexander Hamilton Concerning the Public Conduct and Character of John Adams, Esq.* (New York, 1800), p. 7; Mercy Otis Warren to John Adams, August 1, 1807, *Massachusetts Historical Society Collections* (Boston, 1878), IV, 396. Sedgwick to Alexander Hamilton, October 16, 1788, in Harold C. Syrett and Jacob E. Cooke, eds., *The Papers of Alexander Hamilton* (New York, 1962), V, 226.

15 Paul Wentworth to William Eden, December 22, 1777, in B. F. Stevens, ed., *Facsimiles of Manuscripts in European Archives Relating to America 1773–1783* (25 vols.; London, 1889–95), II, no. 234.

16 Lance Banning, "Republican Ideology and the Triumph of the Constitution, 1789 to 1793," *William and Mary Quarterly*, 3rd ser., XXXI (April 1974), 171.

17 James K. Martin, *Men in Rebellion: Higher Government Leaders and the Coming of the American Revolution* (New Brunswick, N.J., 1973), p. 34; J. G. A. Pocock, *The Machiavellian Moment* (Princeton, N.J., 1975), pp. 507–8; Gordon Wood, "Rhetoric and Reality in the American Revolution," *William and Mary Quarterly*, 3rd ser., XXIII (January 1966), 25; see also Wood, *The Creation of the American Republic* (Chapel Hill, N.C., 1969), p. 17.

18 Peter Shaw, *The Character of John Adams* (Chapel Hill, N.C., 1976), pp. 64–66, 150–51, 186–91.

19 The quotations in this paragraph are, in order of their appearance, from Hutson, *Adams*, pp. 52–53, 73, 88, 74, 110, 101.

20 *Ibid.*, pp. 92–93.

21 *Ibid.*, p. 111.

22 J. W. Schulte Nordholt, *Dutch Republic* (typescript), 22–24; I. Leonard Leeb, *The Ideological Origins of the Batavian Revolution* (The Hague, 1973), p. 141.

23 Schulte Nordholt, *Dutch Republic*, p. 23.

24 Hutson, *Adams*, pp. 98, 108–9.

25 *Ibid.*, pp. 105–6.

26 *Ibid.*, p. 104.

27   *Ibid.*, pp. 104–8.
28   Schulte Nordholt, *Dutch Republic*, p. 225.
29   Hutson, *Adams*, p. 110.
30   *Ibid.*, p. 102.
31   Adams to Mercy Otis Warren, July 30, 1807, *Massachusetts Historical Society Collections*, IV, 386.
32   Schulte Nordholt, *Dutch Republic*, pp. 226–30
33   Lyman H. Butterfield, ed., *Adams Family Correspondence* (Cambridge, Mass., 1973), IV, 338.

The Founding Fathers and the Two Confederations

The United States of America and the United Provinces of the Netherlands, 1783–89

· ⚜ ·

LAWRENCE S. KAPLAN

THERE is a long-standing sense of kinship between the United States and the Netherlands rooted in a romantic tradition encapsulated in the preface of John Lothrop Motley's *Rise of the Dutch Republic:* "The maintenance of the right of the little provinces of Holland and Zealand in the sixteenth, by Holland and England united in the seventeenth, and by the United States of America in the eighteenth centuries, forms but a single chapter in the great volume of human fate; for the so-called revolutions of Holland, England, and America are all links of one chain."[1] This common history and destiny became all the more meaningful when England was temporarily separated from that chain in the American Revolution. The Dutch then became co-belligerents of Americans in that conflict, served as bankers of the new nation after the war, and were perceived as fellow sufferers for the cause of republicanism and democracy throughout the Revolutionary era.

The Netherlands, therefore, loomed large in the minds of the founding fathers, particularly John Adams, minister to Great Britain and commissioner to the Netherlands, and Thomas Jefferson, minister to France, in the 1780's. Through their eyes such statesmen as John Jay, Secretary of Foreign Relations, and James Madison, leading Virginia critic of the Confederation, perceived events in the Low Countries. The role that the Dutch played both as symbol and as substance in the fashioning of the federal union is worth examining for the example their experience with confederation offered to the founding fathers of the struggling transatlantic republic. The bicentennial year of the Netherlands' recognition of the independence of the United States and its signing of a treaty of amity and commerce is an appropriate occasion for a review of their connection.

It is often forgotten that next to France the financial support and fate of the Low Countries preoccupied Adams and Jefferson from their respective perches in London, Paris, and—at one point in 1788— jointly in Amsterdam. They knew better than their colleagues at home the significant position Dutch bankers were occupying in the life of the American Confederation in the 1780's. In Jefferson's case the success of his mission in Paris depended, he believed, upon the ability of the United States to pay interest on its debts to the powerful French patron, and this could be accomplished only through the assistance of Amsterdam bankers. Failure to secure new loans would damage the Republic's credit rating in the world, perhaps irreparably, and could even be a harbinger of the failure of the republican experiment itself. Consequently, they watched with painful fascination the upheaval in the Netherlands, the struggle between the Francophile and Americanophile Patriot Movement against the Anglophile stadtholderate which in so many ways seemed to be a proving ground for republicanism against monarchy in the eyes of friends and enemies of America.

Self-interest mingled with and perhaps predominated over the appreciation of the Dutch legacy to America when John Adams in his memorial to the States General of April 19, 1781, petitioning for their recognition of the United States, pointed out that "if there was ever among nations a natural alliance, one may be formed between two republics." Their origins "are so much alike, that . . . every Dutchman instructed in the subject, must pronounce the American revolution just and necessary, or pass a censure upon the greatest actions of his immortal ancestors."[2] Although the horizons of his expectations from this "natural alliance" may not have stretched beyond beneficial commercial relations with the Dutch West Indies and loans and advances on generous terms in a joint war effort, such practical considerations did not detract from the importance of the Netherlands to the future of the American republic.

However manipulative Adams' intentions may have been in linking the destiny of the two nations in 1781, guile seemed almost wholly absent a few years later when he sensed the dawning of a new age in the Dutch Patriots' challenge to the House of Orange. In 1786 his language sounded as hyperbolic as Jefferson's was to be over a similar stirring in France: "In no Instance, of ancient or modern history, have the People ever asserted more unequivocally their own inherent and

unalienable Sovereignty."[3] Just as for Jefferson in Paris at the beginning of the French Revolution, the achievement of the Dutch would
reflect America's service to a new and better Old World.

When this brave new world was stifled at birth, Jefferson's and
Adams' mourning for the Patriot cause was deeper than it would have
been for a business partner or a military ally. Years later in his autobiography Jefferson recalled with bitterness and regret the fall of
Holland, "by the treachery of her Chief, from her honorable independence, to become a province of England; and so also her Stadtholder, from the high position of the first citizen of a free Republic
to be the servile Viceroy of a foreign Sovereign."[4] Jefferson's sentiments
about the fate of his friends victimized in the Netherlands in the
1780's and in France in the 1790's were in character. Jefferson rarely
could abandon a friend. These sentiments took on special significance
when they appeared in the comments of the harsher John Adams.
Repeatedly he expressed his pity by identifying the victory of the
Prince of Orange with "rigorous persecutions and cruel punishments
of the Patriots in Holland, which are held out in terror."[5] Abigail
Adams shared her husband's sorrow. She wrote to their son John
Quincy that "history does not furnish a more striking instance of
abject submission and depression" than the conquest of the Netherlands "by a few Prussian troops, a nation that formerly withstood the
whole power and force of Spain."[6]

Genuine as these moods were, veering from unbridled optimism to
the most despairing gloom, they did not characterize the substance of
either Jefferson's or Adams' concerns about Holland during their min-
istries in Europe in the 1780's. Understandably, the dominant theme
and most insistent subject of communications across the Atlantic was
the state of America's debt to Dutch bankers and the continuing need
to float loans in order to sustain the shaky fiscal structure of the
Confederation. Given the critical nature of the problem, the attention
of diplomats abroad had to center on coping with its implications.
Adams had labored under enormous handicaps to initiate loans in
the first place, in the face of the unwillingness of the Orangists to
embarrass the British by supporting rebellious colonists as well as of
cautious bankers concerned about the safety of their investments. Not
until the States General had recognized the United States in 1782 were
American sympathizers—and France's friends—in the financial community of Amsterdam able to respond to Adams' importunities.
America's chief banker was the van Staphorst family, who also served
as the agent of Versailles. Of the 10 million dollars in foreign debt,
by 1788 almost half was owed to Dutch creditors.[7] In short, the credit
of the United States abroad rested as much in Dutch hands as in those
of America's original benefactors, France. The difficulties of a con-

federal government in New York unable to collect sufficient revenues to pay even the interest on its debts plagued its diplomats abroad throughout the life of the Articles of Confederation.

In this context philosophical speculation about the virtues of Dutch republicanism, or even gratitude for past favors, had to yield to the bleak reality of recommending that Dutch financiers be encouraged to purchase American debts to France on the assumption that defaulting to France would be more dangerous to America than defaulting to private bankers in Amsterdam. As Jefferson put it in 1786, "If there be a danger that our payments may not be punctual, it might be better that the discontents which would thence arise should be transferred from a court of whose good will we have so much need to the breasts of a private company."[8] At the same time Jefferson and Adams were uncomfortable in their knowledge that Dutch speculators had exploitive interests in the American economy. If they were able to buy up the domestic debt as well, they could control the direction of America's economic future. Congress, concerned about the risk of American credit in Holland, turned down the plan.[9]

The problem of excessive dependence was illustrated by the sluggishness of Dutch bankers in floating a new loan in 1786 and 1787 at a time when the Congress of the Confederation could not pay interest on earlier loans. Jefferson was left with the burden of finding ways of meeting unfulfilled payments to French veteran officers of the Revolution as well as the expenses of his own establishment in Paris. The solution suggested in Amsterdam was to seek payment of a year's interest on certificates of the American domestic debt held by Dutch speculations as a precondition for the completion of the current foreign loan.[10] These issues provoked a crisis in 1787 for the two American diplomats, and particularly for Jefferson, who felt intimidated by the intricacies of money questions and who was discomfited further by the prospect of Adams leaving him alone with them by returning to Massachusetts in the midst of the crisis. It appeared that the friends of America in Amsterdam—the Willink brothers and the van Staphorst brothers—had maneuvered the diplomats into a corner.

Adams did leave Europe in April 1788 but not before meeting his distraught colleague Jefferson in March at The Hague (where Adams intended to pay a farewell courtesy visit as American commissioner to the Netherlands) and at Amsterdam. There they managed to win a reprieve of three years for the United States in the form of a new loan to meet pressing obligations in Europe. Despite anger on Adams' part and anguish on Jefferson's there was little doubt about the outcome. The Amsterdam bankers had too much at stake to permit the destruction of American credit, as Adams recognized. Moreover, they were well aware that a new government then coming into being in America would repay their investment at full value.

There was a happy ending to the problem of American credit in Holland, and certainly a satisfactory arrangement for those financiers who anticipated the redemption of debts by the new federal government. But they were not achieved before Jefferson, the first Secretary of State in the new government, became thoroughly troubled and not a little confused by financial machinations, American as well as Dutch, he witnessed around him. In New York in 1790 he claimed that he always had been of the opinion that "the purchase of our debt to France by private speculations would have been an operation extremely injurious to our credit; and that the consequence foreseen by our bankers, that the purchasers would have been obliged, in order to make good their payments, to deluge the market of Amsterdam with American paper and to sell it at any price, was a probable one."[11] The Secretary of State obviously had changed his mind since 1786, when he thought that such an arrangement was worth making. His education in the mysteries of high finance yielded some cynical insights by 1789. He reported to Jay that bankers would be able to borrow to fill subscriptions just enough to pay interest, "just that and no more or so much more as may pay our salaries and keep us quiet. . . . I think it possible they may chuse to support our credit to a certain point and let it go no further but at their will; to keep it so poised as that it may be at their mercy."[12] Small wonder that Jefferson had an animus against speculators and feared their influence on the economy. It is in this context that he cried out his belief that "the maxim of buying nothing without money in our pocket to pay for it, would make our country one of the happiest on earth."[13]

It was in keeping with his personality that Jefferson's difficulties would be articulated more in generalizations over the evils of speculation than in ad hominem diatribes against the Dutch as speculators. With a more lively paranoiac streak to push him, Adams would spell out what Jefferson would only touch lightly. To Adams the troubles over loans were "a mere pretence, and indeed the whole appears to be a concerted Fiction." He wanted to alert Jefferson against "the immeasurable avarice of Amsterdam."[14] Dutch behavior, he claimed, was a product of a national character; they were "a Nation of Idolators at the Shrine of Mammon," he had exclaimed in 1780 when he encountered resistance to his efforts to win Dutch recognition during the war.[15] These slurs were delivered in moments of frustration, but they suggest an unflattering national stereotype functioning in the American psyche. The stereotype appeared more benevolently in Benjamin Franklin's discussion about the facts behind paper money in 1767 when he admonished innocent Americans to observe that "Holland, which understands the Value of Cash as well as any People in the World, would never part with Gold and Silver for Credit."[16] It was a short step from this pejorative appreciation to Franklin's assertion in 1781 that "Holland is no longer a *Nation* but a great *Shop;* and I begin to think it has no other Principle or Sentiments but those of a Shop-keeper."[17]

How much of this sentiment represented the essence of American feelings about the Dutch? How much did it reflect the mood of a crisis, the normal reaction of an impotent debtor to an apparently powerful manipulative creditor? There is no simple answer to these questions. It is worth noting, though, Adams' point that as heartless men of commerce they were even "worse than the English."[18] But the English after all presented more than a legacy of Mammon to Americans. So did the Dutch. In a quiet moment in 1783 Adams confessed that his vexations over loans were as much the product of "clashing interests—English, French, Stadholderian, Republican, and American" —as anything else.[19] And while merchants, bankers, and speculators sought their own advantages from the parlous condition of American finances, the dramatis personae contained Americans as well as Nether-landers. More significantly, there was none of the ideological malice and threat from the major Amsterdam creditors which would have been found among the British or the Orangists.

Similar ambivalent feelings may be found in American views of commercial relations with the United Provinces. Holland's role in the American Revolution as carriers of war supplies and as co-belligerents against Great Britain initially offered ground for optimism over the future of Dutch-American commercial ties. Jefferson had been excited over the prospects since 1776. And as he negotiated for a commercial treaty in The Hague, Adams seemed to share this optimism. He con-vinced himself at least that Pieter Johan Van Berckel, en route to the United States as first minister of the United Provinces, had concurred in his generalization that those West Indian islands would flourish most "which had the freest intercourse with us, and that this inter-course would be a natural means of attracting the American commerce to the metropolis."[20] Recognizing the inability of France to be flexible in its navigation laws, Adams believed that "we must make the most we can of the Dutch friendship, for luckily the merchants and regency of Amsterdam had too much wit to exclude us from their islands by treaty."[21]

Reality soon intruded to return Adams and his colleagues to their more normal skepticism. The Netherlands, it was obvious, was not different from any other European nation. If the most-favored-nation clause in the commercial treaty of 1782 had any meaning it was only in the symbolic value granted by the fact of an agreement itself, not by a Dutch departure from the restrictive economic system of Europe.[22] Madison was convinced that the British example would dominate Europe. Given the weakness of Congress's power to regulate commerce under the Confederation, France and the Netherlands would do as the British had done: play off one state against another, thereby encouraging disunion as they freely discriminated against American shipping.[23] On occasion the Dutch even appeared more obdurate than their European rivals. Hamilton indulged in the conventional stereotype when he observed that the Netherlands' "pre-eminence in the knowledge of trade" has led them to adopt commercial regulations "more rigid and numerous, than those of any other country; and it is by a judicious and unremitted vigilance of government, that they have been able to extend their traffic to a degree so much beyond their natural and comparitive [sic] advantages."[24] Jefferson seemed to agree with this judgment when he noted gloomily that "Holland is so immovable in her system of colony administration, that as propositions to her on that subject would be desperate, they had better not be made."[25] John Jay added that the Dutch fear of competition made it "look as if the Dutch regret our having found the Way to China, and that will doubtless be more or less the Case with every Nation with whose Commercial Views we may interfere."[26]

But these comments were hardly final judgments of American policy makers during the Confederation about the role of the Netherlands in America's future commercial relations. They were manifestations of unhappiness over the weakness of both the American confederation and its potential European partners which permitted Britain to exploit American trade without fear of retribution. To the end of this period Jefferson still nursed hopes that France or Holland would eventually replace Britain as America's chief trading partner, if only out of their self-interest. Hence, he deplored the actions of individual states in violating treaty agreements with the continental nations and deplored the provisions in the Articles of Confederation that permitted states to pass their own navigation acts;[27] they would provide excuses for Europeans to continue in their old ways. He continued to assume that British excesses and arrogance in its control of the American market would stimulate the Dutch or French to liberalize their trade policies with the United States. Although hoped-for lower freight rates and reduced tariffs from their European allies never materialized, the Americans persisted if only because increasing British hostility fostered the illusion of impending change.[28]

Unwilling or unable as it was to respond to American pleas, the United Provinces shared a community of economic interest with the United States, which was visible to Louis-Guillaume Otto, the astute

Eerste Gehoorgeeving aan den Afgezant VAN BERCKEL
in America.

The reception of the first Dutch envoy by the
Congress of the United States at Princeton, N.J.—
engraving by Reinier Vinkeles

secretary to the French minister to the United States from 1779 to 1784. "The Americans' connections with the United Provinces," he wrote, "will remain all the more firm, as they are based on a large conformity of political principles, on an equally strong passion for commerce without a great deal of rivalry, on a similarity of mores and customs, and perhaps also an equally strong hatred for England."[29] Otto envisaged a role for his nation in its benevolent interest in exploiting Dutch and American Anglophobia to link the two republics each to the other and both to France.

The French diplomat was correct in identifying continuing American antipathy toward the former mother country. He failed, however, to anticipate the inability of France to play its part as defender as well as exploiter of the two smaller countries. In 1785, when Otto was writing his memoir, France appeared to waver in its support of the Francophile Dutch Patriots as the Austrians threatened war with Holland over the firing on an imperial ship on the Scheldt. At that time a coalition between France and Prussia on behalf of the Dutch was in the making against Austria and Russia, with England as a neutral in this conflict. Unsuccessful French mediation left the Netherlands with a war penalty of 10 million florins. Two years later the partners in the diplomatic minuet shifted. Austria would play a small role in concert with France against a more powerful British-Prussian combination which was far more serious both to the Dutch and to the Americans.

In 1787 Prussia invaded Holland to avenge an insult to the Princess of Orange, the King's sister, by the Francophile Patriots. The Patriot party, a combination of aristocrats and democrats, intellectuals and businessmen, looked to America for inspiration and to France for sustenance. Once again France failed its Dutch friends; the French, intimidated by British influence with the Stadtholder and by the ineptness of the Patriot defense, repudiated their alliance. The aristocratic elements among the Patriots then deserted to the Orangists, and the pro-American republicans were sentenced to defeat and exile.

The impact of this event upon Jefferson and Adams was traumatic. It underscored the growing concern about the interference of the major powers in Dutch affairs which was the subject of so much of Jefferson's correspondence to America from 1785 to 1788. If the Netherlands' plight moved them it was not only because the victims were identified as friends of America and the oppressors as supporters of the Anglophile Stadtholder; it was also because the troubles of the Dutch confederation could become the troubles of the American confederation; civil war invited foreign intervention.

Jefferson initially displayed considerable sangfroid when the crises began in 1785. He regarded the kindling of the "lamp of war" in the Low Countries as a species of European power politics which would be worrisome to Americans only because peace terms with England had not been fully executed. "That done," he felt, "their wars would do us little harm."[30] Even the Prussian occupation of Holland on behalf of the Stadtholder did not fully jar him; he recognized as much as any diplomat the distressing state of France's finances, and understood intellectually their reasons for conciliation.[31] As late as October 1787, after the Stadtholder had been reinstated and Britain was obviously triumphant, he still would write that it was "possible, and rather probable," that France would eventually go to war to restore the Patriots to power and humble England once again.[32]

But this was the last shred of wishful thinking. He was no longer above the scene in the summer of 1787 as he reflected on Holland's fate—"a British navy and Prussian army hanging over Holland on one side, a French navy and army hanging over it on the other."[33] No longer did he look upon a foreign war as outside America's concern. He recognized in the summer of 1787 that any war threatening to damage the position of the French ally would endanger the United States.[34] And when France formally announced to the British its intention not to fullfill its obligations to its Dutch ally, Jefferson's panic was complete. He was moved to note an "important lesson, that no circumstances of morality, honour, interest, or engagement are sufficient to authorize a secure reliance on any nation, at all times, and in all positions. A moment of difficulty, or a moment of error may render for ever useless the most friendly dispositions in the king, in the major part of his ministers, and in the whole of his nation."[35]

The experience of the Netherlands was a powerful argument to American witnesses of the evils of the balance of power and the inadequacies of alliances with great powers. Europe is a dangerous place, and its history a warning to America. While there may be temporary advantages in joining one side or another, or occasionally imperative reasons for it, it is always perilous and never to be sought after by the smaller power. "Wretched indeed is the nation in whose affairs foreign powers are once permitted to intermeddle!" Jefferson exclaimed in 1787.[36] Holland was that wretched nation, a "frog between the legs of two fighting bulls," as Adams saw it.[37] And but for the grace of God and the width of the Atlantic Ocean the fate of Holland could be America's as well.

Yet with all the empathy felt for the failed Patriots by Adams and Jefferson there was concomitantly a smugness, a sense of superiority that derived from the Dutch status as Europeans. If they failed, part of that failure was their own doing. Americans at home shared this conceit. The source of many of their impressions of the United Provinces in the 1780's were two diverse personalities: Charles W. F. Dumas, a diplomatic agent for both the French and the Americans and a devoted client of the Patriot cause; and Gijsbert Karel van Hogendorp, a nephew of Minister van Berckel and advocate of the Stadtholder's position. Although the former was closer to Jefferson and Adams personally and professionally, the youthful van Hogendorp presented sufficient counterbalance to Dumas to stimulate American doubts about the anti-Orange forces.[38] There was division among the Patriots between aristocratic regents who wished only to reduce prerogatives of the House of Orange and the more democratic elements who wished to render magistrates more responsive to the popular will and to emulate the activities of the American Revolution, and this was well known to American observers. It was the ineptitude of the latter and the fickleness of the former that colored their judgments. Adams characterized the friends of America as "unskillful and unsuccessful asserters of a free government" who knew too little about history and less about government. "They have, therefore," mourned Adams, "been the dupes of foreign politics and their own indigested system."[39]

If it was not a case of "plague on both your houses," at least there was a distancing of Americans from even the best-intentioned of the Dutch allies. Distinctions between Orange and Patriot were blurred, for if their old friends the Patriots were to be pitied, "so are their deluded Persecutors."[40] Weighing van Hogendorp against Dumas, Jefferson claimed to be "disposed to wish well to either party only as I can see in their measures a tendency to bring on an amelioration of the condition of the people, an increase in the mass of happiness."[41]

These caveats, however, did not exclude the possibility of reclaiming and rehabilitating the "poor Patriots of Holland," as Washington called them.[42] It was just that their rescue would have to be accomplished by removing them to America and to freedom.[43]

Despite the Olympian tone adopted by the American diplomats, the fate of the United States in 1787 was hardly as secure as their language made it seem. Was the American confederation in better shape than the Dutch? Would the new constitution just then being framed be the solution for the ills which beset the Congress of the Confederation? The statesmen on both sides of the Atlantic could not be certain of the outcome. While the United Provinces was an example to them as they went about creating a federal union, the example was susceptible to differing interpretations.

The initial lesson for Jefferson was the threat to liberty inherent in the elevation of a monarchical prince which made even a weak and divided federation a happier arrangement. The Prince of Orange was "a half king, who would be a whole one," as he wrote Abigail Adams, a villain in the sense that George III was to the American colonies.[44] Employing a bestiary image he was to use frequently in the future, he warned against hereditary magistrates and wished "to besiege the throne of heaven with eternal prayers to extirpate from creation this class of human lions, tygers, and mammouts called kings."[45] Benjamin Franklin shared Jefferson's fears, from his base as delegate to the Constitutional Convention in Philadelphia. To him "a single head," the projected federal President, may be sick or malevolent, or responsible for the destruction of a country, as in the case of Holland under the Stadtholder, the "Source of all the present Disorders in Holland." If the United States did need a strong executive, he should be, as the Stadtholder was not, subject to impeachment.[46] Jefferson's concern about the conditions for an American presidency was even stronger; he worried over the length of the executive's term and the danger of indefinite tenure. The behavior of the Stadtholder "would have sufficed to set me against a Chief magistrate eligible for a long duration, if I had ever been disposed towards one."[47]

Advocates of the Constitution conceded that the stadtholderate contained monarchical qualities but either dismissed them as inapplicable to the American executive on the grounds that the president was to be elected periodically or converted the model into an argument against confederation. Madison made a point in the Virginia convention of locating the evils of the Stadtholder in the structure of the Dutch confederation itself. Given its inherent weaknesses, he claimed that the Prince at least served to keep the faltering nation togther.[48] In New York, Alexander Hamilton went further in ascribing merit to the Stadtholder; only he was in a position to give "energy to the operations of this government which is not to be found in ours."[49] So, unhappy as the experience of the Dutch may have been, at least its system contained a leader with authority lacking in any officer of the American confederation. The Constitution, according to this line of reasoning, would grant the new President those powers which had made the Stadtholder effective while withholding those which could make him a tyrant. Even Jefferson and Franklin ultimately accepted this judgment.

Consistency was not a dominant element in the roles which the United Provinces played for America at the time of its Constitutional Convention and the ensuing debates in state ratifying conventions. It served as a useful metaphor, mentioned, in fact, no fewer than thirty-seven times in 1787 and 1788, to be summoned, as were the Amphictyonic Council and the Germanic confederation, to serve debaters' points.[50] Whether the elaborate re-creation of Dutch history, as presented by both sides at the conventions, was accurate was immaterial. What counted was the usefulness of Dutch history—real, imagined, or just misinformed—as grist for argumentation. Nor did it matter if the precedent reflected favorably or unfavorably upon the Netherlands. At one time, Madison noted Holland's failure to make constitutional changes after four attempts; at another, its success in getting its way with the other provinces through the corrupt influence of its wealth. In the former instance, Holland was the victim of the principle of unanimity; in the latter, the bully of the smaller members of the confederation.[51]

In the end the Dutch proved to be a more serviceable foil for the Federalists than for the anti-Federalists. Not that the enemies of the Constitution did not try to build up a Netherlands in their own image. One method, employed by William Grayson in the Virginia convention debates, was to claim that Dutch problems were not the consequence of misgovernment: "Holland, we are informed, is not happy, because she has not a constitution like this. This is but an unsupported assertion." Moreover, the Dutch had "a fellow-feeling" toward Americans, according to the Virginian, and were willing to continue to loan money to the United States because "they were in the same situation with ourselves." As proof he suggested that their willingness to allow American debts to pile up stemmed from the fact that they have not yet paid their debts to France dating back to the days of Henry IV.[52] Melancton Smith in the New York convention took a similar tack in claiming that the Netherlands, despite so many defects, "yet existed; she had, under her confederacy, made a principal figure among the nations of Europe, and he believed few countries had experienced a greater share of internal peace and prosperity."[53] These were vain gestures. The anti-Federalists' defense of the Dutch experiment was no more successful than their defense of their own Articles of Confederation. There was a consensus among most of the founding fathers that the Netherlands was a species of failed confederacies—Greek, German, Swiss—which the American confederation too closely resembled.[54]

But the Dutch republic was not simply a negative model which the founding fathers of the federal union sought to avoid. If they were ignorant of or indifferent to the inner workings of Dutch history and government, their knowledge of the events of their own time was full and accurate and important to them. Madison and Monroe, Washington and Jay, knew explicit details from Adams and Jefferson, and their responses were far more perceptive and compassionate than they would have been if the Netherlands were only another case study of an aristocratic republic. The words of the American diplomatists in Europe as well as those of their correspondents at home betrayed an anguish over the sufferings of a kindred people with kindred institutions.

These sentiments were reciprocated in full. Inevitably, considerable Dutch sympathy for the American cause in the Revolutionary War had been dictated by an opportunity to capture lost West Indian trade, by anticipated land speculation in the Ohio and Susquehanna valleys, and by the expectation of profits from American securities. But there was additionally a political and ideological content to the economic gamble Amsterdam financiers and businessmen made in their American investment. It was not coincidental that the leading figures in these transactions, such as the financier Nicolas van Staphorst and the tobacco merchant Jan de Neufville, were participants in the Patriot Movement. They equated the victory of America over Great Britain with the defeat of the Anglophile Orange forces and regarded the emancipation of America from the British Empire as a replication of their own secession from the Spanish Empire in the sixteenth century. George Washington was William the Silent redivivus.[55]

There was probably greater sentimentality about the relationship on the Dutch side than there was on the American. The latter were frequently annoyed at the Dutch goals and methods, were convinced that their ambitions were beyond their capacities, and were skeptical of their ability to acquire the kind of self-government Americans possessed. Yet their annoyance appeared to mask fears that American behavior might have been the same in their situation, or even could be in future situations. Hence, the sufferings of Holland provided "a crowd of lessons," as Jefferson put it: "Never to have an hereditary officer of any sort: never to let a citizen ally himself with kings: never to call in foreign nations to settle domestic differences: never to suppose that any nation will expose itself to war for us, etc."[56]

More than fear of a common fate inspired their reactions. The friendship with Patriot leaders evoked emotions greater than the sum total of American self-interest. Adams and Jefferson were deeply affected by the similarities in the direction the Dutch Patriots, or at least the Americanophile segment of them, were traveling. They wished them well even as they doubted their potential to succeed. And when they failed, their American friends beckoned them to be born again in the New World. There they could participate in a political and social order to which they could only aspire in the Old World.

NOTES

1   John Lothrop Motley, *The Rise of the Dutch Republic: A History* (2 vols.; New York, 1898), I, iii-iv.

2   Charles F. Adams, ed., *The Works of John Adams* (10 vols.; Boston, 1850–56), VII, 399–400.

3   Lyman H. Butterfield et al., eds., *Diary and Autobiography of John Adams* (4 vols.; Cambridge, Mass., 1961), III, 201.

4   Alexander A. Lipscomb and Albert E. Bergh, eds., *The Writings of Thomas Jefferson* (20 vols.; Washington, D.C., 1904), I, 115–16.

5   Adams to Jefferson, October 28, 1787, in Julian P. Boyd, ed., *The Papers*

of Thomas Jefferson (Princeton, N.J., 1950), XII, 292; Adams to Jay, November 15, 1787, *Works of John Adams*, VIII, 460.

6 Abigail Adams to John Quincy Adams, October 12, 1787, in the Adams Papers, reel 370.

7 See Merrill Jensen, *The New Nation: A History of the United States during the Confederation, 1781–1789* (New York, 1950), p. 383.

8 Jefferson to John Jay, September 26, 1786, in Boyd, *Papers*, X, 406.

9 James C. Riley, "Foreign Credit and Fiscal Stability: Dutch Investment in the United States, 1781–1794," *Journal of American History*, LXV (December 1978), 672 ff.; Merrill D. Peterson, *Thomas Jefferson and the New Nation* (New York, 1970), pp. 362–63. *Journals of the Continental Congress*, XXIII, October 2, 1787, 590–93.

10 Willink and van Staphorst to Jefferson, January 31, 1788, in Boyd, *Papers*, XII, 542 ff.

11 Jefferson's Opinion on Fiscal Policy, August 26, 1970, *ibid.*, XVII, 425.

12 Jefferson to Jay, March 12, 1789, *ibid.*, XIV, 645.

13 Jefferson to Alexander Donald, July 28, 1787, *ibid.*, XI, 633.

14 Adams to Jefferson, February 12, 1788, *ibid.*, XII, 581.

15 Adams to James Warren, December 9, 1780, in W. C. Ford, ed., "Warren-Adams Letters," *Massachusetts Historical Society Collections*, LXXIII (Boston, 1925), II, 154.

16 "Facts Concerning American Paper Money," 1767, in Albert H. Smyth, ed., *The Writings of Benjamin Franklin* (10 vols.; New York, 1907), V, 9.

17 Franklin to Charles W. F. Dumas, August 6, 1781, *ibid.*, VIII, 292.

18 Adams to Warren, December 9, 1780, "Warren-Adams Letters," II, 154.

19 Adams to Robert Morris, May 21, 1783, *Works of John Adams*, VIII, 59.

20 Adams to Livingston, July 23, 1783, *ibid.*, VIII, 112.

21 Adams to Livingston, July 7, 1783, *ibid.*, VIII, 85.

22 Madison to James Monroe, June 21, 1786, in William T. Hutchinson and William M. Rachal, eds., *The Papers of James Madison* (Chicago, 1962) IX, 82.

23 From *The North-American*, No. 2, October 8, 1783, *ibid*, VII, 321.

24 From *The Continentalist*, No. V, April 18, 1782, in Harold C. Syrett and Jacob E. Cooke, eds., *The Papers of Alexander Hamilton* (26 vols.; New York, 1961) III, 78.

25 Jefferson to Jay, October 11, 1785, in Boyd, *Papers*, VIII, 608.

26 Jay to Jefferson, July 14, 1786, *ibid.*, X, 135.

27 Jefferson to Adams, November 19, 1785, *ibid.*, IX, 43.

28 Jefferson to Monroe, December 11, 1785, *ibid.*, IX, 95.

29 Paul G. Sifton, ed., "Otto's *Mémoire* to Vergennes, 1785," *William and Mary Quarterly*, XXII (October 1965), 643.

30 Jefferson to Madison, November 11, 1784, in Boyd, *Papers*, VII, 506; Jefferson to Samuel Osgood, October 5, 1785, *ibid.*, VIII, 589.

31 Jefferson to Jay, June 21, 1787, *ibid.*, XI, 491; Jefferson to Edward Carrington, August 4, 1787, *ibid.*, XI, 679.

32 Jefferson to John Sullivan, October 5, 1787, *ibid.*, XII, 209.

33 Jefferson to Benjamin Vaughan, July 2, 1787, *ibid.*, XI, 533.

34 Jefferson to George Washington, August 14, 1787, *ibid.*, XII, 37–38.

35 Jefferson to Jay, November 3, 1787, *ibid.*, XII, 310.

36 Jefferson to Vaughan, July 2, 1787, *ibid.*, XI, 533.

37 Quoted in Edward Handler, *America and Europe in the Political Thought of John Adams* (Cambridge, Mass., 1964), p. 115.

38 See commentary in Boyd, *Papers*, XIII, xxxiii.

39 Quoted in Handler, *America and Europe in the Political Thought of John Adams*, p. 112.

40 Adams to Jefferson, November 10, 1787, in Boyd, *Papers*, XII, 335.

41 Jefferson to G. K. van Hogendorp, August 25, 1786, *ibid.*, X, 299.

42 Washington to Henry Knox, February 5, 1788, in J. C. Fitzpatrick, ed., *The Writings of George Washington* (19 vols.; Washington, D.C., 1931–44), XXIX, 401.

43 Washington to Reverend Francis Adrian Vanderkemp, May 28, 1788, *ibid.*, XXIX, 505; Adams to Jefferson, November 10, 1787, in Boyd, *Papers*, XII, 335.

44 Jefferson to Abigail Adams, July 1, 1787, *ibid.*, XII, 33.

45 Jefferson to David Humphreys, August 14, 1787, *ibid.*, XII, 33.

46 *Writings of Franklin*, June 30, 1787, IX, 603; Max Farrand, ed., *Records of the Federal Convention*, July 20, 1787 (4 vols.; New Haven, Conn., 1937), II, 68. This point is repeated in Patrick Henry's comments on June 9, 1788, during the debate on the Constitution at the Virginia state convention, in Jonathan Elliot, ed., *The Debates of the State Conventions* (5 vols.; Philadelphia, 1836–45) III, 160.

47 Jefferson to William Stephens Smith, November 13, 1787, in Boyd, *Papers*, XII, 356.

48 June 12, 1788, *The Papers of James Madison*, XI, 126.

49 June 17, 1788, Elliot, *Debates*, II, 234.

50 See William H. Riker, "Dutch and American Federalism," *Journal of the History of Ideas*, XVIII (October 1957), 495.

51 Farrand, *Records*, June 29, 1787, I, 478; *ibid.*, June 28, 1787, I, 457. Madison underscores Holland's special influence in the *Federalist*, No. 20.

52 Elliot, *Debates*, June 12, 1788, III, 290; *ibid.*, June 11, 1788, 275.

53 *Ibid.*, June 17, 1788, II, 224.

54 See J. W. Schulte Nordholt, "The Example of the Dutch Republic for American Federalism," *Bijdragen en Mededelingen Betreffende de Geschiedenis der Nederlanden*, XCIV (1979), 437–49.

55 See Simon Schama, *Patriots and Liberators: Revolution in the Netherlands, 1780–1813* (New York, 1977), p. 61; Robert R. Palmer, *The Age of the Democratic Revolution: The Challenge* (Princeton, N.J., 1959), pp. 325 ff.; J. W. Schulte Nordholt, "Gijsbert van Hogendorp in America, 1783–1784," *Acta Historiae Neerlandicae*, X (1978), 139, found van Hogendorp one of the few disappointed Americanophiles, preferring the Constitution to the Articles.

56 Jefferson to Adams, September 27, 1787, in Boyd, *Papers*, XII, 189.

Financial and Economic Ties

The First Century

· ᏋᎌᎧᏠᏕᏅ ·

JAMES C. RILEY

W HEN the foreign associations of the United States in the late eighteenth and the nineteenth century are considered, it is customary to think first of the close American association with Great Britain. This is natural, for the British and the American people shared much in background and outlook that encouraged and sustained close ties. Even in a period of occasional discord and strained relations, a period that began in conflict and was marked once again, in 1812, by open war, Britain provided the Americans with their closest diplomatic associate. In trade too American tastes continued to reflect habits and attitudes carried over from or acquired during the colonial era. Other states, not least the Dutch and the French, imagined that the War of the American Revolution signaled more than the political detachment of the thirteen colonies. But to a large extent they were wrong, as both the Dutch and the French realized during the 1780's.[1]

Nevertheless, the Anglo-American association can easily be given exaggerated weight. In the first place, of course, there were important points about which the two peoples differed. Even after the War of 1812 there were many in America who considered another conflict imminent, and inevitable.[2] Such feelings found expression again during the American Civil War, when influential Britons, including the editors of the London *Times*, sided with the Confederacy and threatened to carry their antagonism toward the federal government into open conflict. At the level of interpersonal relations the persistence of discord between the two countries might suggest all the more strongly the basic closeness of the relationship.

But there is another area in which this natural tendency to think of the closeness of the United States and Britain is misleading. Although willing to trade with the Americans, to the mutual benefit of both economies, and willing also to associate diplomatically with the Americans, although often as a superior rather than an equal partner,

[49]

the British were slow to develop an appetite for investing in the United States. In three critical phases of the first century of the American Republic—during the War of the American Revolution, immediately thereafter during the peacetime years of the Confederation government and the early years of the new federal government of 1788, and during the American Civil War—foreign credit was required in order to sustain the financial stability of the American government. Of course, we should not expect the British to have helped finance the American Revolution, even if acts of such a nature were not wholly unheard of in that era.[3] But we might reasonably expect a close associate to have assisted the young republic in gaining financial stability, particularly by 1790, when the war was no longer fresh and there was an active pro-British faction in the American government. And we might all the more readily expect the British to have chosen to support the Union during the American Civil War. On both occasions some investment capital made its way from Britain to the United States, but slowly and in comparatively small amounts.

A similar surprise awaits us when we consider British investment in the economic rather than political infrastructure of the United States. Desperately in need of investment capital, the American economy customarily offered higher yields than were available in Europe, and seemed, in most judgments of the day, to have a prosperous future. (Europeans were much impressed with the land area and rate of population growth of the United States.) British investors were clearly willing to invest abroad. Beginning in the 1790's they supported massive loans for the Austrian monarchy,[4] indeed the largest loans to my knowledge ever (to that point) extended to a foreign power. After the Napoleonic wars the British shifted more and more attention toward investments in the economic development of foreign territories until, by the latter decades of the nineteenth century, many Britons were worried about the ramifications of massive and continuous capital exports.

When public and private authorities in the United States sought capital for social overhead improvements and venture opportunities, they customarily looked to London as well as to other foreign capital markets. But here too the British responded slowly, and with amounts considerably less than would be expected on grounds of the otherwise close relation between these two peoples.

The fact of the matter is that in this one area at least there was no fundamental harmony between the two peoples. It is not that they were at odds so much as that they were detached from one another. In government borrowing and in capital investment for economic development the Americans had much more in common with another people, another people who showed time and again that in their judgment the United States offered an attractive financial climate. These people were the Dutch. I propose to examine the financial associations of the Americans and the Dutch, to try to discover why in finance and economic development the closest working relationship existed between these two peoples.

In the realm of public finance these contacts may be traced to the darkest period of the American rebellion against Britain. To finance a war fought at least in part over the very issue of taxation, the Americans sought to avoid any overt assessment of war costs. Drawing on extensive experience with fiat money, an experience acquired as a result of the perpetual shortage of specie in the colonial era, the Confederation Congress sought first to finance the war by issuing paper currency. From 1775 through 1783 paper money provided more than half (57 percent) of the constant dollar income of the new government —that is, taking into account the real value of this paper at the time of its issue.[5] Revenues from taxes, in contrast, brought in no more than 9 percent.

But, of course, the utility of fiat money financing was limited, in the first place because of the quickly declining value of money issued in excessive quantities, and second because the continental dollar could not be used directly to acquire war supplies from abroad. Foreign loans and credits provided only 12 percent of the specie value of wartime revenues. But their impact was greater than this proportion suggests because the foreign loans contributed neither to the hyperinflation of the continental currency nor to the unfavorable international balance of payments the Americans faced.

The earliest financial assistance obtained abroad came from France and Spain, allies of the United States in war against Britain. But as the costs of that conflict mounted, both allies found themselves forced to curtail support to the Americans. The French, who dominated this alliance, turned then to the Amsterdam capital market in search of additional credits. The fr5 million loan opened in November 1781 carried with it sufficient guarantees to persuade investors to come forth. The guarantees, however, were provided by France and the Dutch States General rather than by the Americans, so that it is difficult to see how this loan constituted any sort of success for the Americans among Dutch lenders. Certainly the political climate in the Dutch republic tended to favor the Americans; there was considerable good will toward the American cause and antagonism toward Britain, which helps explain the unusual guarantee extended by the States General.

Nevertheless, in 1782 the American representative in the Dutch republic, John Adams, opened a fr3 million loan (later increased to fr5 million) on the credit of the United States alone. The Dutch lacked detailed information about the Americans' financial position, but they knew enough to respond cautiously to this loan. Although opened in 1782 it was not fully subscribed until 1786. In the meantime another loan was floated (for fr2 million in 1784) and a third planned (for fr1 million in 1787).[6] The financial association had been established, even though Dutch credits delivered directly and indirectly to the Americans played only a secondary role in war finance.

The era during which Dutch credits were of particular importance covers the first decade of peace, from 1784 through 1794. In those years the United States had two successive governments, neither of which had established a working taxation apparatus that delivered enough domestic revenues to sustain even the minimal functions of peacetime government. The first of those governments, the Confederation, lacked the authority to force the states to meet the levies assessed them, so that its weakness was a weakness in fundamental law. That problem was corrected in the constitution drafted in 1787 and ratified in 1788. The new law provided Congress with adequate authority to tax. But, of course, the abstract authority could not quickly be transformed into actual tax revenues. In fact, the new federal government (in the American context, of course, "federal" now means centralized; then the term meant "relating to a compact") acted with all deliberation to exercise its financial prerogatives. Not until the middle 1790's were taxes collected in amounts sufficient to meet the ordinary expenditures of government.

In the interim the Americans floated a number of loans in Amsterdam (and one in Antwerp), raising a total of fr32.5 million, of which fr22,450,000 was supplied the new federal government from Amsterdam between 1788 and 1794. The importance of these credits can be understood properly only when they are compared to other revenue sources (Table 1).[7] During the organizational years of the new government, 1789 through 1791, foreign loan receipts (of which Dutch loans formed the largest part) provided some 43 percent of total central government revenues, and in 1792, 35 percent. For the entire period of the loans, through 1794, foreign credits provided 26 percent of central government revenues. The new American government depended in its early years on Dutch loans. Much is often made of the importance of foreign credits during the Confederation, but this later era of dependence is seldom recognized. In fact, Alexander Hamilton turned to Dutch credit as an essential, if largely unavowed, element of his plan for organizing the finances of the new government. As I have said elsewhere, "Hamilton's was a sound program that dealt cleverly and fairly with conflicting views in the United States about the federal and state debts and about use of the revenue authority theoretically available to Congress under the Constitution. But it could

TABLE 1

Foreign Loans and Central Government Revenues and Expenditures, 1789–94
(in thousands of dollars)

	4 March 1789–31 Dec. 1791	1792	1793	1794	Totals
Revenues					
Ordinary revenues	4,419	3,670	4,653	5,432	18,174
Domestic and foreign loan revenues	5,791	5,071	1,068	4,609	16,539
Foreign loan revenues (by estimated date of availability for disbursement)	(4,410)	(3,042)	(386)	(1,146)	(8,984)
Total revenues	10,210	8,741	5,721	10,041	34,713

not have succeeded on the strength of the resources available within the United States alone."[8]

If the Americans depended on foreign credit to a degree unprecedented among other governments of the day, how were they able, given the weakness of their political and financial position, to persuade the Dutch to lend so much? Although not well informed about American financial and political issues, and before 1786 lacking even much fundamental information, there were several things that attracted Dutch bankers and investors to the American loans.[9] In the first place, many of the Dutch found the American experiment in representative government admirable, and felt also a sense of community with another people who had fought for a republican style of government. On many counts there was not much similarity between the federal republic of 1788 and thereafter and the Dutch republic. But Dutch attitudes toward the Americans were formed in the era of the Confederation, a government very similar in nature to the Union of Utrecht and possessed, although in more glaring form, of some of the same weaknesses as the Dutch republic.

That the American loans were a factional matter became clear to Adams in his first efforts to line up an issuing house. Orangist bankers were not interested, perhaps because they shared little of this sympathetic attitude, and perhaps also because the American government did not meet even their rather undemanding standards for debtor states. Adams finally succeeded with a group of firms, W. & J. Willink, N. & J. Van Staphorst, and De la Lande & Fynje, that had little standing in the community of firms organizing foreign government loans. Van Staphorst and De la Lande & Fynje were partisans who found the American loan congenial on political grounds. Willink, in contrast, was apolitical. Like their associates, however, this firm's partners could presumably see certain opportunities in the American loan. It offered a chance to enter into a privileged and lucrative field of banking, that in which loans were organized for foreign powers usually with generous commissions for the issuing house. In the customs of the Amsterdam market, firms tended to acquire control over the loans issued by one or another borrowing power. That held true here, as Van Staphorst and Willink (De la Lande & Fynje suspended payments in 1785) directed other issues after 1782. Commissions on these loans were distributed among several parties, but the bankers got the largest share of what were, especially in the early U.S. loans, generous commissions. In short, the negotiation of these credits offered Van Staphorst and Willink a chance to expand their business and profits. And they did what they could to preserve this association. When Congress was forced to issue new loans in order to meet service payments on earlier credits, something that amounted implicitly to insolvency, the bankers were able to withhold knowledge of this from the investing public.

Factional attitudes and business opportunity will help us understand how the Americans found the way to issue loans, but they will not explain why Dutch investors lent so much. To grasp that we must first recognize that the American issues offered yields somewhat higher than those available from most competing loans. The difference, about 1 percent, will not strike us as imposing, but in the terms of the day it constituted a 25 percent premium (5 as against 4 percent) over what the most creditworthy foreign governments paid in loans floated in Amsterdam. The advantage was still greater when compared to yields offered in Dutch government loans. Investors obviously judged that this was a sufficient risk premium. On some occasions, when they responded eagerly rather than cautiously to new issues, they evidently deemed the yield on American issues to be more than sufficient. But it is true also that the Americans wanted to borrow large sums when Europe was at peace and when, by coincidence, the refinancing of old loans and fresh loans to European governments required less capital than was available in Amsterdam to be lent.

Still there was considerable hesitation on the part of investors, as the slow subscription of the 1782 loan demonstrates. What finally persuaded them was, in my judgment, the punctuality with which the Americans serviced their loans. Above all else Dutch investors evaluated debtors according to the standard of punctuality. Therefore when Van Staphorst and Willink took sufficient care to arrange the payment of interest, even to the point of borrowing more to do so, debtors became content with the risks involved in these loans. My explanation of this phenomenon differs somewhat from Professor van Winter's, but the conclusion we reach is identical: the Dutch lent to the Americans, and Dutch bankers organized the American loans, chiefly because these loans seemed to make good business sense. And in retrospect we can see that they did.

From the first there were overtones in the Dutch-American financial relationship of a community of outlook, especially on certain political issues. But most people did not lend money then any more than they do so now for such reasons. The financial association developed because it was mutually advantageous, and because each party in the relationship recognized, and was prepared to seize, such an advantage. The commercial relationship that the Dutch had hoped would develop with the Americans had not emerged. But a close financial relationship had developed, a financial relationship with its own economic implications.

To see these economic implications we should gaze in two directions, first toward the Dutch republic and then toward the United States. In the Netherlands these loans contributed significantly to the financial sector of a broadly diversified economy. Together with the Russians, who borrowed to fight the Turks and to refinance earlier loans, the Americans raised immense sums on the Amsterdam market in the late 1780's and early 1790's, at a time when the traditional leading borrowers—Britain and France—were largely out of the market for credit. This thriving financial sector reflected an economy seeking to reorient itself away from types of activity, especially the staple market trade and textile processing, at which the Dutch were no longer competitive. It has been customary to doubt whether the growth of the financial sector compensated for shrinkage elsewhere, and especially to wonder whether employment opportunities held up as the economy shifted orientation.[10] But an examination of the best available percapita income estimates reveals that the Dutch remained the wealthiest people on the European continent and, if not also the wealthiest in the world, second and then only slightly to the British. How was such a position sustained in an economy putatively undergoing decline?

In my judgment, part of the answer is furnished by Peter Klein's recently expressed doubt that the "rise of the financial sector would have decreased employment opportunities."[11] And part is furnished by the realization that our measurements of Dutch economic trends have tended too often to focus on testing whether formerly prosperous sectors continued to thrive rather than testing how the economy as a whole performed. Other types of commerce, some manufacturing, but especially the large and thriving realm of commercial and financial services, continued to prosper (although not during the revolutionary

Alexander Hamilton, by John Trumbull (1756–1843)
(*Courtesy of the National Gallery of Art, Washington, D.C.*)

and Napoleonic wars). In terms of a national income measurement, they compensated for deterioration elsewhere, and sustained the republic's position as a pocket of unusual prosperity.[12]

After new American loans ceased to be issued, the old loans still required financial services. They were not fully paid off until 1809. In the meantime they continued to make an *economic* contribution, and they also preserved this part of Dutch assets from the depredations of the period of French domination of the Dutch Netherlands.

Turning our gaze now to the West, we can see that these loans had another set of economic implications as well. Having become accustomed to the idea of U.S. issues on the capital market, and having been persuaded of the reliability of the United States as a debtor, Dutch investors turned to consider first other forms of investment in American government securities and then non-government investments also. In buying domestic government securities, the Dutch sought the extraordinary yields available from heavily depreciated paper. By buying it, however, they helped drive its price back toward par. Thus Hamilton's program, which sought to re-establish the domestic credit of the United States, was aided substantially by Dutch demand for these securities.[13]

This paper, which was called "liquidated debt"—a misleading term that did no harm to its reception among European investors— was bought chiefly in the United States by a circle of particularly enterprising Amsterdam banking and brokerage houses, among them Van Staphorst and Willink, but also the firm of Pieter Stadnitski. Stadnitski had earlier helped pioneer the single-unit investment trust, using in that case French royal securities. Beginning in 1787 he set out to apply this format to the market for American securities, offering Dutch investors the chance to buy into a trust holding as its only asset a bloc of this domestic debt paper. Between 1787 and 1793 twenty-eight trusts were formed by several houses; through them investors acquired between $7 and $10 million in these securities. As a result of these and other purchases, by 1803 the Dutch held a total of $13.1 million, some 22 percent of the total domestic debt of the United States. Besides contributing in an important way to the success of Hamilton's plan for financial stabilization, these purchases had the additional effect of shifting large amounts of capital into American hands. Whereas the Americans had formerly paid a premium for European goods, a premium expressed in a low dollar value against European currencies, this massive shift of investment capital created a temporary dollar premium.[14] It also provided capital to an economy previously held back by a shortage of investment capital, and at the same time strengthened the monetary position of the United States.

The Dutch also invested directly in the American economic

infrastructure. Again they followed the lead of Pieter Stadnitski, who saw that as domestic debt reached par other backing would have to be found for new investment trusts. In association with the Parisian-Swiss banker Etienne Clavière and an Amsterdam associate, Théophile Cazenove, Stadnitski dispatched J.-P. Brissot de Warville to the United States to investigate unsettled land. As this interest became more serious, Cazenove himself was sent to the United States as resident agent for what was now a circle of Amsterdam houses: Stadnitski, Van Staphorst, P. & C. Van Eeghen, and Ten Cate & Vollenhoven, soon to include as well the Willinks and R. J. Schimmelpenninck as investor, attorney, and adviser.[15] Stadnitski again fashioned single-unit trusts which in 1793 offered Dutch investors the opportunity to buy shares in two one-million-acre land development schemes that would take advantage of rapid population growth and westward movement in the United States.

At the same time this group of houses bought vast tracts in upstate New York and Pennsylvania—the famous Holland Land Company and its purchase. There are interesting stories still to be told about these land development schemes, but here it is necessary to synthesize their contribution to American economic development. Like Dutch purchases of American domestic debt, the land transactions provided Americans with more of the wherewithal to achieve some of the optimistic economic projects under consideration in the 1790's. Once they had become large-scale landowners, these firms found additional investments would be necessary in order to attract settlers and provide them with a chance of prospering. Over the years, until they sold out, more money was put into these tracts. This story is usually told from the perspective of the Holland Land Company papers. Thus it accentuates the difficulties the Dutch had in making any profit out of the enterprise, and how they came to rue Stadnitski's enthusiasm for innovative financial ventures. It might also be told from the perspective of these territories themselves, in which case the history of the company might be seen as a history of ineffective management and of the tardy seizure of development opportunities. How much did absentee company ownership hold back the growth of a region that might, under local and individual landownership, have been more adept at taking advantage of opportunities before it?

On the one hand, then, some Dutch firms and rentiers invested heavily in American land in the expectation that population growth would bring it into demand. When the land did not sell quickly they found themselves obliged to invest further in its development, and to contribute to such allied projects as the Erie Canal, which promised to increase the value of this land and to assist the economic development of the region. On the other hand, these and other Dutch investors became interested during the 1790's also in projects intended to improve transportation in the United States and in specific endeavors such as the Society for Establishing Useful Manufactures (S.U.M.), which was originally an industrial undertaking but became mired in the speculative ambitions of some of its participants. In this way capital flowed into the United States for the Union Canal, the Santee River Company, the James River Canal Company, the Bank of the United States, the Bank of North America, the real estate development of Washington, D.C., the land purchases and speculations of other Dutch firms, and many other ventures.

What had been for a time a pointedly focused path of investment fragmented. And this fragmentation continued, after a hiatus during the dismal business conjuncture in the Dutch Netherlands of 1809 to 1814. In the interim, in 1804, the Dutch firms of Hope & Co., Willink, and R. & Th. de Smeth opened a loan in Amsterdam to provide the United States with part of what it owed France for the purchase of the Louisiana Territory.[16] But the federal government did not for a long time seek money abroad, so that after the 1790's, investors had to search for opportunities across a broad front. After the Napoleonic wars the fragmentation continued, now as individual American states sought credit to finance development projects. Once again premium yields proved attractive to Dutch and other European investors, but there was considerable exaggeration in many of these projects. As Professor van Winter discovered, the Americans were free to propose whatever they wished, and many ventures partook of the wildly speculative nature of early American land transactions.[17]

Altogether, foreign investments, in which the Dutch played now a significant but no longer a leading role, were concentrated in the years 1825–40, "when, directly or indirectly, they provided more than ninety percent of the funds invested" in canal-building projects.[18] Although Dutch investment and merchant banking seem now to have become relatively passive, it is still the case that van Winter's brief epilogue remains the standard source on Dutch participation in these ventures. In the United States, state and local history has recently engaged more attention from academic historians, but many topics remain to be explored.

Nevertheless, there is no doubt that the British took an increasingly active role in economic development projects, beginning especially with London's participation in financing the Louisiana Purchase and the interest that the firm of Francis Baring & Co. took in American opportunities. More and more frequently in the 1820's and 1830's Americans turned to the London rather than the Amsterdam market. Large sums moved still from the Kingdom of the Netherlands toward the United States, although now sometimes through the intermediary of non-Dutch firms. For the sake of this essay, however, it is enough to call attention to these contacts, and to the continuing lack of detailed research on many of their aspects.[19]

But one episode in the Dutch-American financial association remains to be noticed. Once again, in a time of crisis, it was Dutch credit that led the way and provided essential assistance for a program of financial stabilization. On this occasion it was not a crisis of building but one of preserving the Union.

When the American Civil War began, neither side was prepared. The South hoped to win before the superior manpower and resources of the Union could be brought to bear, and perhaps also with foreign assistance. In 1861, however, neither combatant could count on taxation as the chief means to finance the conflict, and both turned instead to paper currency finance. This was the kind of taxation Benjamin Franklin had had in mind when he explained about the currency of the Revolutionary era that it "pays and clothes troops, and provides victuals and ammunition, and when we are obliged to issue a quantity excessive, it pays itself off by depreciation."[20]

The Union effort to finance the Civil War with domestic credit began in July 1861, when Salmon P. Chase, newly appointed Secretary of the Treasury, anticipated extraordinary expenditures of no less than $217,169,000 in a total budget just short of $320,000,000.[21] Before the end of the year, Chase found this estimate too optimistic, began a shift away from interest-bearing loans toward demand notes, and allowed, on December 30, the suspension of payments in specie by state banks. The Union government found itself in the awkward position of having to fight a costly war that was going badly at the head of a public many parts of which had little enthusiasm for the conflict. By January 1863, Congress had authorized the issue of $450 million in greenbacks, plus additional sums in fractional currency and interest-bearing paper that also circulated as legal tender.[22] Measured by gold, the greenbacks already in circulation had fallen to 69 percent of face value, and seemed likely to fall further as long as the Union's fortunes in the conflict continued to wane. And as James S. Pike, the American representative in The Hague, reported to Secretary of State William H. Seward, European distrust of American financial policies moved in harmony with the fall of prices on U.S. securities.[23]

What disturbed Europeans was the method Chase had adopted to finance the war. From the conservative financial perspective of mid-century, a paper currency means of providing revenues brought to mind such unsettling experiences as French and Austrian experiments during the revolutionary and Napoleonic wars. There was some concern with the slavery issue but, as Pike reported in February 1863, "the interest and solicitude in regard to our war is now turned almost exclusively upon its financial aspect. The opinion has become very general—almost universal—that it must soon terminate unless brought within more manageable compass and placed on a broader basis of taxation."[24]

But merely two weeks later, on February 25, Pike reported: "The money men of Holland have begun to buy our government securities."[25] It was their opinion that federal finances had bottomed out, and that Chase's new tax program would reverse the prior trend. In fact, there had been no dramatic shift in Union tax policy, but proceeds from existing levies, especially the income tax of 1861, did increase during the war. Once established, the hopeful attitude toward Union creditworthiness prevailed, and prices on American securities on the Amsterdam market began to rise with purchases, a trend duplicated in Frankfurt. For the rest of the winter, throughout the spring, and into the summer of 1863, Pike continued to report rising prices and purchases. By summer the Europeans believed also that the Union would win, since, with the battles of Gettysburg and Vicksburg, its superior resources were telling. But we should notice that they began to buy before the prospect of a Union victory was evident, before the Emancipation Proclamation, and certainly before it could be said that federal finances were secure.

Why then did the Dutch begin to buy securities which had long been available to them? On February 18 Pike reported to Seward that a cotton shortage was not developing in Europe and that European trade appeared to be unaffected by American events.[26] The South's strategy and hopes were failing. It was not the strength of the Union but the weakness of the Union's opponent that, judging from Pike's insights, reoriented Dutch thinking about federal securities. Later, early in March, Pike found an opportunity to comment further on this point: "The Dutch capitalists, unlike many of the English, have no prejudices against us, and have larger and more liberal views in regard to our resources, and belief in our ability as well as disposition to pay."[27]

It would be unrealistic to argue that Dutch, or even Dutch and German, investment in federal securities turned the tide of the war and altered the history of American political geography. Nevertheless, this reversal of investors' attitudes toward federal government securities inaugurated a series of foreign purchases which by March 1865 reached, according to Matthew Simon's estimate, £60 to £80 million.[28] And what had begun during the war continued thereafter, for European financial interest in both government securities and economic development projects grew sharply after 1865.[29] In this case, however, the Dutch lead in exploiting financial opportunities in the United States was held only briefly. Before the end of the war Britain was again dominant.

During three periods in the early history of the American republic, Dutch investments figured importantly in preserving the financial stability of this republic. Much might be made, especially in the celebration of Dutch-American ties, of ideological or political reasons for these close financial contacts. But I believe, with Professor van Winter, that it is easy to exaggerate the role of partisanship and political sympathy. It is rather in Pike's insight that we are to find the more persuasive explanation for these actions. In language reminiscent of William Short, who in an earlier day had reported to Alexander Hamilton about the attitudes and intentions of Dutch investors and bankers, Pike noticed that "Dutch capitalists, unlike many of the English, have no prejudice against us." Enlarging on this, what Pike detected was that the Dutch calculated their interests coolly. They invested in the United States in 1863 in part because they were familiar with it from earlier exposures, but in the final analysis they invested once again because they expected to make a profit. And they invested when they did because, in their calculations, federal credit seemed to have bottomed out. Eighty years earlier Pieter Stadnitski, grandson of an immigrant from Poland, had detected a taste among the Dutch for getting into new ventures earlier than their rivals. Exploiting that insight had enabled him to make his fortune. Among investors, apparently, this preference had not changed.

Throughout the period we have discussed, from the 1770's to the 1860's, financial contacts led economic contacts in the association of these two peoples. For the Dutch the financial contacts remained pre-eminent. Although at times they invested readily enough in projects for economic development of the American republic, it was chiefly financial returns that came forth from these contacts. The American market did not become in any sense a preserve of the Dutch, and in internal American development the Dutch remained largely silent rather than active partners. For the Americans, on the other hand, Dutch capital and credit had both financial and economic consequences. As we have seen, it was above all timely in its appearance, so that on three occasions governments in serious financial difficulties found those difficulties eased not so much by its magnitude as by its availability when no other recourse offered itself. This role is easily detected, for it depends on little more than the examination of American budgetary history. But the contribution of Dutch investments to American economic development remains difficult to specify. Clearly those investments contributed something at several different times to specific infrastructural improvements. Clearly also they redressed a negative trade balance, something especially noticeable around 1790 but evident also in the 1830's. On each of the three occasions they also contributed to monetary stabilization, a consequence with both financial and economic ramifications. And, finally, they also served in a general way to provide resources for economic development. But it is still not possible to establish the weight that should be attached to the role of foreign, or Dutch, investment in the economic prosperity of the United States in this era.

NOTES

1 The standard source on failed commercial expectations, as on much else in the history of the Dutch-American association from the 1770's to 1840, is Pieter J. van Winter, *American Finance and Dutch Investment, 1780–1805, with an Epilogue to 1840* (trans.; 2 vols.; New York, 1977). This is a revised version of *Het Aandeel van den Amsterdamschen Handel aan den Opbouw van het Amerikaansche Gemeenebest* (2 vols.; The Hague, 1927–33). For the period beginning in 1790 it is possible to follow Dutch-American trade, and compare it with Anglo-American trade, in *Statistical Tables Exhibiting the Commerce of the United States with European Countries from 1790 to 1890* (Washington, D.C., 1893), pp. xv, xviii, xxxiii, and xliii.

2 Julius Rubin, "An Innovating Public Improvement: The Erie Canal," in Carter Goodrich, ed., *Canals and American Economic Development* (New York, 1961), pp. 63–64, discussing the views of Vice-President Daniel Tompkins, who sought in 1817 to block passage of a bill providing financing (in part through loans to be raised abroad) for the Erie Canal. Tompkins took the view that "England will never forgive us, for our victories," so that New York should arm for war rather than help finance transportation improvements. This attitude so angered the Federalist chancellor James Kent, otherwise an opponent of the bill pending, that Kent overrode Tompkins' objections, saying: "If we must have war, or have a canal, I am in favour of the canal."

3 Consider, for example, the story Marten G. Buist recounts in so interesting a manner about the mutual association of Britain, France, and Spain to secure and distribute Mexican silver in Europe during the Napoleonic wars, in *At Spes Non Fracta: Hope & Co., 1770–1815* (The Hague, 1974), pp. 284–380.

4 These loans are discussed by S. R. Cope, "The History of Boyd, Benfield & Co.: A Study in Merchant Banking in the Last Decade of the Eighteenth Century" (Ph.D. dissertation, University of London, 1947), and Karl F. Helleiner, *The Imperial Loans: A Study in Financial and Diplomatic History* (Oxford, 1965).

5 Davis Rich Dewey, *Financial History of the United States* (12th ed.; New York, 1968 reprint), p. 35, provides these figures:

paper money issues	$37,800,000
domestic loans	11,585,506
foreign loans	7,830,517
tax revenues	5,795,000
miscellaneous	2,852,802
	$65,863,825

6   See James C. Riley, "Foreign Credit and Fiscal Stability: Dutch Invest-
ment in the United States, 1781–1794," *Journal of American History,*
LXV (December 1978), 654–78, for a summary of these matters, and van
Winter, *American Finance,* for the authoritative treatment in detail. Also
E. James Ferguson, *The Power of the Purse* (Chapel Hill, N.C., 1961).

7   *Report of the Secretary of the Treasury on the State of the Finances for
the Year 1867* (Washington, D.C., 1868), pp. 356–59.

8   Riley, "Foreign Credit," p. 678.

9   Pieter Stadnitski, a merchant and broker, investigated opportunities in
America, and reported optimistically in two pamphlets, *Ophelderend
bericht wegens het fonds, genaamd Liquidated Debt, of vereffende
schulden, ten laste de Vereenigde Staaten* . . . and *Omtrent de natuur
en soliditeit van welk fonds de directeur Pieter Stadnitski een omstandig
bericht gegeeven heeft,* both lacking place or date of publication. I believe the first appeared in 1787.

10   The fullest and most recent discussions of these matters appear in Johan
de Vries, *De Economische Achteruitgang der Republiek in de Achttiende
Eeuw* (2nd ed.; Leiden, 1968), *passim;* A. M. van der Woude, "Demogra-
fische Ontwikkeling van de Noordelijke Nederlanden, 1500–1800," in
Algemene Geschiedenis der Nederlanden, ed. D. P. Blok et al. (Haarlem,
1980), V and J. A. Faber, "De Noordelijke Nederlanden van 1480 tot
1780: Structuren en Beweging," in *ibid.,* V, 197–249.

11   P. W. Klein, "The Dutch Regents and the Changes of the Economic Bases
of Their Power in the 17th and 18th Century," an unpublished paper
given at the Istituto Internazionale di Storia Economica in Prato, April
21, 1980, p. 3.

12   See my "The Dutch Economy after 1650: Decline or Growth?," forthcoming in the *Journal of European Economic History.*

13   Riley, "Foreign Credit," pp. 671–77.

14   Trade flows may be followed in Douglass C. North, "The United States
Balance of Payments, 1790–1860," in *Trends in the American Economy
in the Nineteenth Century* (Princeton, N.J., 1960), pp. 576–79, 587–601.
Some of North's estimates can now be updated with data on flows between the United States and the Dutch Netherlands.

15   In addition to van Winter, *American Finance,* see Paul D. Evans, *The
Holland Land Company* (Buffalo, N.Y., 1924), and, among published
documents, "The Holland Land Company and Canal Construction in
Western New York . . . ," *Buffalo Historical Society Publications,* XIV
(1910), 3–185.

16   Van Winter, *American Finance,* II, 923 ff.; van Winter, "Louisiana
Gekocht en Betaald," *Bijdragen en Mededelingen van het Historisch*

Genootschap, LXXV (1961), 37–55; and van Winter, "De Verkoop van Louisiana," *Tijdschrift voor Geschiedenis*, XLVII (1932), 41–61. Slightly more than half of the financing for the Louisiana Purchase was arranged in London, although the Dutch bought into that also.

17 Van Winter, *American Finance*, II, 940–93, and Harvey H. Segal, "Cycles of Canal Construction," in Goodrich, ed., *Canals and American Economic Development*, pp. 179–81, 186–92.

18 Segal, "Cycles," p. 180.

19 However, see Reginald C. McGrane, *Foreign Bondholders and American State Debts* (New York, 1935), pp. 10–11, 31–34, 151, 171–75, 185–86, on Dutch interests in the United States during the 1830's and 1840's, and *passim* on foreign interests in general; and B. U. Ratchford, *American State Debts* (Durham, N.C., 1941), pp. 92–95.

20 Quoted by Joseph Albert Ernst, "Currency in the Era of the American Revolution: A History of Colonial Paper Money Practices and British Monetary Policies, 1764–1781" (Ph.D. dissertation, University of Wisconsin, 1962), p. 398.

21 Dewey, *Financial History*, p. 276.

22 *Ibid.*, pp. 288–89.

23 I have consulted the Pike-Seward correspondence of December 1862 through July 1863 reproduced in U.S. Department of State, *Papers Relating to Foreign Affairs of the United States*, Diplomatic Correspondence, 1863 (Washington, D.C., 1864), II, 878–97.

24 *Ibid.*, II, 884.

25 *Ibid.*, II, 886.

26 *Ibid.*, II, 885–86.

27 *Ibid.*, II, 888.

28 Matthew Simon, "Cyclical Fluctuations and the International Capital Movements of the United States, 1865–1897" (Ph.D. dissertation, Columbia University, 1955), I, 88, and II, 684–87.

29 *Ibid.*, I, 122–23, 127.

An Act without Peer

The Marshall Plan in American-Dutch Relations

· 𝕮𝕏𝕏𝕊𝕺 ·

E. H. VAN DER BEUGEL

O N June 5, 1947, during a commencement speech at Harvard University, Secretary of State George Marshall launched the European Recovery Program, rightly and better known as the Marshall Plan.

On April 13, 1948, President Truman signed the Foreign Assistance Act, the legal embodiment of the Marshall Plan.[1]

On April 20, 1948, *The Economist* wrote:

> This week it is fitting that the people of Western Europe should renew their capacity for wonder, so that they can return to the U.S. a gratitude in some way commensurate with the act they are about to receive. For a day or two, the Marshall Plan must be retrieved from the realm of normal day-to-day developments in international affairs and be seen for what it is —an act without peer in history.

I will deal with my subject in three parts.

   I. The political framework in which this act was conceived, with special emphasis on the American perspective.
  II. The impact of the Marshall Plan on the process of European cooperation.
 III. The impact of the Plan on the Netherlands, on American-Dutch relations, and some aspects of the role of the Netherlands in the execution of the Plan.

I

The attack on Pearl Harbor in December 1941 terminated 150 years of American isolationism. The future of the United States became inextricably bound with every part of the globe. Isolationism disappeared both as an option and as a philosophy for the conduct of American foreign policy. Many elements of traditional U.S. foreign policy, however, remained in the attitude with which the United States conducted the war, in its policy at the meetings of the Big Three, and in the way it emerged from the war in 1945. It seems to me that in the period from 1945 till the launching of the Marshall plan in 1947, the change in American foreign policy was more radical than what the shock of Pearl Harbor brought about in 1941.

The policy with which the United States emerged from World War II as a country with a monopoly of political, economic, and military strength was based on the assumption that the wartime alliance between the United States, the United Kingdom, and the Soviet Union would provide the basis of the postwar order. The United Nations would be the guardian of peace. Peace treaties would be concluded with the former enemy states. The world economic order would be restored after an initial period of readjustment. Thereafter, the Bretton Woods institutions and the proposed International Trade Organization would be instrumental in settling worldwide economic problems and in guaranteeing a free flow of trade and finance. The U.S. armed forces would be demobilized to an extent compatible with a normalized world situation.

This was in no way an isolationist program; on the contrary, this program required the full and active participation of the United States on an unprecedented scale. There was an almost pathetic urge to avoid the errors of 1919 and a repetition of political and economic events leading to World War II. On the other hand, there remained a strong urge to return to "normalcy." "The U.S. attempted to remedy the old mistakes of 1919 rather than assess the new problems of 1945."[2] The main remnant of traditional American foreign policy was the deep reluctance to use power in peacetime and in particular unilateral American power.

Between 1945 and 1947, the hopes of the United States for the postwar order were shattered, mainly by a combination of two factors: the collapse of its overoptimistic assessment of the nature of Soviet foreign policy and its underestimation of the near-total collapse of the political, economic, and social structure of most European countries.

> For decades massive historical caravans had been observed moving slowly towards predictable destinations; Great Britain towards loss of Empire and inability to maintain the balance of power in Europe and order in Asia; Western Continental Europe toward instability and weakness; the United States toward economic and military preeminence in political isolation; and the Soviet Union towards a fundamental challenge of Western civilization.[3]

1. As to the first element—the wrong assessment of the nature of Soviet foreign policy—an analysis of the origins of the Cold War would reach beyond the context of this article. Just a few comments on this subject, so closely linked with the concept of the Marshall Plan.

The revisionist school in American history has—it seems to me— one and only one positive element. It forced us to rethink what might have become too easy clichés. For all the rest, I fully agree with Maddox's brilliant analysis of the work of the main revisionist authors and his conclusion that their view of American foreign policy during and immediately after World War II can only be sustained by doing violence to the historical record.[4] I also find myself in complete agreement with Arthur Schlesinger's conclusion that the most rational American policies could hardly have averted the Cold War.[5]

The events leading to the "great revolution" in American foreign policy between 1945 and 1947 are varied and in most cases particular to certain regions and countries. Iran, Greece, Turkey, and Poland are significant examples. What these events had in common was that they showed Soviet policies and actions to be the opposite of what the United States expected and hoped for. They were, however, over-shadowed in importance by the total impossibility of reaching any agreement between the superpowers on the administration and the future of occupied Germany. Varied and particular as these events may be, they led the United States to the conclusion that it had to give up its hope for global stability and peace-keeping through the United Nations. It felt obliged to adopt an active unilateral policy—if necessary a policy of force—to contain the expansionist policies of the Soviet Union.

2. As to the second element leading to the 1947 policy—the threatening economic and social collapse of Europe—the prewar European economic pattern was nearly destroyed by the war.

a. Physical devastation and disruption in Western Europe and in the principal food- and timber-producing zones of Eastern Europe, combined with the dislocation of the European transportation system, caused a paralysis of production.

b. Wartime liquidation of foreign holdings, prolonged interruption of international trade which occurred simultaneously with the loss of income from merchant fleets and foreign investments, led to the exhaustion or diminution of dollar funds at a time when many vital needs could be met only from dollar funds.

c. The loss of millions of lives, human strain and exhaustion after nearly six years of war and enemy occupation, gravely affected the productivity of labor.

d. Internal financial disequilibrium, the inevitable result of a long war, upset the monetary stability of almost all European countries.

e. A grave shortage in the supply of food and raw materials that were vital to the European economy, both for direct consumption and as earners of dollars, existed in Southeast Asia.

f. There was an abnormal increase in population in certain areas resulting from the wartime movement of people.

It was against this background that the Truman Doctrine and the Marshall Plan were born. The policy was formulated by President Truman when he said in his message to Congress on March 12, 1947: "I believe that it must be the policy of the United States to support free peoples who are resisting attempted subjugation by armed minorities or by outside pressures." The Truman Doctrine constituted the political-military tool of the new American policy; the Marshall Plan was its main political-economic instrument.

A relatively short period of preparation by a supremely capable and imaginative group in Washington, with star performers like Acheson, Bonesteel, Kennan, Clayton, Lovett, and Harriman, enabled Secretary Marshall to make his historic speech at Harvard on June 5, 1947. In his speech one can clearly define two objectives. One was the economic rehabilitation and reconstruction of Europe. The second was to use American aid to foster, advance, and promote European cooperation.

I would like to conclude this first part of my introduction with two rather loosely connected comments.

1. Historically, it might be interesting to observe that Secretary Marshall extended his offer of American aid to the whole of Europe, including the Soviet Union. But at a meeting with France and the United Kingdom in June 1947, where the American initiative and the possible European response were discussed, Molotov not only flatly refused Soviet participation but pressed the Poles and the Czechs, who had already decided to respond positively to the American initiative, to cancel their acceptances. The Iron Curtain runs exactly along the line between those countries that participated in the Marshall plan and those that did not, either by their own decision or under pressure from the Soviet Union (with the exception of Spain, which was not invited).

The tragic events in Poland have given rise to a totally distorted picture of the Yalta Conference. The Iron Curtain was not established in Yalta. Poland was not "assigned" to the Soviet Union in February 1945. On the contrary, one of the main bones of contention between the United States and the Soviet Union after Yalta was the way in which the Soviet Union flagrantly broke the agreement on Poland after the Yalta Conference.[6]

2. In the presently fashionable exercise of debunking American foreign policy, it is often stated that the Marshall Plan was launched only because of American self-interest. In general this is an absurd argument. No country and certainly no major country can conduct a foreign policy which is not based on self-interest. The only relevant question is whether the interpretation of self-interest is narrow, egoistic, and geared only to short-term interest or whether the interpretation of self-interest is long-term, imaginative, and constructive. Whereas the first interpretation—the narrow one—was adopted by the European powers in the late 1930's, the Marshall Plan, it seems to me, was a shining example of constructive and imaginative self-interest.

It was in the clear interest of the United States to help Western Europe to become strong again both for economic and for political reasons. But there also was a genuine element of generosity. Let me just quote a paragraph from the report of the Herter committee, the most important congressional committee, recommending the adoption of the Foreign Assistance Act in 1948:

> If we undertake the proposed European Recovery Program we are in effect assuming the responsibility for the revival of Western Europe. Responsibility without power is a situation generally avoided by cautious people. But the alternative in terms of human lives, misery and slavery is perhaps too frightful to permit us the luxury of being cautious. We can only hope that the nations of Western Europe, who have the power over their economic destinies, will themselves realize the responsibilities of their predicament and by actively cooperating with each other, help themselves.[7]

II

The launching of the Marshall Plan initiated a priority in American foreign policy which would be consistently sustained for at least twenty years. Its central theme, supported by five administrations, both Democratic and Republican, was the active support for European unification. Secretary Marshall formulated this priority in his Harvard speech: "The program should be a joint one, agreed by a number of, if not all European nations." This was a muted statement compared to the depth of political and psychological feeling about the subject in American public opinion.

American thinking on the necessity of greater European cohesion was still in its infancy in 1948. Unity, unification, federation, integration, self-help, and mutual efforts were different and sometimes loose terms to express the same objective. This objective, however, was clear and it was there to stay as an integral part of U.S. foreign policy, supported not only by several administrations but also by a broad consensus in public opinion.

Even before the Marshall Plan was launched (during the congressional discussions on aid to Greece and Turkey in March 1947) the Senate adopted the following resolution:

> Resolved by the Senate (the House of Representatives concurring) that the Congress favors the creation of a United States of Europe.[8]

Practically without exception the media all over the country joined the Congress. A few examples:

> Like the famous advice Benjamin Franklin gave to the American colonies, for Europe it is a case of join—or die. (St. Louis *Post-Dispatch*, March 16, 1947.)

> Europe's unification is Europe's last chance. (*Wall Street Journal*, February 3, 1947.)

> Above all the U.S. out of her own wonderful experience of the Union of the States should support a European federation plan. Victory must be translated into new life and that means a continental modern, political, social and economic system. (Dorothy Thompson in the Washington *Star*, February 11, 1947.)

> A United States of Europe could be the means of restoring a decent living to the part of Europe which represents the civilization of which we are a part. It may prove to be the only means. (Miami *Herald*, March 27, 1947.)

> But it is only too true, as statesmen have said so often in one way or another, that Europe must federate or perish. (Editorial, New York *Times*, April 18, 1947.)

> Only a federation holds forth hope of permanent peace and economic well-being in Europe. (Evansville *Courier and Press*, May 18, 1947.)

> The people in the ruins of Europe can take heart from the perils that beset Americans in 1787. (Buffalo *News*, May 22, 1947.)

Historically it is rare for a major power to make the creation of another major power one of its central foreign policy objectives. It is the reverse of the more common maxim of *"Divide et impera."* Without the Marshall Plan no OECD; without OECD no Schumann Plan; without the Schumann Plan no European Community. The process of European cooperation and integration, notwithstanding its slowness and its weakness and notwithstanding its structural and fundamental obstacles, would have been impossible without the active and full support of more than twenty years of American foreign policy, started with the conditions of the Marshall Plan on the issue of greater cohesion of the European countries.

The legitimate question arises concerning the motives behind this

The Marshall Plan—cartoon by Jo Spier (1900–1978)

very outspoken and consistent American policy. The motives were, it seems to me, a mixed bag.

There was the political judgment that only a strong and unified Europe could resist Communist internal and external pressures.

There existed a deep irritation about the fragmentation of the European nations, which had brought the United States twice into a world war.

There was the economic concept of the large, single market which in American eyes was indispensable for a better division of labor and a higher standard of living.

There existed a genuine desire to transplant the blessings of the continent-sized, politically and economically unified state to the old mother countries with which the average American felt close sentimental bonds.

There also were more trivial but very understandable motives— for example, the U.S. administrations had to deal with many different interests and national problems and were desirous of replacing these endless and complicated negotiations with dealings with a single and strong partner.

These were the general motives behind the policy to support and foster European cohesion. There was, however, one particular problem which strongly preoccupied the American policy makers: how to bring Germany back into the Western system.

As early as January 1947, John Foster Dulles, who was the Republican special adviser to Secretary Marshall, expressed the basic elements of this preoccupation. Without the reconstruction of German economic potential there could not be recovery in Europe. Reconstruction in Germany implied unification of the Western Zones of Occupation. But unification of the Western Zones implied unification of Europe. A German settlement should advance European unification, instead of rebuilding the structure of independent, unconnected sovereignties. The industrial potential of Germany should be integrated into Western Europe. It should not be left in the control of Germany. A statesmanlike solution to this political and economic problem, providing safety against German aggression and a more stable and prosperous life for the people in Western Europe, was a positive alternative to the Potsdam policy of imposed pastoralization.[9] "Not only Germans but neighboring people will eventually rebel at trying to cover with manure the natural industrial basis of Europe."[10]

The German problem was aggravated by the huge sums the U.S. occupation authorities had to pump into their zone in order to avoid total chaos and by the subsequent pressure to deal unilaterally with the German problem. The concept of large-scale aid to a unifying Europe solved the dilemma between a bilateral support for the

American Zone, which both domestically and internationally was hardly acceptable, and a complete collapse of the center of Europe.

I find myself in full agreement with John Gimbel when he stresses the vital importance of the German problem from the American perspective in 1947.[11]

In the context of American-Dutch relations it is worthwhile to observe that in all these objectives the United States found a staunch and loyal ally in the Netherlands, not only as the recipient of aid (there the Dutch were as a matter of course no exception) but very strongly in the concept of European integration in general and the solution of the German problem in particular.

III

Under the Marshall Plan, the Netherlands was the recipient of more than $1.1 billion (and those were 1947 dollars). It was the fifth-largest recipient (after Britain, France, Italy, and West Germany). It received the largest amount of aid per capita. After a hesitant start on the repair of the almost unbelievable war damage to the country in 1945, it became clear in the winter of 1946–47 that the reconstruction had to be slowed down or even stopped because of the total absence of foreign currency in general and dollars in particular to finance the vital imports. Only a massive injection of dollars could prevent a sliding back to economic misery.

The Marshall Plan was the dream and the dream came true. Reconstruction could be not only resumed but accelerated through the combination of direct aid to the country and the liberalization of trade and payments in Europe for which Marshall Plan aid was an indispensable condition. Marshall Plan aid laid the foundation for a new industrialization that was essential for the densely populated Holland; it vitally contributed to the repair of the war damage; it was indispensable for the restoration of financial and social stability; it enabled the country to resume its place in international trade, on which it was dependent more than any other European country; it brought its balance of payments into equilibrium; it heavily contributed to the restoration of the exhausted monetary reserves. For those who are interested in the quantification of these observations, I recommend the excellent book published by the Netherlands government as a token of gratitude to the American people.[12]

Allow me to draw attention to what I consider an important and underexposed facet of the execution of the Marshall Plan.

Heavy demands were made on the hundreds of Americans who worked in Europe to supervise the execution of the Plan. They were primarily responsible for what happened to the enormous amounts granted under the aid program; they were responsible to Washington in all its executive and congressional branches. In addition, they were the people who in the countries concerned suddenly would be involved in a vital item of economic recovery and in such a way that they were simply the donors and we were simply the receivers: givers from a sovereign state versus receivers from a sovereign state. Their American responsibility brought them in touch with and made them co-responsible for almost every aspect of the economic, monetary, and social policies of the receiving countries. That also implied an understanding of the political situation in the country to which they were assigned.

This was totally different from our relation to traditional diplomatic representatives. It was not merely a mediating, listening, and reporting function. On the contrary, the Americans found themselves right in the middle of policy making, in spheres which belonged to the privacy of national sovereignty. What an opportunity for giving rise to conflicts, not only in the personal sphere but mainly in the relations between states! One unfortunate word, and it could be regarded as interfering in the business of a sovereign state. One word left unspoken, and it could endanger the responsibility toward the U.S. government. Authoritarian action could bring the reproach that "we do not want any proconsuls"; being too compliant could bring a complaint of slackness from the other side of the ocean. On the one hand, the irritation toward a donor, who in the nature of things is never popular, had to be avoided; on the other hand, one had to take into account that "the U.S. taxpayer's money may never be thrown away." What were needed, therefore, were people who possessed not only first-rate diplomatic qualities but at the same time an extensive knowledge of economics; people who combined wisdom and tactfulness with sufficient toughness and the ability to negotiate. They were the outposts of the new role of the United States in the world. On their behavior mainly depended whether that new and indispensable connection between the western and eastern parts of the Free World could be established and maintained.

Above all, they had to be conscious of the fact that this was not a matter of one bestowing a gift with a royal but dominating gesture and the other accepting timidly and thankfully. The fundamental principle of the Marshall Plan was something far beyond this. It was a joint attempt, a joint venture.

Washington of 1948 succeeded exceptionally well in creating a team which possessed the extraordinary combination of all the needed qualities. The Marshall Plan undoubtedly stirred the public imagination, which helped recruiting. But another reason for the quality of the team was that enviable American flexibility which facilitated the smooth flow of personnel from industry, universities, media, and trade unions to government posts and vice versa. Very few top functions were manned by what one could call the "professional civil servant."

It should go on record that, considering the delicate nature of the task (and I especially refer to the Netherlands), our cooperation has always been characterized by frankness, an ever-growing understanding of our mutual problems, and, from the American side, undivided support for everything which could benefit the Netherlands. It has seldom been the case that foreign representatives had to acquire such complete insight into virtually all aspects of the economic position of the country in which they were serving. There was no end to details which they could demand, indeed had to demand, to be able to perform their duties. The Netherlands has been privileged to welcome Dr. Alan Valentine and Clarence Hunter as chiefs of the ECA mission. Both men have left an unmistakably personal mark on their work. Both, together with their staffs, were constantly in close touch with all branches of economic and political life in the Netherlands. Both have understood this country.

The United States was a generous giver; the Netherlands was an easy and constructive receiver. On all major points there was a great affinity between American and Dutch attitudes. There are—taking into account the huge differences between a major and leading power and a small or medium-sized ally—clear analogies between the historical backgrounds of their conduct and their concept of foreign policy. Both have a tendency to a moralistic approach to foreign policy; both have a missionary drive in their relations with foreign countries; both have a reluctance to employ the element of power in foreign policy; both often confuse the obtainable and the desirable; both had periods in their history when they thought they were too good for the world and other periods when they thought they were too bad.

When Secretary of State Cordell Hull reported to Congress on the Moscow meeting of the three Foreign Ministers and the Moscow declaration of October 1943, he said that "in the post-war period there would be no longer any need for spheres of influence, for alliances, for balance of power or any other of the special arrangements through which, in the unhappy past, the nations strove to safeguard their security or to promote their interests.[13] This "one world" concept without alliances and with the United Nations as the sole guardian of peace was exactly the world in which the Netherlands felt itself at home. Both countries emerged from the war with the same approach to the postwar world order. There was a complete parallel between the changes which took place in the United States between 1945 and 1947 and the turn Dutch foreign policy took in the same period.

After 1947 the United States found Holland at its side both in its urge for greater European cooperation and in the solution to the German problem. In the Committee for European Economic Cooperation (the informal predecessor of the OECD), Holland was among the first in line to defend both issues, aided by the outstanding qualities of its main representatives in the committee, Dr. H. M. Hirschfeld and D. P. Spierenburg, and of course motivated by what it conceived as its interest. Historically, the violent discussions in the hot summer of 1947 in Paris between the Dutch and the French on the German issue are most interesting for a study of the period.

Are there any conclusions to be drawn? A few.

The first is that the Marshall Plan cannot be repeated. The United States' position has fundamentally changed. It is no longer the undisputed and sole source of strength, of political and economic power. It only has two traditions in its foreign policy: one is splendid isolation and one is benevolent hegemony. Both traditions simplified the world outside the United States. It now has to conduct its foreign policy in an immensely complicated world without being able to fall back on either of these traditions.

The Marshall Plan was a typical example of the period of benevolent hegemony. Furthermore, the Marshall Plan could succeed only in the specific area of the world—Western Europe—in which the human, social, financial, and educational infrastructure was uniquely suited to receive the massive injection of aid and use it successfully.

The second conclusion is that it would be understandable but unhelpful nostalgia to hope that anything like the very special circumstances of 1947 could reoccur. The world has fundamentally changed. The United States—still a superpower—has lost its pre-eminence in the economic, military, and political fields. In East-West relations superiority has been at best replaced by parity.

The tenacity of the nation-state proved to be much greater than those who dreamed about European unity in the fifties and the sixties expected. The welfare state—the *"état providence"*—is a national animal and the nation-state has become, more than we expected, the natural framework of loyalty and dependence of the average citizen.

The North-South issue is, if not preponderant, at least a major factor in international relations.

The near-consensus about the main elements of foreign and domestic policy from the fifties and the sixties in the policy-making establishment has broken down.

It would be unrealistic to hope again for a stable and structured Western world built on two pillars—the United States of America and the United States of Europe. The maximum we can achieve and hope for is what Miriam Camps has called a reasonable management of interdependence.[14]

Finally, in American-Dutch relations the two main questions are whether in the United States wisdom and long-term interest will prevail over fully understandable short-term irritation, and in the Netherlands whether sensible and active participation in the Western system will prevail over an irrelevant neutralist-pacifist tendency, so intimately linked to our history.

Nostalgia is neither a political nor a historical category. I feel it, however, when I think of 1947.

NOTES

1 Full texts of both are in *In Quest of Peace and Security: Selected Documents on American Foreign Policy, 1941–1951* (Department of State Publication 4245, 1951).

2 Barbara Ward, *The West at Bay* (London, 1948), p. 85.

3 Joseph M. Jones, *The Fifteen Weeks* (New York, 1955), p. 9.

4 R. J. Maddox, *The New Left and the Origins of the Cold War* (Princeton, N.J., 1973), p. 164.

5 Arthur Schlesinger, "The Origins of the Cold War," *Foreign Affairs*, XLVI (October 1967), 52.

6 See, among others, M. C. Brands's excellent analysis of the Yalta Conference in *NRC Handelsblad*, January 13, 1982.

7 *What Western Europe Can Do for Itself*, Preliminary Report No. 14 of the House Select Committee on Foreign Aid, February 13, 1948.

8 *Congressional Record*, 80th Congress 1st session, pp. 2418, 2425.

9 John C. Campbell, *The United States in World Affairs, 1945–1947* (New York, 1947), p. 471.

10 *Ibid.*

11 John Gimbel, *The Origins of the Marshall Plan* (Stanford, Calif., 1976), pp. 267–80.

12 *Road to Recovery: The Marshall Plan, Its Importance for the Netherlands and European Cooperation* (The Hague, 1954).

13 Campbell, *The United States in World Affairs*, p. 28.

14 Miriam Camps, *The Management of Interdependence* (Washington, D.C., 1974).

ADDITIONAL REFERENCES

ACHESON, Dean. *Present at the Creation.* New York, 1969.

ARKES, Hadley. *Bureaucracy, the Marshall Plan and the National Interest.* Princeton, N.J., 1972.

BELOF, Max. *The United States and the Unity of Europe.* Washington, D.C., 1963.

VAN DER BEUGEL, Ernst H. *From Marshall Plan to Atlantic Partnership*. Amsterdam and New York, 1966.

BROWN, William Adams, Jr., and Redvers Opie. *American Foreign Assistance*. Washington, D.C., 1953.

DIEBOLD, William, Jr. *Trade and Payments in Western Europe: A Study in Economic Cooperation, 1947–1951*. New York, 1952.

"EUROPEAN and Atlantic Cooperation: The Dutch Attitude," special issue of *International Spectator* (The Hague, April 1965).

FERRELL, Robert H. *George C. Marshall*. New York, 1966.

DE FEYTER, C. A. "The Selling of an Ideology," in Rob Kroes, ed., *Image and Impact: American Influences in the Netherlands since 1945*. Amsterdam, 1981.

GARWOOD, Ellen Clayton. *Will Clayton: A Short Biography*. Austin, Tex., 1958.

HARRIS, Seymour E. *The European Recovery Program*. Cambridge, Mass., 1948.

HOFFMAN, Paul G. *Peace Can Be Won*. Garden City, N.Y., 1951.

JENKINS, Roy. "The Marshall Plan Memorial Lecture June 3, 1977." German Marshall Fund, 1977.

KENNAN, George F. *American Diplomacy, 1900–1950*. Chicago, 1951.

OECD. *From Marshall Plan to Global Interdependence*. OECD, 1978.

PRICE, Harry Bayard. *The Marshall Plan and Its Meaning*. Ithaca, N.Y., 1955.

TRUMAN, Harry S. *The Memoirs of Harry S. Truman*. 2 vols.; Garden City, N.Y., 1955–56.

VANDENBERG, Arthur H., Jr. *The Private Papers of Senator Vandenberg*. Boston, 1952.

WHITE, Theodore H. *Fire in the Ashes: Europe in Mid-Century*. New York, 1953.

WILSON, Theodore A. *The Marshall Plan, 1947–1951*. Washington, D.C., 1977.

American-Dutch Political Relations since 1945

What Has Changed and Why?

· ⬥⬥⬥ ·

ALFRED VAN STADEN

AN account of the evolution of the political relations between the United States and the Netherlands since World War II is much like the story of two disappointed lovers making a sentimental journey. To be sure, at this moment, both partners are still together, tied by undeniable military and economic bonds, but the former marriage of the heart has broken down and turned into one of convenience, if not a case of living-apart-together. Indeed, mutual feelings of solidarity and attachment have weakened and given way to coolness and reproaches to and fro. Looking at recent, sharp disputes on important security issues, one is almost tempted to think—not for the children's sake but out of a desire not to besmirch the parents' memory—the two parties have decided not to part. Of course, the American-Dutch estrangement, grown since the late sixties and particularly perceptible at the level of political opinion leaders, is being muted and disguised by the polished language of official diplomacy. Nevertheless, it is but too real and, I venture to say, potentially dangerous for the future relationship between both countries.

It is the purpose of my lecture to explore the nature and dimensions of the changes which have taken place, as well as to shed some light on their causes. At the outset I must make two preliminary points. First, the subject under discussion has a built-in imbalance of some sort. Postwar U.S.-Dutch political relations are inherently asymmetric, because they are about the interactions of a superpower and a small country. Nobody would argue the contrary. This means, among other things, that what is important or even vital from a Dutch point of view may be rather marginal or insignificant in American eyes. Second, as I was born, bred, and socialized in Holland, the perspective of my observations is inevitably a Dutch one, and rather than deal with

American attitudes toward the Netherlands, I shall concentrate on Dutch attitudes toward the United States.

Let me take your minds back to the international situation just after the end of the war. Both nations were on the threshold of a fundamental change in their external orientation, breaking with established and at the same time cherished, prewar foreign policies, which, incidentally, bear a striking similarity. The leading themes of those policies, isolationism on the one hand and neutrality on the other, share a common aversion to entangling alliances. And just as American isolationism was not a total abstinence from world affairs, Dutch neutrality did not preclude an active involvement in matters of international trade and finance or travel and humanitarian concern.

Both concepts were no longer considered to be viable policy options in 1945, even though the forces of isolationism were still surprisingly strong in the United States. Because of its crucial role in the liberation of Western Europe and, afterward, its large-scale economic assistance through the Marshall Plan, the United States enjoyed a tremendous popularity in Dutch society. Nevertheless, in the immediate postwar period, political relations between the United States and the Netherlands were not particularly close and cordial. One reason lies in the divergent approaches of both countries to building a new international system. It seems worth dwelling awhile on this point.

As early as the war years, the Dutch government had repeatedly spoken of the need for political and military cooperation with powerful and like-minded countries once the war was over. There is no doubt that the government was thinking first and foremost of Great Britain and the United States. Thus, in May 1942, Foreign Minister van Kleffens, having reflected on the foundations of a postwar world order, submitted a plan to his Norwegian and Belgian colleagues, Lie and Spaak, for the formation of regional security organizations unifying all non-aggressive states and to be led by those Western powers.[1] In late 1943, speaking before a BBC microphone, he outlined the idea of a Western bloc with North America and the Dominions as the arsenal, Great Britain as the base, and Western Europe (France, Belgium, and the Netherlands) as bridgehead.[2]

Since the permanent involvement of the United States in European security affairs was a main feature of van Kleffens' suggestions, the reaction on the part of the American administration was naturally essential. During his visit to the United States in the summer of 1942 and after (by the way, American-Dutch diplomatic relations had been elevated to the level of ambassadors; as a matter of fact, the United States was the first country to grant the Netherlands this honor![3]), the Dutch Foreign Minister discussed the idea of regional security organizations with Secretary of State Cordell Hull and his deputy, Sumner

Welles. Both Americans agreed to the principle of Atlantic cooperation, but clearly refused to commit themselves. They promised to have
van Kleffens' scheme studied and worked out by panels in the State
Department and the War Department.

I would certainly strain historical truth if I suggested here that
the exercise started by this produced a noticeable effect on the planning
of postwar American foreign policy. As the war continued Washington
joined London in the latter's outspoken preference for a more exclusive
approach to the building of a new world. It supported the so-called
Four Power Plan, basically meaning that the four Great Powers (the
United States, the Soviet Union, China, and Great Britain) had to
arrive in concert at common proposals prior to consulting other
governments. As a result, small nations such as Holland were to lose
any substantial influence upon important postwar blueprints such as
the framework of the United Nations Charter. Nor were they able to
place their marks on the United Nations Relief and Rehabilitation
Administration,[4] which was created in 1943 and functioned until 1947.

The initial American enthusiasm for a system of collective security
within the UN framework put the Dutch government in a difficult
position. At the end of the war, it was still strongly in favor of a
security policy based on an alliance with the other democratic
countries of Western Europe and it also wanted the United States
to be involved in the protection of the Old World. Van Kleffens, in
particular, considered it of the utmost importance that no policy
should be pursued which might alienate the United States from
Europe. The Dutch government was not in a position, however, to
make the American administration change its mind on its predilection
for the new world organization. Moreover, it feared that by pushing
too hard in the direction of an alliance in Western Europe, an isolationist backlash might be produced in America. So, in spite of its own
inclinations toward a regional security arrangement, backed up by the
United States, the Netherlands—at least for the time being—could not
but base its security policy on the international cooperation that was
supposed to take shape in the United Nations.[5]

As it happened, this policy, born of necessity, was in several ways
rationalized by the Dutch government. For one thing, Soviet ambitions
in Eastern Europe were being played down. Thus, for example, in
November 1945, van Kleffens tried to reassure members of the Dutch
Parliament by saying: "I am able to state that the government of
Russia by no means harbors imperialist ambitions but that it is trying
in its own way to ensure its security."[6] For another, the dangers of
the formation of blocs were suddenly emphasized. It was suggested
on several occasions that the creation of an alliance might provoke

the Russians to mold a counter-coalition, as well as damage cooperation on a global scale and cause international tensions.[7]

Let me now return to my starting point. There is another and
probably more important reason why the political relations between
the United States and Holland were not particularly close in the first
years after the war. This reason relates, of course, to disagreements on
the ongoing struggle for independence in Indonesia. Those disagreements were very profound indeed and gave rise to bitter explosions in
Holland against what was regarded as undue American interference.
At first, though, American policy with regard to the acrimonious
conflict between the Dutch and the Indonesian nationalists had been
one of hands off. But in June 1947, when alarming reports on the
situation in the Netherlands East Indies were reaching the State
Department from Batavia, the United States concluded that the time
had come for a more active participation in Indonesian affairs.[8]

In light of American anti-colonial traditions and in view of
widespread sympathies in Congress for the cause of Indonesian
nationalism, it was very hard, if not impossible, for the U.S. government to take the Dutch side in the escalating conflict. In addition, the
Cold War having broken out, this very conflict had become a function
of East-West rivalries, and for fear of driving them into the arms of
Moscow, America did not want to antagonize the forces of nationalism
in Asia and the Middle East. Especially after the prompt suppression
of the Communist rebellion at Madiun, in September 1948, the
Indonesian nationalist movement was perceived by the United States
as a bulwark against the rising tide of international Bolshevism. From
this point of time, American-Dutch relations became outrightly
strained, reaching their nadir during and just after the second Dutch
police action of December 1948. The United States was among those
who sharply critized this action.

In the same month that the Indonesian nationalists crushed their
Communist countrymen, the new Dutch Foreign Minister, Dirk U.
Stikker, had an interview with Secretary of State George Marshall.
Stikker was given a cold reception by Marshall. He had been plainly
given to understand that there would be no American support whatsoever for the Dutch. They were expected to confer independence on
the Indonesian population on short notice, and, on top of it, the
Republic of Indonesia was to get American help. In his memoirs,
Stikker indulges in bursts of collective self-pity over Marshall's snub.
He reminds us of the Battle of the Java Sea (February 1942), in which
the Dutch fought shoulder to shoulder with the United States (and
for that matter Britain too) against the Japanese navy, and accuses
the Americans of showing a "we know better" or "holier than thou"

attitude.[9] (It is ironic, at the least, that the same notes are now being struck on the other side of the Atlantic.)

Resentment on the part of large sections of the Dutch population grew as the Americans decided to apply pressure. Immediately after the beginning of the second police action, Marshall aid for Indonesia was cut short. The United States even threatened to withhold the weapons needed by the Dutch for their contribution to the Western defense system, as provided for by the Treaty of Brussels.[10] In March 1949, one year after the signing of this treaty and only shortly before the signing of the North Atlantic Treaty in Washington, Stikker, who happened to be in Paris for a meeting of the Organization for European Economic Cooperation, received an official call by Averell Harriman. The latter, acting under instructions from the State Department, made it perfectly clear that the United States, while prepared to create an Atlantic alliance and to give military aid to its future allies, would not be willing to give such aid to allies such as the Netherlands, as long as they had not solved their colonial difficulties.

Stikker's testimony on this important new development is most surprising. He claims that had he explained the American attitude to the Dutch Parliament (either in public session or in private committee meetings), Holland would not have joined NATO. He, therefore, decided to see the party leaders individually. They agreed that if the Americans were to withdraw their threat before the signing of the North Atlantic Treaty in early April, they would probably be willing to vote in favor of ratification.[11] There is reason to call Stikker's assessment into question with respect to the likelihood that the Netherlands might not have entered NATO as a consequence of its colonial perils. Indeed, it is remarkable that in his *Present at the Creation* Harriman's superior at the time, Dean Acheson (a close personal friend of Stikker's), makes no mention whatsoever of the entire affair, while the official record of American foreign policy, the well-known *Foreign Relations of the United States* compilation, devotes relatively little attention to the point at issue.[12] (Of course, both may be ascribed to the asymmetry of interest which I spoke of earlier.)

In any case, the irritation and hard feelings on the part of Stikker, one of the Dutchmen who turned out to be firm Atlanticists, are a perfect illustration of the poisoned political climate in the Netherlands on the eve of the creation of the Atlantic Alliance. As late as 1974, in a personal letter to Philip Jessup (who as U.S. representative had strongly denounced the second Dutch police action in the Security Council), he wrote he still believed that "the U.S. government knew nothing about the Indonesians, about their charm or complicated character, and had little regard for their small ally (stubborn as it may be) that was in 1948 at the brink of collapsing after having suffered five years of Nazi occupation at home and in the awful Japanese concentration camps in Indonesia."[13]

Military alliances are mainly based on common perceptions of threat and identity of interests. It was thus hardly the long historical ties that brought America and Holland together in NATO. But once the Indonesian issue was settled (I am not speaking of New Guinea yet), both countries started to join hands, or better: the United States was allowed to press the Netherlands to its bosom and successive Dutch governments, as well as the overwhelming majority of Dutch population, were quite happy about that. In fact, during the fifties and the sixties, the United States found in Holland one of its most loyal allies and staunchest supporters. For example, in 1950, the Dutch gave wholehearted support to U.S. policies in the United Nations concerning the Korean War. In sending a combat unit composed of volunteers, the Netherlands was one of the fifteen countries that joined America in the UN forces to help South Korea to repel the attack from the north.

Similarly, on the recurrent question of which Chinese government should represent the state of China in the UN, the Taiwan-based nationalist regime or the Communist regime holding power on mainland China, Dutch voting behavior in the General Assembly of the world organization was dictated by the wish not to deviate too much from the United States.[14] Even though the Netherlands had formally recognized the government of the People's Republic of China in 1950 and continued to maintain diplomatic relations with this government, it successively abstained on the seating of the PRC in the UN. By supporting American moratorium resolutions which marked the Chinese question an "important matter," thus requiring a two-thirds majority, the Dutch actually contributed to keeping Peking outside.

Thus, on the long and tiring road to the unity of Europe, Dutch willingness to collaborate with the other Western European countries was subordinated to the principle of Atlantic cooperation, being the cornerstone of Dutch foreign policy. In contrast to economic integration, the Netherlands has been very lukewarm toward politico-military cooperation with its European partners; it defended keeping the European Community open to the Atlantic world and it effectively opposed schemes that could have sent Europe drifting away from America. In the early sixties, Joseph Luns, the former diplomat who dominated the Dutch foreign policy scene for a long time and who had stubbornly refused to go along with the French plan for the creation of a European Political Union (which would have performed military tasks as well), was perceived by President De Gaulle as a caretaker of Anglo-American interests. Next to power-balancing considerations as regards France and West Germany, a main motive behind Dutch insistence on Britain's entry into the Common Market was related to the conviction that the participation of the United Kingdom would sustain the Community's Atlantic orientation.[15]

On matters of strategy within NATO, the Dutch have displayed a remarkable readiness to leave the major responsibility for Europe's nuclear protection to the United States.[16] Also, from the moment the United States itself became vulnerable to the nuclear weapons of the Soviet Union, the Netherlands continued to trust in the American President to make all decisions to use nuclear weapons in full accord with the defense needs of Europe and those of America. In fact, statements or opinions expressed in the larger European countries which voiced doubts concerning the reliability or credibility of the so-called strategic guarantees of the United States to Europe were regarded by successive Dutch governments as both improper and dangerous because of their potential for self-fulfilling effects.[17] Dutch decision makers denied the existence of any basic conflict of security interests between the United States and its overseas allies. For this reason, the formation of an independent European nuclear force was also firmly rejected. Highly characteristic of the Dutch position on nuclear affairs during the period under discussion was the fact that the Netherlands was in 1957 the first NATO country to react positively to an American offer for the deployment of tactical nuclear weapons on European soil and for placing these weapons at the disposal of the European NATO armies.

Finally, in return for American military protection and as a clear sign of solidarity, Holland lent all but unconditional support for political and military actions taken by the United States throughout the world. In the years America, because of Vietnam, was overwhelmed with criticism and almost ostracized by the international community, the Dutch government was one of those few governments which refused to leave Washington in the lurch. To the detriment of his popularity in the Netherlands, Foreign Minister Luns resisted strong appeals on the part of the Dutch Parliament to press the U.S. government to discontinue the bombardments of North Vietnam without prior conditions. As late as 1970, the Dutch government was in sympathy with President Nixon's decision to expand U.S. military operations to Cambodia. Elliot Richardson, the Undersecretary of State at the time, declared on American television that Holland was the sole country which had instantly supported the controversial American move.[18]

The enumeration of examples should not, of course, be a substitute for sound, exhaustive historical research, but it is beyond doubt that in the fifties and sixties the basic attitude of successive Dutch governments toward the United States was one of loyalty and faithfulness, if not outright docility. Only the New Guinea[19] dispute in the early sixties put a temporary damper on American-Dutch political relations. To a certain extent, we may notice in this case some of the features of the collision between the two countries on the eve of Indonesia's independence more than ten years earlier. The Dutch, and especially Mr. Luns, profoundly misjudged power realities in the world and clutched at an American promise of logistical support for possible Dutch military operations which had been made by John Foster Dulles on a special occasion in 1958[20] but turned out to be worthless at the very moment the Netherlands actually became engaged in hostilities with Indonesia. The Americans, for their part, as always preoccupied with their worldwide confrontation with the Soviet Union, were hoping to wean Sukarno away from Moscow by gratifying his special desire (the ceding of Dutch New Guinea to Indonesia) and put pressure on the Dutch government.[21]

Like Mr. Stikker before him, Foreign Minister Luns was very disappointed in the U.S. administration. He vented his spleen particularly on President Kennedy's brother Robert, who played an important part in the outcome of the New Guinea dispute. Indeed, in an interview Mr. Luns stated:

> I have always had the feeling that if he [President John Kennedy] had not been so much under the influence of his brother Robert, his policies would have been better. Also with regard to the Netherlands. The President reversed his course on the question of New Guinea on the advice of his brother. Robert Kennedy was in Indonesia for three or four days during the period of conflict. He was so much impressed by Mr. Sukarno's charm that after his return he was firmly convinced that Indonesia would immediately become an ally of the United States if only New Guinea was turned over to Sukarno. Obviously, as happened to so many others, he was deceived by Sukarno. Moreover, he assumed that he could do anything to the Netherlands without us protesting or doing anything about it. He was right in that assumption, by the way.[22]

However, the American-Dutch rift on the New Guinea issue is an exception rather than the rule of warm and friendly political relations during the period under discussion. The fact that the issue caused only a temporary diplomatic chill and did not produce lasting hard feelings demonstrates the fundamental pro-American disposition of Dutch policy makers. It may be wondered why the Netherlands was attached and wedded so much to its American ally. It is hard to distinguish here between considerations of self-interest and ethical principles. On the one hand, perceiving a real Soviet threat, Dutch policy makers were absolutely convinced that the Western European countries were not able to defend themselves and thus were entirely dependent upon American military protection. In such circumstances those countries could not afford to damage political relations with their powerful life-insurer. The willingness of the United States to assist Western Europe in the event of war, with all the means at its disposal, was assumed to depend upon the extent to which the European allies were showing solidarity.

On the other hand, Dutch loyalty to America also had moral overtones. It was partly the expression of the debt of gratitude which Holland owed the Americans for their role in World War II and of the belief that a small country ought to display respect to the state on whom it is dependent for its continued existence. It was felt that gratitude and respect obliged Dutch politicians to criticize the Americans only in the careful and moderate tone one uses with a dear friend who has taken the wrong path in life.

The departure of Joseph Luns from Dutch political life in 1971 symbolized the end of an era of close American-Dutch political cooperation. Since then, the Netherlands has become increasingly critical and independent vis-à-vis the United States. Thus, when around Christmas 1972 the American government decided to resume the bombing of North Vietnam as ferociously as before, Mr. Luns's successor at the Foreign Ministry, Norbert Schmelzer (certainly not a political radical), publicly denounced the American decision in most certain terms. The contrast with previous official reticence was most striking. In *The White House Years* Henry Kissinger strikes very bitter notes in describing the criticism of Holland and other European countries at the time. He writes:

> The Swedish government compared us with the Nazis (having, of course, been neutral during the Second World War). The Danish, Finnish, Dutch and Belgian governments also castigated the alleged bombing of cities. The French Foreign Minister made allusively critical comments. Not one NATO ally supported us or even hinted at understanding of our point of view—especially painful from countries who were insisting in their own defenses on a strategy involving massive attacks on civilian targets.[23]

Similarly, one year later, many Dutchmen accused the United States of involvement in and covert support for the military coup in Chile which ended the Allende regime. The political left in Holland came to worship the deposed Chilean President as a hero and a martyr of social justice, overthrown by outside imperialist forces. The left-of-center Den Uyl cabinet, in power from 1973 to 1977, irritated the Americans by giving development aid to Cuba and North Vietnam.

In late 1973, this cabinet was embarrassed by a generous American offer to help the Dutch overcome the consequences of an oil embargo imposed upon them by the Arab members of OPEC as a penalty for allegedly pro-Israel sympathies. Referring to Dutch reluctance to make use of the offer, a leading Dutch newspaper wrote: it appeared the Netherlands government had received an indecent offer.[24]

Then, in 1977, the Netherlands led the drive against President Carter's intention to produce the so-called neutron bomb and to introduce this weapon into Western Europe. Well over one million Dutchmen signed a petition against it.[25] Two years later, in December 1979, the Dutch government disappointed the United States very much (and for that matter other NATO countries too) by having reservations concerning its share in the deployment of 572 new nuclear delivery systems in Western Europe. In December 1981, it again refused to commit itself on that score. One month before, an unprecedented number of about 400,000 demonstrators had marched through the streets of Amsterdam in protest against an imminent new nuclear arms race in Europe. The term "Hollanditis" was coined and, whether a misnomer or not, became common currency as an international symbol of European neutralism and people's resistance to nuclear armaments. In the meantime, the Dutch government, in the person of its present Foreign Minister, Max van der Stoel, took pride in being a critical rather than, as in the old days, a faithful ally of the United States.

After having led up gradually to the subject, I have now come to the main question of my lecture: what is the nature and what are the causes of the changed political relationship? At the outset, I must emphasize that the changes in American-Dutch political relations during the past decade are by no means unique and may be seen as part of a more general pattern of estrangement between America and Europe. Still, I do not hesitate to say that the Netherlands began to dissociate itself from U.S. actions and opinions earlier and more strongly than, for instance, West Germany and that, in addition, the current gap between Holland and America on security matters and— not to be forgotten—on Third World issues is wider than that between the United States and other Western European countries.

Indeed, recent Dutch pleas for arms control agreements regardless of Soviet behavior in Afghanistan, Poland, or elsewhere, as well as calls for the reduction of the role of nuclear weapons in NATO's military strategy and for unilateral restraint in the production of new weapons systems, contrasted violently with Reaganite views—rhetoric or not—on regaining military strength, bargaining chips, and linkage. And so did Holland's commitments to human rights policies, large-

scale development assistance, and sympathies for reforms of the international economic system as opposed to American support of rightist
military dictatorships and beliefs in the value of laissez-faire liberalism
and the free-enterprise system as a universal remedy for problems of
economic development.

Yet what counts perhaps even more for the present and future
relations between the two countries is not merely the fact that America
is no longer seen in the Netherlands as a nation without sins, or as
the blameless leader of the free world, but that many Dutch opinion
leaders (and some foreign policy makers as well) have come to speak
without hesitation of characteristics common to superpowers as
though their similarities go much further than parallel nuclear might
and their differences add up to little more than ideological dazzle-
painting. A strong tendency of creeping neutralism has arisen in
Holland in recent years—a tendency to put the foreign policy behavior of the United States on the same footing with the external
behavior of the Soviet Union, to equate American dealings with
Central and Latin American republics and Russian actions in Eastern
Europe. Concomitant with the rise of a U.S.-Soviet mirror image is the
spread in Dutch society of feelings of moral superiority regarding
both superpowers, a feature fitting so very well in deeply rooted
foreign policy traditions of Holland.

Certainly, a clear majority of the Dutch population is still in
favor of NATO membership and continuation of military cooperation
with the United States. But what is this to mean when at the same
time an almost equal majority is very reluctant to accept the consequences of this cooperation and responsible Dutch politicians (not
only of the left) are keeping themselves at a distance from American
strategies and view the United States and the Soviet Union with an
attitude of "a plague on both your houses"? Although it would be
incorrect to confuse the growth of anti-Americanism in the Netherlands with any increase in sympathy for Soviet Communism, it is
amazing to observe well-meaning idealists focusing strongly on the
outrages of so-called American imperialism on the one hand and being
agnostic about Soviet foreign policy goals and apparently unaware of
a Soviet military buildup on the other hand.

This is the situation we find in Holland at present and, following
up this description, I shall finally discuss the factors that made the
country change from its former role of loyal ally to one of reluctant
ally. As little as the transformation of American-Dutch political relationships is a phenomenon confined to the relations between Holland
and the United States only, neither are its underlying causes entirely
typical of the Dutch foreign policy setting and merely to be understood as national idiosyncrasies. Thus, American-Dutch political rela-

tions have also been affected by a new war scare prevailing in many countries of Western Europe, widespread feelings that the development of military technology has outrun the control of statesmen, that the modern balance of terror is too fragile, and that Europeans could be incinerated in a war between the superpowers. To many of them, nothing seemed worse than the prospect of a possible nuclear holocaust.

Indeed, it was genuine fear and anger at the prospect of a nuclear war leaving little more of Europe than the ashes and radiation where 350 million people now live which swelled the so-called peace movement beyond its traditional constituencies in the Netherlands, as well as in other Western European countries. One would, therefore, deceive oneself in interpreting the rise of this movement in terms of a Communist conspiracy or calling it a gimmick to restore sagging church attendance. And, of course, whether in reality chances of war have increased or not is rather irrelevant. As the saying goes, if men define situations as real, they are real in their consequences.

It is evident that American-Dutch political relations have also been influenced by the advent of new generations of voters and a new political elite whose images of the world and of America bear the marks of quite different historical experiences from those of previous generations. I realize that this is a terribly obvious and commonplace explanation, but we should not forget that many platitudes contain elements of truth. Equally those relations underwent the influence of what has been described as the "dialectics of détente" between the East and West.[26] It is true, the process of détente in the first half of the seventies created new realities meaning quite different things to Europeans and Americans. Many Europeans like the word "détente," have come to associate it with more stability, economic advantage, and normalization of East-West relations. On the contrary, to many Americans "détente" means: spectacular growth of Soviet military capabilities, Soviet geopolitical offensives in Africa and western Asia, and, last but not least, a decline in the U.S. power position.

As to the latter, it has been suggested that the relative weakening of American economic and military strength is a main cause of Western rift and tensions. This I do not believe. Such an explanation presupposes that Western European countries are seeking, at the expense of relations with the United States, a policy of accommodation toward the Soviet Union out of fear of Russian military superiority. The point is simply that not many Europeans still regard the Soviet Union as basically dangerous to their freedom. It is the development of weaponry, the ongoing nuclear arms race rather than Russian intentions, that frightens most people. Bert Röling, a Groningen peace researcher with a great following in Dutch society, once wrote:

The danger that threatens us is not the deliberate attack by the Soviet Union, but the war unsought by both blocs, arising out of misperception or miscalculation, or the getting out of control of a crisis. In such a case of inadvertent war . . . weapons are being used that have been deployed to prevent the use of arms by deterrence.[27]

Even though more general European conditions, touched upon earlier, also explain the changed American-Dutch relationship to a large extent, no explanation seems to be complete without taking into account more specific factors. It is these factors, stemming from the Dutch national situation, that may account for the relative precocity and intensity of strains between both countries. For a better understanding, the following may serve.

Up to the middle of the sixties Dutch society had been profoundly stable. The social invention that held together a religiously divided country was "pillarization" (verzuiling). Each major religious and secular grouping formed a "pillar"—a separate social order in which its social, religious, and political institutions were closely interwoven. Dutch politics was the politics of accommodation (pacificatiepolitiek), characterized by overarching cooperation at the elite level and a strong deference of the rank and file to the bloc leaders, as well as a great deal of political passivity and non-participation on the part of the public at large.[28] As for foreign policy in particular, though this field was pre-eminently the exclusive domain of a handful of diplomats and other professionals, its basic tenets rested nevertheless on a broad, permissive consensus in the country. Dutch foreign policy was national or transpartisan policy and stood outside daily political stirrings. It was, in that sense, depoliticized.

Almost all observers of Dutch political and social life agree that in the second half of the sixties Dutch society underwent major changes. With journalistic hyperbole Walter Laqueur, in his famous "Hollanditis" article, even speaks of a cultural (or pseudo-cultural) revolution taking place at the time.[29] What we are witnessing, in fact, is a partial breakdown of the pillarization model, a strengthened process of secularization, efforts to expose political differences, as well as an unmistakable shift among younger people from acquisitive values to a post-materialist life style. The latter did not fail to exercise its influence upon the appraisal of America, the symbol of unfettered capitalism and of the so-called achieving society.

What we are also seeing is a rebellion against the establishment and a drive for more political participation, culminating in a gulf of democratization which did not halt at the borders of foreign politics. And all of this happened in the years when ordinary people, for the first time in their lives, were confronted with moving and dramatic television coverage of the less pleasant side of American society—race riots in the big cities and U.S. involvement in the Vietnam War. It is the interaction of these external and internal developments that provides clues for understanding the transformation of Dutch foreign policy and, derived from it, the change in American-Dutch political relations.

The process of democratization in Holland had two interrelated effects, namely a domesticization and an ideologization of foreign policy.[30] As far as the first outcome is concerned, Dutch foreign policy became more and more the object of internal political strife and a main issue-area in interparty coalition bargaining. In addition, a welter of "action groups" made their appearance on the foreign policy stage. These rather informal promotional groups (as distinguished from more long-standing and established goal organizations such as the Dutch section of the European Movement, the Atlantic Committee, and associations supporting the United Nations) were to use unorthodox methods and levers for political action outside the normal institutional channels. As Dutch foreign policy ceased to be the exclusive hunting grounds of a small band of experts, the postwar consensus crumbled away.

The process of democratization, which had made political authorities both very nervous and responsive to political demands coming from almost all sectors of Dutch society, also led to an ideologization of foreign policy. It enabled radical groups, whose members generally came from the middle and lower classes and whose impulses were most often missionary, to carry political weight. What we know of the relationship between foreign policy attitudes and social position suggests that people occupying high social positions tend to hold pragmatist and gradualist foreign policy opinions, whereas people with low social positions are inclined to espouse moralist and absolutist ideas on international questions.[31]

Indeed, in Holland, moralist ideas permeate pre-eminently the thinking of groups who had not been part of the traditional foreign policy establishment and who began giving dissenting opinions on Dutch foreign policy. The inclusion of representatives of those groups in the policy-making process that democratization brought about, in juxtaposition with the impact of heavily religious thinking for centuries, offering them fertile ground, is highly responsible for the augmented ideological loading of Dutch foreign policy since the early seventies.

What is the relevance of these remarks to American-Dutch relations? Ideologization of foreign policy is tantamount to the application of rigid moral standards to the making of foreign policy decisions. It comes down to the judging of international developments in terms of good and evil, rather than in terms of what is feasible and what is not. In the eyes of many Dutchmen, U.S. foreign policy no longer answered their elevated expectations as to how the leader of a democratic alliance ought to behave in international affairs. The impact of Vietnam can hardly be underestimated in this regard. Jerome Heldring, a leading foreign policy analyst in Holland, struck home when he wrote:

> When the big protector America, whose "faithful ally" the Netherlands has always been, is caught—indeed thanks to the American communications media and American democracy itself—in the atrocities and backstairs work it has committed in the Vietnam War, one has to be a seasoned "Realpolitiker" not to be shocked by it and not to draw certain lessons from it. And the Dutch people . . . were not exactly educated in and by their past to such a "realpolitische" outlook on international politics.[32]

May I add that a great part of the interested public in Holland has failed to recognize that a powerful nation like America, to a large extent because of its responsibility for protecting the independence of dozens of states, was forced to dirty its hands? Many years ago, Irving Kristol asserted that the championing of a highly idealistic, morally clean foreign policy could be the privilege of only small countries.[33] Indeed, unlike great powers, which are entangled in a web of responsibilities from which there is no hope of escape, small states can afford the luxury *not* to act and to pursue a pseudo-foreign policy based upon solemn exhortations to the rest of the world to save itself. It was H. A. Lorentz (1853–1928), the Dutch physicist and Nobel laureate, who once stated he was glad he belonged to a nation which was too small to commit any major blunders.[34]

In the beginning of my lecture, I airily compared the current state of American-Dutch relations to a certain development of married life. Thinking of the strained relationship between these countries, perhaps some would like to recall the American saying that a good marriage is rooted in creative tensions. Even though it is tempting to accept its underlying wisdom in this American-Dutch bicentennial year, I shall resist the temptation. The point is, I do see many tensions, but—unfortunately—less creativity.

NOTES

1   A. E. Kersten, "Van Kleffens' Plan voor Regionale Veiligheidsorganisaties" ("Van Kleffens' Plan for Regional Security Organizations"), *Jaarboek van het Departement van Buitenlandse Zaken, 1980–1981 (Year-*

book of the Ministry of Foreign Affairs, 1980–1981) (The Hague, 1981), p. 157.

2 S. I. P. van Campen, *The Quest for Security: Some Aspects of Netherlands Foreign Policy, 1945–1950* (The Hague, 1958), pp. 13–14.

3 For this item, see Albert Kersten, *Buitenlandse Zaken in Ballingschap: Groei en Verandering van een Ministerie (Foreign Affairs in Exile: Growth and Change of a Ministry) 1940–45* (Alphen aan den Rijn, 1981), pp. 137–38.

4 Kersten, "Van Kleffens' Plan," p. 164.

5 H. A. Schaper, "The Security Policy of the Netherlands, 1945–1948," in J. H. Leurdijk, ed., *The Foreign Policy of the Netherlands* (Alphen aan den Rijn, 1978), p. 91.

6 *Proceedings of the First Chamber, Interim Session, 1945*, p. 31.

7 See, for instance, *Proceedings of the Second Chamber, 1946–1947*, National Budget for 1947, 3rd chapter, Memorandum of Reply, p. 15.

8 P. J. Drooglever, "The United States and the Dutch Applecart during the Indonesian Revolution," in Rob Kroes, ed., *Image and Impact: American Influences in the Netherlands since 1945* (Amsterdam, 1981), p. 34.

9 Dirk U. Stikker, *Men of Responsibility: A Memoir* (London, 1966), pp. 115–18.

10 Drooglever, "Dutch Applecart," p. 43.

11 Stikker, *Memoir*, pp. 145–46.

12 Dean Acheson, *Present at the Creation* (New York, 1969) and *Foreign Relations of the United States, 1949, Vol. VII: The Far East and Australasia* (Washington, D.C., 1976), *passim*.

13 Letter of Dirk U. Stikker to Philip C. Jessup, September 26, 1974 (copy given to the author by Mr. Stikker).

14 Joris J. C. Voorhoeve, *Peace, Profits and Principles: A Study of Dutch Foreign Policy* (The Hague, 1979), p. 209.

15 For Dutch European policies, see Susanne Jonas (Bodenheimer), "The Denial of Grandeur: The Dutch Context," and Robert S. Wood, "Europe and the Communitarian Image in Dutch Foreign Policy," in Leurdijk, ed., *The Foreign Policy of the Netherlands*, pp. 235–303.

16 Robert W. Russell, "The Atlantic Alliance in Dutch Foreign Policy," in *ibid.*, p. 170.

17 A. van Staden, *Een Trouwe Bondgenoot: Nederland en het Atlantisch Bondgenootschap, 1960–1971 (A Faithful Ally: The Netherlands and the Atlantic Alliance, 1960–1971)* (Baarn, 1974), pp. 81–121.

18 Van Staden, *Een Trouwe Bondgenoot*, p. 78.

19 The Indonesian name for this territory is West Irian.

20 J. G. de Beus, *Morgen, Bij het Aanbreken van de Dag: Nederland Driemaal aan de Vooravond van de Oorlog (Tomorrow at Dawn: The Netherlands Three Times on the Eve of War)* (Rotterdam, 1977), pp. 272–88. See also on this subject *De Volkskrant*, August 29, 1981.

21 De Beus, *Morgen*, pp. 334–403, and Arend Lijphart, *The Trauma of Decolonization: The Dutch and West New Guinea* (New Haven, Conn., 1966), p. 278.

22 Han J. A. Hansen, ed., *Luns, Drees, De Quay, Marijnen, Cals over Luns (Luns, Drees, De Quay, Marijnen, Cals on Luns)* (Hilversum and Maaseik, 1967), pp. 44–45. Translated from the original Dutch.

23 Henry Kissinger, *The White House Years* (Boston, 1979), pp. 1453–54.

24 *NRC Handelsblad*, December 1, 1973.

25 Philip P. Everts, "Reviving Unilateralism: Report on a Campaign for Nuclear Disarmament in the Netherlands," *Bulletin on Peace Proposals*, I (1980), 40–56.

26 M. C. Brands, "The Dialectics of Detente and the Involution of the Netherlands," in Kroes, ed., *Image and Impact*, pp. 80–90.

27 B. V. A. Röling, *Het Wapenprobleem (The Problem of Armament)* (Assen and Amsterdam, 1977), p. 27. Translated from the original Dutch.

28 Arend Lijphart, *The Politics of Accommodation: Pluralism and Democracy in the Netherlands* (2nd rev. ed.; Berkeley, Calif., 1975).

29 Walter Laqueur, "Hollanditis: A New Stage in European Neutralism," *Commentary*, August 1981, pp. 19–21.

30 J. L. Heldring, "Between Dreams and Reality," in Leurdijk, ed., *The Foreign Policy of the Netherlands*, pp. 317–18. For a comparison of the foreign policy processes in Holland and America, see Bernard C. Cohen, "Political Systems, Public Opinion and Foreign Policy: The United States and the Netherlands," *International Journal*, XXXIII (1977–78), 195–216.

31 See, for example, Johan Galtung, "Foreign Policy Opinion as a Function of Social Position," in James N. Rosenau, ed., *International Politics and Foreign Policy: A Reader in Research and Theory* (New York, 1969), pp. 551–72.

32 J. L. Heldring, "De Nederlandse Buitenlandse Politiek na 1945" ("Dutch Foreign Policy since 1945") in E. H. van der Beugel et al., *Nederlandse Buitenlandse Politiek: Heden en Verleden (Dutch Foreign Policy: The Present and the Past)* (Baarn, 1978), p. 39. Translated from the original Dutch.

33 Irving Kristol, "American Intellectuals and Foreign Policy," *Foreign Affairs*, XLV, No. 4 (July 1967), 602.

34 As quoted by Amry Vandenbosch, *Dutch Foreign Policy since 1815: A Study in Small Power Politics* (The Hague, 1959), p. 303.

Part Two

· ·

DUTCH
IMMIGRATION
AND SETTLEMENT
IN THE
UNITED STATES

The Dutch in New Netherland

· ❦ ·

HENRI AND BARBARA VAN DER ZEE

REACHING the top of the World Trade Center one evening four years ago was an experience we will not soon forget. It was a few days after the publication of our book *A Sweet and Alien Land*, the story of Dutch New York, New Amsterdam. But from the restaurant's windows up on the 110th floor, it was almost impossible to see that little corner of Manhattan that had preoccupied us, as authors, for so long. Stretching away to the horizon we could see a vast modern city; but what had once been New Amsterdam itself was now almost hidden away at the foot of this towering symbol of modern New York.

When we walked for the first time through Lower Manhattan, three years earlier, the Dutch past had seemed closer. It was Labor Day, and the streets were deserted—just like any Dutch town on a Sunday. The old warehouses, decrepit and neglected, that still stood between newer skyscrapers might have been in Leiden or Delft, although they were built in the eighteenth and nineteenth centuries, long after New Amsterdam became New York.

But what was even more striking was the fact that the streets still ran according to the old plan laid out by Master Kryn Fredericks, the engineer from Amsterdam who arrived in Manhattan in 1625. He was sent by the newly formed West India Company, which had received a charter for this first Dutch settlement in the New World and was now anxious to protect its province, a promising source of the precious beaver furs.

A fort was, understandably, the first priority and Fredericks brought with him a grandiose design. Starting an American tradition perhaps, it was to be a pentagon in shape; its circumference would measure more than 1,000 feet and the moat surrounding it would be eight feet deep. In the middle of the fort enclosure, there was to be a marketplace; around it, houses for the Council and the town notables, as well as a schoolhouse, church, and hospital all under one roof; and there were plans for a small town outside the fort.

The project was never fully carried out, and the fort was never the size Fredericks had intended. But the street names in Lower Man-

hattan today show that at least the outline of his town planning survived: Pearl Street was once Paerelstraat; Water Street is Waterstraat
anglicized; and Beaver Street is English for Beverstraat, named after
the small Dutch colony's most important source of income.

It is fascinating to stroll around that little patch of New York City
today. On the corner of Stone Street and Bridge Street once stood the
first stone houses to be built in New Amsterdam; and Stone Street itself
was the first in New Amsterdam to be cobbled in true Dutch style.

Broad Street, unusually wide for this part of town, was once New
Amsterdam's first canal, the Heerengracht: and just like the canals in
old Amsterdam, it was so extensively used as the city's sewer that in
1662 a lock was built to keep it artificially filled with water, so that,
as the ordinance said, "the great and unbearable stench may be suppressed which arises daily when the water runs out."

The casual visitor will notice very little of the former Dutch pres-
ence in this corner of New York. He is probably unaware that the
Customs House on Bowling Green was built where once Fort Amster-
dam stood; that the Bowling Green itself was once het Marcktveld,
the Market Field; and that on the corner of Whitehall Street and State
Street once stood the splendid mansion of the last Dutch governor of
New York, Peter Stuyvesant, which the first English governor, Sir
Richard Nicolls, rechristened Whitehall.

In a recent interview with Jan van Wieringen of *De Volkskrant*,
Professor Bert Salwen, an anthropologist at New York University, remarked that until the beginning of the 1970's—only ten years ago—it
was generally believed that continuous building in New York had
destroyed all trace of the Dutch occupation.

In recent years, however, historians and archaeologists have discovered that underneath modern New York much of New Amsterdam
still survives. An old pair of shoes found in 1969 on a building site
near Water Street aroused curiosity and the diggings by the Division
for Historic Preservation of the state of New York that followed turned
up a treasure trove of seventeenth-century pipes, wooden spoons, wine-
glasses, bottles, and china.

Archaeology, unfortunately, is an expensive business for devel-
opers, who are in a hurry to get their buildings up. But the discoveries
of 1969 marked the first of a new series of diggings, which have been
greatly helped by the present economic slump. The most important
dig so far was concluded only a year ago, when a team of archaeologists
and students were able to work on the site of the Dollar Savings Bank
on Water Street. They discovered the foundations of New York's first
City Hall, a building that began its life more frivolously as New Amsterdam's official Town Tavern and was raised to the dignity of Stadt
Huys when the town got its city charter in 1653.

The archaeologists who toiled on this site for eight months came up with an astonishing haul. Before the bulldozers moved in, no less than four tons of Dutch history was dug up. At the moment it is stored at New York University awaiting thorough examination, and it is hoped that the New York City Landmarks Preservation Commission will produce a first report very soon.

But even before the archaeologists went to work in the soil of modern New York, it was possible to paint a vivid picture of the Dutch in New Amsterdam. The city with its capital port was never very big, but it welcomed a steady stream of visitors, many of whom wrote down eyewitness accounts of what they saw.

The diarist Nicolaes van Wassenaer was the first to take note of these accounts, in his *Historie van Europa*, and in 1626 he was able to write that Fort Amsterdam was already "very large." The Comptoir, the Counting House, he went on, was a stone building roofed with reed, while the other houses were made of bark. They were in fact dugouts, made in haste by the first settlers to arrive, before winter found them homeless; six or seven feet deep, their sides were cased in with wooden planks, the floor covered with thick bark, and the roof made of branches covered with more bark or with slices of turf.

By the time the West India Company started to build its fort, the colonists were beginning to emerge from their holes to build the earliest proper houses, made of wood. We must, however, wait till the early 1640's for the next eyewitness account of the small settlement on Manhattan Island, then governed by the dictatorial and brutal Willem Kieft.

Rather surprisingly, the man who in 1643 visited the predominantly Protestant community was a French missionary, Father Isaac Jogues, who had been saved by the Dutch from torture at the hands of the Mohawk Indians. They helped him to escape from North New Netherland to Manhattan, and walking around it, Jogues observed the small lively port with keen interest. A place with the "arrogance of Babel" was his impression; it had no more than 400–500 inhabitants, yet, as Kieft told him, eighteen different languages were spoken there.

The primitive hamlet of the 1620's and 1630's had grown into a fair-sized village, dominated by the Counting House, built inside the fort. Although an English visitor described this four years later as "a castle of great use for keeping the natives at a distance," Jogues obviously had had a closer look and noticed that the four bastions were crumbling away and that the original moat had filled up with earth.

When Jogues left New Amsterdam a year later, inside the fort work had begun on the building of a church. Until that time, the New Amsterdamers had had to make do with a room over the horse mill of Francis Molemaecker. Later, a small chapel had been built, near the East River, but this was no more than a "mean barn," as someone described it. And Governor Kieft decided—or rather was pushed into it—that it was high time New Amsterdam had a proper church.

The big problem was how to raise the money to pay for it. The West India Company felt it had spent enough on the colony and the settlers were still relatively poor. But with the cunning that was Kieft's most characteristic trait, he seized the perfect occasion to part the colonists from their savings—a wedding party, in this case for Sarah Jansz, stepdaughter of the pastor of the city, Dominie Bogardus. Kieft waited till the punch was flowing freely. Then he struck—"after the fourth or fifth round of drinking," as one of the guests later hazily recalled. His fund raising was startlingly successful—"all then with light heads subscribed largely, competing one with another."

How the wedding guests felt about their enforced generosity the following morning can be easily imagined. But nobody was allowed to get out of paying up, the same guest indignantly recorded. Kieft kept them all to their word.

Perhaps Kieft's enthusiasm for the building of this first church can be explained by guilt. Several years earlier, he had already finished building the Stads Herberg, or Town Tavern, a fine stone building where the many visitors to New Amsterdam could now be accommodated. Until it was finished, he told a visiting Dutchman, Captain David de Vries, "he suffered great annoyance" from the stream of visitors because he had to put them up and entertain them in his own house. The Town Tavern was a two-story building, outside the town facing the East River, and—as we now know for certain—standing where Pearl Street crosses Hanover Square.

The Town Tavern weathered some stormy years before it was given the prestigious new title of Stadt Huys, or City Hall. Its first host, Philip Gerritsen, lasted only three months before he died of a stab wound from one of his customers.

The incident was by no means unusual. In the rough pioneering society of New Amsterdam, brawls and fights were so common that Kieft and his successor, Peter Stuyvesant, were constantly increasing the fines for its disorderly citizens.

The Town Tavern was far from being the only inn in town. One report in 1648 stated that a quarter of the city buildings were grog shops. And the previous year Dominie Backerus, the new pastor who had arrived in Amsterdam with Peter Stuyvesant, wrote back disapprovingly to the Church Council in Amsterdam that he had counted seventeen public houses—enough to make the citizens "very much inclined to intoxication."

One of the most popular inns was het Houten Paerd, the Wooden

Horse, run by a lively Parisian, Philip Geraerdy. The inn's name was a tongue-in-cheek commemoration of his brief military career in the New World. This had been abruptly terminated by his being sentenced to "ride the wooden horse" a standard punishment for soldiers who had been absent on leave without permission. Like other offenders, Geraerdy had been forced to sit for hours at a time on a crossbar with heavy weights hanging from his feet, a drawn sword in one hand—and a pitcher in the other.

But this brawling, vigorous, and in fact, for a pioneering city, normal life was already doomed by Kieft's folly. When he sailed for Europe in 1647, much of this once thriving town had gone up in smoke. The governor with his usual lack of judgment had declared war on the Indians, with disastrous consequences for the colonists, and New Amsterdam and its surroundings were now little more than "piles of ashes from burnt houses and barns." Stuyvesant arrived to find it no better than a slum, with cows and goats grazing on the ruined walls of the fort, streets like cow paths, and a few straggling buildings dotted about. The clean lines of Kryn Fredericks' ground plan were, as Stuyvesant reported to Holland, now blurred "by the disorderly manner hitherto and now daily being practiced in building and erecting houses."

He tackled the situation with great energy and thirteen years later New Amsterdam was once more demonstrably a town; in September 1660 a visiting ship's captain wrote enthusiastically to his employers in Amsterdam: "This place, the Manhattans, is quite rich of people and there are at present full over 350 houses so that it begins to be a brave place."

In that year the city surveyor counted precisely 342 houses, in which lived 1,500 citizens. Even the English were envious of this thriving and bustling port, strategically sited between the Hudson and the East River, "the whirlpool which the Dutch call the Hellgat." One of these Englishmen was a certain Samuel Maverick, who sang the praises of the Dutch capital in a report to London: "very delightsome and convenient for situation, especially for trade . . . with an excellent harbour."

By that time, the days of pioneering and Kieft's Indian wars were a thing of the past. The New Amsterdamers now lived in a degree of luxury of which Stuyvesant's own family mansion, built in the mid-1650's on what is now the corner of Whitehall Street and State Street, was a fair example. He had spared no expense. The plot that Stuyvesant had confiscated from a rich English merchant, Thomas Baxter, after his defection from New Amsterdam during the most recent Anglo-Dutch war, had been leveled with 9,000 tons of sand. And eyewitness accounts tell of "an expensive and handsome building" made of stone,

(TOP) West India House, Amsterdam, Holland
(*Copyright Museum of the City of New York*)

(BOTTOM) The Hartgers drawing of New Amsterdam—
the earliest known view of the port of Manhattan
(*Copyright J. Clarence Davis Collection in the
Museum of the City of New York*)

with a gabled façade, surrounded at back and sides by lawns and a formal Dutch flower and vegetable garden. Its front overlooked the market, while a flight of stairs went down to the river, where the governor's personal barge was moored.

Stuyvesant was never very rich, but the interior of his house was said to be opulent, full of solid Dutch furniture, silver, and china shipped over from Europe. And he was certainly not the only Dutchman who lived in such style in New Amsterdam. Next door was the house of Captain Nicholas Varleth, a wealthy shipowner, who had married Stuyvesant's sister Anna, and New Amsterdam counted in the last years of its existence as a Dutch city several inhabitants who nowadays could be called millionaires: men such as Cornelis Steenwyck, Oloff Steven van Cortland, and Pieter Couwenhoven, names still around in New York today.

As the recent diggings have demonstrated, they lived extremely well. "The Dutch seem to have had a taste for luxury," Dr. Nan Rothchild of New York University said recently. "We came across some particularly fine glass and china, for instance." Another discovery that impressed the archaeologists was that, unlike the English, the Dutch brought over their own livestock, cows and pigs included. According to our own researches, the first cattle arrived as early as 1625, when the West India Company sent over ships freighted with horses, cows, and hay. Later in the same year, they sent a flyboat carrying sheep and hogs. The cattle were unloaded first at Governor's Island, and then shipped over to Manhattan, where twenty of them died. But the rest settled down happily in their new home, and no wonder: each one had it own attendant and separate stall during the long voyage.

The desire of the Dutch to go on enjoying their own traditional food suggests more than just good appetites. It was symptomatic of the general attitude of the settlers in New Netherland, who tried by every means to re-create the life style they had enjoyed in Europe. The United Provinces was one of the richest and most powerful nations in the world at this time, and the Dutch in general lived comfortably. It was a perennial problem for the big Dutch trading companies to find people ready to abandon their comfortable homeland for an unknown country peopled, as they saw it, by naked pagans. And those who were adventurous enough to give it a try had a single aim: to turn New Netherland into a Dutch province, and New Amsterdam into a Dutch town.

It goes without saying that when in 1657, under pressure from the city fathers of New Amsterdam, Governor Stuyvesant introduced the Burgher-recht, it was an instant success. More than 200 citizens immediately enrolled as so-called small burghers, a rank which for the sum of 20 guilders was open to any man born in the city or who had lived there for at least a year and six weeks. The great Burgher-recht—for members of the government, magistracy, clergy, or officers—was less popular: it cost 50 guilders, and only twenty inhabitants at first claimed great burgher status, among them Stuyvesant himself.

The introduction of the burgher-right did not, of course, mean that from one day to the next New Amsterdam was transformed into a city of solidly respectable citizens, and nothing makes this clearer than the records of the court of New Amsterdam. Established by Stuyvesant, the court sat every Monday morning in the Stadt Huys, presided over by the burgomaster and the schepens, the aldermen. Its records reveal a bawdy, boisterous society in which rumor and gossip were rife. And the very first case that opened the court's first session, on February 10, 1653, was eloquent of New Amsterdam morals. It involved a certain Allard Anthony, a somewhat unpopular alderman, who was actually sitting as one of the judges. According to several witnesses, Anthony had had an affair with the wife of one Joost Goderis, a weigh-house employee. Half a dozen men taunted Goderis with his wife's infidelity, telling him that he ought to wear horns. The desperate man lashed out at one of his persecutors, who then stabbed him with a knife. The case trailed on for weeks, and the luckless Goderis—continually harassed by his highly public woes—grew more and more desperate; in the end he lost both his wife and his job.

This was certainly not the only case of adultery on record. In a port like New Amsterdam, there were plenty of bored housewives ready to oblige a passing sailor—although New Amsterdam was notorious for its prostitutes—and there were many unsavory court cases as a result. In one, a sailor was hauled before the court because he had been spotted in the bushes with the wife of Willem Beeckman, an important Company employee. Straight-faced, the sailor told the magistrates that he had received such a kiss from Mevrouw Beeckman "that I could scarcely compose myself." It was, according to gossip, the price for his silence, since he had surprised her with another man, the rich storekeeper Cornelis Steenwyck. One malicious woman told her neighbors that the sailor had been given money as well, and that he bitterly regretted that he had not taken the gold ring from Mevrouw Beeckman's finger into the bargain. The case was dismissed after the main witness retracted her story, pleading for "forgiveness if she had repeated one word to the injury of Mme Beeckman."

Another sailor, discovered in the bushes with another housewife, was let off since the woman in question was decidedly eccentric. As the New Amsterdamers related with relish, she had once been seen visiting a public house "clad in men's clothes, having a pair of whiskers painted black," and had ordered a pint of beer.

Most of the cases heard by the court had to do with property, but those concerned with impropriety in any form drew by far the biggest audiences. New Amsterdam had no playhouse and the court was the best substitute. A particularly sensational case involved the wife of one Hendrick Sluyter. After a fight with another woman she had, "in the presence of respectable company, with their wives, hoisted her petticoats up to her back and showed them her arse." Since this, according to the records, was an offense "not to be tolerated in a well-ordered province," she was shipped home to Holland, despite her ingenious plea that she had lifted her skirts at her husband, not at the bystanders.

Annetje Bogardus, widow of a minister, got off lightly by comparison. She was accused of exhibitionism, having displayed her ankle in public. A friend came to the rescue, testifying that Annetje, passing the blacksmith's shop, "placed her hand on one side, and drew up her petticoat a little so as not to soil it since the road was muddy." She was acquitted.

The sentences handed out in New Amsterdam were harsh by modern standards. Before Stuyvesant's time, executions were fairly common, but during his term of office, the court confined itself to flogging, scourging with rods, and banishment. Sometimes the punishment was completed by cutting off the right ear or branding on the cheeks. In one talked-about case, however, the court ordered a death sentence to be carried out on a Company Negro, Manuel Gerritsen. He was one of a group of nine who had confessed to the murder of another slave, and he was chosen by lot to be hanged as an example. It turned out that he was not nicknamed Manuel the Giant for nothing: the gallows on the Strand had not been built for his size and weight, and when the cord broke and he crashed to the ground, the bystanders asked for mercy, which, it was noted in the records, "was accordingly granted."

Prison life in New Amsterdam was certainly no picnic, but it was quite humane. The dark, damp prison in the fort was hardly ever used; instead, most of the prisoners were kept in cells under the Stadt Huys. And the laxness of security was demonstrated by one prisoner who, after getting his jailer drunk, disappeared up the chimney. Despite this, the jailers still received permission in 1658 "to lay in beer, wine and spirits for the prisoners, free of excise, likewise fire and light gratis." There was only one condition: that this should not lead to "any parties directly or indirectly."

In its attitude toward prisoners, as in its care of paupers and orphans—tolerant and humane—New Amsterdam reflected society as it then was in the Netherlands, hundreds of miles away on the other side of the Atlantic. Small wonder that the English in Massachusetts and Connecticut studied the thriving Dutch community with bewilderment and envy, but to many of them, quite the most enviable feature of New Amsterdam was its broad-mindedness in matters of religion. This was certainly not the official policy of Stuyvesant. Together with the Protestant ministers, he devoted plenty of time and energy to combating the presence of dissenters such as the Lutherans and Quakers, and he strongly objected to the arrival of the first Jews. He received, however, very little support from the directors of the West India Company. As C. R. Boxer remarks, in his excellent book *The Dutch Seaborne Empire*, the Heeren XIX were convinced that religious toleration would be as advantageous for New Netherland as it had been for Amsterdam.

They told him in numerous letters that he was not to be too strict with Protestant dissenters, since this might discourage immigration and induce people already living there to leave. They went so far as to give him the typically Dutch practical advice to connive at non-Calvinists celebrating their own forms of worship, providing that they were discreet about it and caused no annoyance to their orthodox neighbors.

Such an attitude was in strong contrast to that of New England, where women were still being charged with witchcraft—as was Judith Varleth, sister of Stuyvesant's brother-in-law Captain Varleth, in 1662. She was fortunate enough to be acquitted after Stuyvesant wrote urgently to John Winthrop, governor of Connecticut, protesting that she was innocent of such "a horrible crime," but many women were less lucky and ended their lives at the stake.

Witchcraft was far from being the only "irregularity of morals" on which the unbending Puritans pounced, as John Underhill discovered. This Englishman, who had learned the arts of war in the army of the Stadtholder Prince Frederick Hendrick and married a Dutch girl, arrived in 1630 in America. He visited New Netherland and liked it, but decided to settle in New England, a decision he regretted bitterly when in 1638 he was charged with adultery with a certain Mistress Wilbore, at whom he had been seen to gaze admiringly during a long lecture in a Boston church. Underhill lightheartedly admitted his crime, pleading that "he had not looked with lust at the said miss." When one of the judges asked him why he had not looked at the other ladies present, Underhill flippantly replied, "Verily they are not desirable women." What more proof of guilt could a Puritan court demand? Underhill was excommunicated, and when he asked by which law he was condemned, he was sternly assured that it would certainly be possible to devise a law "against this very sin."

Not long afterward, Underhill left for New Amsterdam, where he was to play a key role in Kieft's Indian wars. Many other Englishmen followed him, to get away from oppressive Puritan New England and build a new life for themselves in the more liberal Dutch society.

It must be said, nevertheless, that although the Dutch attitude toward religious refugees from neighboring European communities was one of tolerant welcome, their behavior toward the Indians was much less admirable.

Initially, Dutch-Indian relations had been cordial. Bearing in mind the Company's instructions that the natives were to be treated both fairly and kindly, Peter Minuit, the first director-general or governor, paid in 1625 a fair price for Manhattan. This island had been discovered in 1609 by Henry Hudson, an Englishman employed by the Dutch East India Company, and for this piece of real estate the Indians were quite satisfied with goods to the value of 60 guilders. Among them were 10 dogs, 80 pairs of stockings, 10 guns, and one copper pan—in fact, as one historian later remarked: "it was the best buy in the world."

The Dutch, unlike the English, were also perfectly willing to learn from the Indians, for whom they felt neither dislike nor contempt. Minor clashes were, of course, inevitable, in particular after the Indians had been introduced to alcohol, previously unknown to them, and discovered they liked it.

Under the despicable government of Kieft the relationship, however, soured. Kieft—a "mean fellow" according to the Indians—decided that the Indians must pay taxes like the Dutch, and when they protested he forgot the Company principle " 'Tis better to rule by love and friendship than by force" and attempted to impose the taxation. The situation deteriorated rapidly, until the colony was a battlefield.

A horrified witness to one of the bloodiest episodes was Captain David de Vries, a humane Dutch businessman, who had traveled all over the world, but who, deeply shocked, wrote in his journal that he had never seen anything like the massacre of innocent Indians organized by Kieft in 1643. "Infants were snatched from their mothers' breasts and cut to pieces in sight of the parents, and the pieces thrown into the fire and into the water; other sucklings were bound to wooden boards and cut and stuck or bored through and miserably massacred, so that a heart of stone would have been softened. . . . Some came to our people on the farms with their hands cut off; others had their legs hacked off and some were holding their entrails in their arms."

Both Kieft and the colony were to pay dearly for such barbarism, and the relations between the "Swannekens" and the "Wilden" were never the same in spite of Stuyvesant's efforts to establish a new understanding with the savages. They remained restless and over the years

(TOP) The only known portrait of
Peter Stuyvesant, probably by
Hendrick Couturier, (active 1661–1674)
(*Copyright New York Historical
Society, New York City*)

(BOTTOM) Coat of arms of
New Amsterdam, 1654
(*Copyright Museum of the
City of New York*)

murdered a total of fourteen settlers. But the governor forbade the Dutch to retaliate. It was in vain, and when in 1655 he had to leave New Amsterdam for some weeks, the simmering hostility on both sides suddenly came to the boil. Hundreds of Indians in canoes, on their way south to wage war on another tribe living on Long Island, landed on Manhattan in search of food. It was the moment the resentful settlers had waited for, and when an Indian woman broke into an orchard to pick a peach, she was shot dead by its owner. Another bloody war broke out.

By the time Stuyvesant had hurried back to restore order, over 300 Dutchmen had been killed and 100 carried off prisoner. It was years before he was able to rebuild the colonists' confidence in their future.

There were other Dutch-Indian clashes, but further from New Amsterdam another serious—and, as it turned out, fatal—threat to the colony demanded more urgently the attention of Stuyvesant and his people.

From the very beginning, the English had always refused to recognize the existence of the small Dutch settlement. James I and his son Charles I had frequently protested against the intrusion of the Dutch on what they considered their property, on the strength of some beautiful pieces of parchment. And the New Englanders had never hesitated to encroach on the boundaries of New Netherland and help themselves to whatever they wanted. The West India Company, under constant pressure from their governors in the New World, had from time to time made tentative efforts to establish their rights. But they received little official support from the Dutch government—and no satisfaction at all in London.

When Stuyvesant arrived in New Netherland in 1647, he had found a colony that had shrunk to a shadow of its former self. Initially, it had stretched from the Delaware River in the south to Cape Cod in the north. Now it was little more than the island of Manhattan; parts of Long Island; one outpost on the Connecticut River and another on the Delaware; and Fort Orange in the north, now Albany. Stuyvesant, urged by the Company, did everything he could to come to an agreement with New England, knowing all too well that the few Dutch settlers were no match for their already numerous English neighbors. Three years after his arrival, he even traveled to the capital of Connecticut, Hartford—built on what officially was still Company property—in an effort to settle the border question, but although he formally ceded large areas of the province to them, they had no intention of sticking to their side of the bargain.

Over the years they pushed forward relentlessly into Dutch territory, and when Charles II returned in triumph to London in 1660, he gave away various parts of New Netherland with a generous hand to those who had remained faithful to him during his years in exile. One of the most important beneficiaries was his brother James, Duke of York, who in 1664 received a charter that conferred on him all the territory of New Netherland, New Haven, and much of Connecticut.

The fact that his new fief was still in Dutch hands was a slight disadvantage, but easily remedied, and in May 1664 a small expeditionary force left Portsmouth under the command of Colonel Richard Nicolls. Their departure was reported to The Hague, where Raadspensionary Johan de Witt protested to the despised English ambassador Downing. "I know of no such country, but only in the mapps" was Downing's indifferent reply. The Dutch ambassador in London, meanwhile, equally protesting, had to be content with a bland assurance from Charles II that he had "no desire to damage the understanding he had with the Dutch."

That de Witt went so far as to make an official protest was in itself a new development. Certainly, he was not moved by love for the West India Company, whom he rightly considered both inept and impotent. But he was now very much concerned for the colony itself. After years of indifference, the persistent interest of the English in this prime site on the Hudson had made it clear to the Dutch government at The Hague that they had a priceless possession in the New World. Not only had the colony great potential in its own right; it was also excellently situated for the contravention of the dreaded new Navigation Acts by which England was slowly but surely sapping Dutch commercial supremacy. And de Witt now began drawing up plans for a drastic reorganization of the Company, with emphasis on New Netherland, which would at last give the colony almost complete autonomy.

These plans were warmly welcomed by Stuyvesant, who from being the Company's loyal servant had slowly changed, over the years, into a dedicated New Netherlander who chafed at the leading reins in which the Heeren XIX kept him and the settlers. He had begun to love the country he governed, and he had every intention of staying there and keeping it Dutch. When Nicolls' fleet was sighted in the Hudson, he already knew of the English intentions and began at once to prepare the defense of New Amsterdam. It was an impossible task. Nobody in New Amsterdam was prepared to sacrifice his life for the sake of the Company that had neglected the colony for years, and the crumbling fort itself had only twenty-four rusting pieces of artillery, most of them useless.

The nearest New Amsterdam came to putting up a fight was a moving but useless gesture made by Stuyvesant himself on the last day of the brief siege. As two of the ships closed in on the city, the one-legged governor limped hurriedly up to the wall of the fort, where a gunner stood ready with a lighted match. The appalled citizens stared up at him while he paused before giving the order to fire. Suddenly two of their number, Dominie Megapolensis and his son Samuel, went up to him, and taking him gently by the arms, led him away.

It was the end of New Netherland. On the following day—Monday, September 8, 1664—the Act of Capitulation was signed in Stuyvesant's "Bouwerij." And fifty-five years after Henry Hudson discovered Manhattan for the Dutch, thirty-nine years after Peter Minuit bought the island from the Indians, and eleven years after New Amsterdam received its city charter, Stuyvesant put his signature to the papers that surrendered New Netherland to the English. A few days later, the burgomasters reported the fact to the West India Company with the final words of reproach: "Meanwhile since we have no longer to depend on your Honors' promises of protection, we with all the poor, sorrowing and abandoned Commonalty here must fly for refuge to the Almighty God. . . ."

The peace terms agreed at the end of the second Anglo-Dutch war, in 1667, settled the fate of New Netherland. Together with other "places, cities and forts which during the war had been taken" it passed into British hands, to remain there—with a brief interruption in 1673—until American Independence in 1776.

But Dutch influence lingered on in New York long after the end of British rule. The Dutch language was common in New York right up to the end of the nineteenth century, and dozens of Dutch names still testify to a Dutch past, while the famous Holland Society refuses to accept as members those who cannot claim direct descent from Dutchmen who came to America before 1672. Architecturally, too, Dutch influence was strong, and for years houses continued to be built with a high stoop as in old Amsterdam—although the danger of flooding in New York was nonexistent. The latest diggings also tell us that the Dutch continued to import their own glass and china until well into the eighteenth century.

There is little visible trace of this Dutch influence today, apart from the four tons of archaeological finds, a handful of Dutch names for streets and neighborhoods—Brooklyn, Harlem, the Bowery, Flushing—a few mansions in the Hudson Valley built in the Dutch style, and the tomb of Peter Stuyvesant in the somewhat dilapidated church of St. Mark's in the Bowery, built on the site of Stuyvesant's onetime garden chapel.

But material souvenirs are not always the most lasting. And the spirit of the old Dutch city has perhaps turned out to be even more durable than its Delft. New Amsterdam was an anarchic, lively, polyglot, turbulent place—just like New York today. It was founded for the express purpose of doing business—rare at the time—and though its aims were materialistic, they bred the virtue of tolerance. As in old Amsterdam, almost anything was permitted so long as it was not bad for trade—and that is still true of the New York we know today.

To us, New York feels much more like a Dutch city than an English one. It has the same aggressive thrust as Amsterdam. And like the Dutchman, the New Yorker is a direct, no-nonsense person.

Perhaps that is the heritage we left behind—to survive long after the English in turn moved out.

The American Dutch,
Their Church,
and the Revolution

JAMES TANIS

FROM the outset of the American Revolution, the British rightly realized that their hope for victory lay in dividing the northern colonies from the middle and southern colonies by controlling the Hudson River valley. Little could Henry Hudson have realized in 1609, as he sailed up the river that was to bear his name, that the Dutch who were to take up his claim would provide the backbone of resistance to the British cause 170 years later.

These middle colony Dutch—those who spoke the language, worshipped mostly in the Reformed Church, and exemplified the Dutch heritage in their homes and manners—were by no means limited to those of Netherlandish blood. Some, like the House of Orange itself, were German in origin; others were Swiss; some were French; and some had even come from Britain. A few were assimilated in the colonies; but most had "become Dutch" in the old country itself. A typical example was the boy Robert Livingston, who, with his family, migrated to Rotterdam from Scotland among a group of religious refugees at the time of the Stuart restoration. In 1673, having adopted the Dutch culture of his neighbors, nineteen-year-old Robert sailed for the New World, where he was to become one of the richest and most powerful men in New York. In Albany he married the widow Alida Schuyler van Rensselaer, and their offspring for generations were among the leaders of the Dutch community. The ancient Dutch hospitality to foreigners was a part of the cultural pattern that these "new Dutch" absorbed and brought with them to America.

The pivotal role of the Hudson Valley in American history became most powerfully clear in the 1750's, at the time of the French and Indian War. Archibald Kennedy, married to the widow of a Dutch settler, was an astute American political observer of the time. He noted that "Hudson's River is the Center and Key of the Continent; it is the basis of all our trade and connections with our own and foreign Indians: And if ever we lose it, we may fairly bid adieu to the Whole."[1] His observations were not limited to the river valley but included its inhabitants, as he referred to the "brave Batavians, and united too, whose Ancestors have so gloriously distinguished themselves in History for their noble Exploits in Defence of their Liberties and Country."[2]

The Dutch example, which became an important symbol for the colonists at the time of the Albany Congress in 1754, embraced the two Willems—Willem the Silent, Prince of Orange and the George Washington of the Netherlands, and his great-grandson, Willem III of the Netherlands, King William III of Great Britain. The union achieved by the Dutch in the sixteenth century became a paradigm for American colonists in the eighteenth century. Though the ideas of union and independence may long have lain in the hearts and minds of many Dutch settlers in America, those ideas were first openly discussed among the English settlers during the decade of the French and Indian War. It was during that war and among the colonial clergy of the Reformed tradition that the rhetoric was forged that was later to serve so decisive a role in kindling and stirring the fires of revolution. At first the focus was on union. At the time of the Albany Congress, Jonathan Mayhew, pastor of Boston's West Church, sharpened the point for his congregation in a sermon preached on the anniversary of the election of His Majesty's council for the province. The enemy at that point, of course, was France—not England—but later the argument was easily adapted to Britain. "No one that is not an absolute stranger to [French] ambition, to their policy, to their injustice, to their perfidiousness, can be in any doubt what they aspire at. . . . Their late conduct may well alarm us; especially considering our disunion, or at least want of a sufficient bond of union, amongst ourselves; an inconvenience which, it is to be hoped, we shall not always labour under. And whenever all our scattered rays shall be drawn to a point and proper focus, they can scarce fail to consume and burn up these enemies of our peace, how faintly soever they may strike at present. What *union* can do, we need only look toward those Provinces, which are distinguished by the name of the *United*, to know."[3] Since the rhetoric was aimed at France, and at the Catholicism which France represented, the resultant appeal was not only to Willem the Silent and to the Dutchmen's war of independence but also to their prince, Willem III, who had saved both the Netherlands and England from the "wicked and ambitious designs" of Louis XIV. In 1755, in *A Discourse Delivered at New-Ark*, the evangelical Presbyterian pastor Aaron Burr noted that "divine Providence prevented their total Overthrow, which seemed inevitable, by sundry favourable Interpositions.

Heaven rais'd up at that time, the great Hero of the Day, King William, then Prince of Orange, who, by his singular Wisdom and Valour, put a stop to that Torrent, which seemed to threaten Europe."[4] In a 1755 sermon, *Religion and Patriotism*, the New Jersey Presbyterian Samuel Davies reminded his listeners of the ancient Anglo-French enmity—"the French, those eternal Enemies of Liberty and Britons." He went on to note that God, "even that same gracious Power, has formed and raised up . . . a William."[5] That same year an old sermon of Francis Makemie was reprinted with its high praise of William III.[6] Burr, Davies, Makemie—all evangelical Presbyterian neighbors of the Jersey Dutch—found "Dutch Willy" a valuable symbol of Reformed patriotism. Their appreciation of the House of Orange added strength to the image of the Dutch as forerunners of liberty and freedom.

In the two decades between the Albany Congress and the outbreak of the Revolution, however, the focus shifted increasingly away from King William III to Willem the Silent and from the Glorious Revolution of 1688 to the struggle for Dutch independence in the sixteenth century. The analogies had strong religious implications, though at first largely limited to anti-Catholic sentiments appropriate to the facts of the French and Indian War. During the same period, however, colonial efforts for a non-denominational college for New York resulted instead in an Anglican establishment, King's College, now Columbia University. From the outspoken objections of pietistic Dutch clergymen, a clear anti-Anglicanism emerged, reviving feelings that had flared up earlier in the century when Lord Cornbury had attempted to exert his influence and authority over the Dutch church. As the Revolution neared, the religious antagonisms shifted more and more from the Church of Rome to the Church of England and to the imagined threat of an American bishop and a state church.

Among the settlers of the middle colonies, there was much more to the religious issue than the specter of Anglicanism. There was an inherent struggle within the various churches of the Reformed tradition, between the revivalistic pietistic evangelicals who were to become revolutionary Whigs and the more staid and orderly orthodox who were to become loyalist Tories. Nowhere was this division more clear than among the Dutch Reformed, where its roots had early been articulated by the patriarch Theodorus Jacobus Frelinghuysen. Indeed, it was his son Theodore who led the Albany Dutch against the establishment of King's College.

Early in the nineteenth century this division was most clearly set forth in *A Lamentation over the Rev. Solomon Froeligh*, recently deceased revivalist dominie and earlier an aggressive patriot leader: "There was between the two people [of Dutch New Jersey] the difference . . . of Whig and Tory during the American revolution, and,

To the Honourable

RIP VAN DAM. Esq

PRESIDENT of His Majesty's Council for the PROVINCE of NEW YORK

This View of the New Dutch Church is most humbly

Dedicated by your Honours most Obedient Serv. W.m Burgis

The New Dutch Church—engraving by William Burgis
(active 1716–1731)
This church in Nassau Street was completed in 1731
and torn down in 1882
(Courtesy of the Bryn Mawr College Library)

twenty-one years before the declaration of independence, there was the difference of *coetus* and *conferentie*. [The terms will be explained later.] But the trouble in the Dutch Church in America did not begin in 1755, although it raged then . . . ; it began 35 years before that. In 1720, in January, the Rev. Theodorus Jacobus Frelinghuysen came to this country from Holland, and settled in the four Raritan [New Jersey] congregations. He was the first experimental Dutch preacher in this country. The commencement of faithful preaching was the source of blessings, and the signal for war. The dissention and rent began in his societies, and, as godly ministers increased, spread throughout the Dutch churches. Whatever the exterior form the dissention may have put on, the radical ground of the whole difference was, nature and grace, the kingdoms of darkness and of light, the children of God and of the devil, the friends or foes of the saving work of the Holy Ghost. These things have from the beginning divided men, and will divide between them for ever!"[7]

If, as this essay contends, the American Revolution was vitally affected by the support of pietistic Dutch Calvinists, particularly the clergy, the motivating ideas behind them form the crucial base for the contention. Behind the banners of "Liberty" and "Independence" were deeply held convictions concerning religious experimentalism with its emphasis on rebirth, millenarianism with its emphasis on the coming of the Kingdom in America, and holy living with its emphasis on introspection and judgment. It is from these fundamental ideas that the revolutionary theology of 1776 took shape—and not only the theology of the War of Independence but much of its political ideology as well.

Aspects of pietism's message had found earlier expression in New Netherland, but from the time Frelinghuysen arrived in 1720 until his death during the winter of 1747–48 he provided the focus and the leadership for the increasingly influential experimental pietists. In addition to his own five natural sons, he led a group of spiritual sons into a single-minded commitment to the rebirth of colonial America. Though directed most immediately to their own congregations, these enthusiastic dominies frequently itinerated, preaching their fiery gospel in other towns and villages. Antagonisms aroused were seen as marks of vitality, and controversies were viewed as signs of alertness. Frelinghuysen's impact was not limited to the Dutch Reformed either. His close friendship with the Presbyterian Gilbert Tennent led to numerous contacts among the Scots-Irish and English Presbyterians, influencing directly the course of revivalism among them. Even George Whitefield, the most famous evangelist in colonial America, visited Frelinghuysen and attested to his influence. Whitefield, a methodistic Calvinist clergyman of the Church of England, found the doors of the

American Anglican churches shut against him, though he was eagerly welcomed by evangelistic Calvinists in other colonial churches. Of his stay with Frelinghuysen and his associates in New Brunswick, New Jersey, Whitefield recorded in his journal: "To me the Meeting seemed to be like the Meeting of the Twelve Tribes, when they came from different Parts to worship the Lord at Jerusalem. Among others that came to hear the Word, were several Ministers whom the Lord had been pleased to honour, in making Instruments of bringing many Sons to Glory. One was a Dutch Calvinistical Minister, named Freeling Housen. . . . He is a worthy old Soldier of Jesus Christ, and was the Beginner of the great work . . . in these Parts. He has been strongly opposed by his carnal Brethren, but God has always appeared for him in a surprising Manner, and made him more than Conqueror, thro' his love. He has long since learnt to fear him only who can destroy both Body and Soul in Hell."[8]

Frelinghuysen was not alone in being opposed by carnal brethren. The clergy of the Great Awakening, as the tumultuous intercolonial revival of the 1740's was known, were generally opposed by those clergy in their own denominations who found their religious enthusiasm offensive and their experimental theology untenable. The traditionalists were troubled by their opponents' informalities of worship and by the liberties they took with the liturgy. The increasing role of the laity among the enthusiasts was also deplored. As the anti-enthusiasts became more vocal, the revivalists responded by finding them "wanting in true religion." Whitefield came to believe that the majority of Episcopal clergymen were unconverted. Gilbert Tennent blasted the churches with his sermon *The Danger of an Unconverted Ministry*. Frelinghuysen mirrored his colleagues' sentiments and gave expression to his own Old World tradition when he cried: "Worthless, foolish pastors. Woe unto you, unfaithful watchmen."[9]

Frelinghuysen's diatribes were not reserved for the clergy. Indeed, his sermons regularly decried the lack of spirituality among his parishioners as well as among those outside of his congregation. One can well imagine the consternation of the elders who opposed him when they rose to partake of the Lord's Supper only to be met by Frelinghuysen's wail: "Behold the swine approach the table." A studied categorizing of Christians, a methodology which placed the pastor in the role of judge, was a central belief among the exponents of experimental godliness. Excesses of judgmental Christianity soon divided those congregations shepherded by pietistic clergy of Frelinghuysen's stripe. And it proved a surprisingly short step from the pastors' judgmental role in dividing the regenerate from the unregenerate of the Great Awakening to their judgmental stance in assaying between the Whigs and the Tories of the Revolution. Nor was the course of enthusiasm in New England far different from that of the middle colonies, though it was fed by slightly different rhetoric.

The Dutch Reformed in America were under the oversight of the Classis of Amsterdam. This bond was all the more significant because the Dutch churches of the middle colonies did not have the direct political interaction with the local government that marked the home churches. All theological and ecclesiastical problems had to be referred to the old country for resolution. All candidates for the ministry were expected to return to the Netherlands for final training and ordination. In all consequential matters, the Classis retained firm control, in spite of its lack of financial support. Given the hazards of sea travel and the great length of time required for even a letter to go from New York to Amsterdam and for its answer to be returned, life in the colonial churches was often difficult in the extreme. Frelinghuysen's disaffected parishioners, for example, first turned to pastors in New York City to plead their case. They in turn wrote to the Classis. Charges and countercharges were sent back and forth for years. An incalculable amount of time and energy was expended in this tripartite battling, energy that was desperately needed for upbuilding the churches in the wilderness of America. The Classis, too, was driven to frustration. It sought a plan from the churches "which might tend to promote the union of the Dutch churches . . . in doctrine and ecclesiastical business, according to the church-order, and the resolutions of Synod— but without impairing our correspondence—either by holding a yearly convention, or in such other way as you may think best."[10] A *coetus* was proposed. The *coetus* was to be an ecclesiastical body, subordinate to the Classis of Amsterdam, which in turn was subordinate to the Synod of North Holland. In the colonies, the *coetus* was to be given the power to ordain as well as to carry out certain routine matters for the local churches belonging to the body. The pietists welcomed this move as a step forward; but Frelinghuysen's longtime opponent, the conservative New York dominie Henricus Boel, led an opposition movement to the *coetus*. Again the Classis sought to adjudicate the matter from the other side of the sea. Ten years of tension and controversy passed before the first meeting of the *coetus* was finally held in September 1747—a few months before the death of the aged and ailing Frelinghuysen. Yet even Frelinghuysen's death scarcely created a lull in the storm. In a memorial note one of his former students wrote of him: "Numerous and fearful are the vicissitudes to be expected by the children of God. For comfort's sake, this is added."[11] It was cold comfort.

Boel's opposition to the *coetus* continued and his cohorts became known as the *conferentie*, considering themselves conferees of the Classis of Amsterdam. Boel, one who "warmed himself by the fire of

THE FRELINGHUYSEN HOMESTEAD.

(TOP) The Repeal, or The Funeral of Miss Ame-Stamp—
pro-American cartoon on the repeal of the Stamp Act,
issued in London and Philadelphia. Typical of
the shift from anti-Catholic to anti-Anglican sentiment
(*Courtesy of the Library Company of Philadelphia*)

(BOTTOM) The Freylinghuysen Homestead—
engraving made about 1750
(*Courtesy of the Bryn Mawr College Library*)

controversy," led the *conferentie* until his death in 1754, when his small but determined group of followers took over. In the meantime, the Classis of Amsterdam withdrew its earlier permission to examine and ordain students for the ministry. This led to new confusions, so the *coetus* went over the head of the Classis of Amsterdam and proposed to the Synods of North Holland and South Holland that the charter be amended so that the *coetus* might become a classis with the clear right to ordain.

At the same time the *coetus* controversy raged, the college issue mentioned earlier came to a head. The proposed non-denominational college of New York was being created as an Episcopal establishment, in spite of the fact that "nine-tenths of the population were non-Episcopal." In arguing for its non-denominational character against "so pernicious a Scheme" as the one proposed by the Episcopalians, William Livingston, grandson of patriarch Robert and a very active Reformed layman, again claimed the heritage of William III. "In the Reign of King James II of arbitrary and papistical Memory, a Project jesuitically artful, was concerted to poison the Nation, by filling the Universities with popish-affected Tutors; and but for our glorious Deliverance, by the immortal William, the Scheme had been sufficient, in Process of Time, to have introduced and established, the sanguinary and anti-Christian Church of Rome."[12] In a circular letter he appealed to "the Dutch Church": "Gentlemen of the Dutch Church . . . trace the Renown of your Progenitors, recollect their Stand, their glorious and ever memorable Stand against the Yoke of Thraldom, and all the horrors of ecclesiastic Villainy, its inseparable Concomitants. . . . Impell'd by their illustrious Example, disdain the Thoughts of a servile Acquiescence in the usurped Dominion of others, who will inevitably swallow up and absorb your Churches."[13]

The conservative Dutch clergy of New York ignored their fellow layman's appeal and petitioned for a chair of Reformed theology in this "Party-College," but their plan aroused even the ire of their own congregation. The pietistic clergy, meanwhile, were working to establish a Dutch Reformed college in New Jersey. Dominie Theodore Frelinghuysen of Albany took the lead by visiting the individual churches, seeking support for both the college and the American classis. In 1755 a meeting of the *coetus* was held in New York, largely attended by those sympathetic to the movement for a college and a classis. Those attending voted to restructure themselves as a classis and proceeded to assume the rights and prerogatives of a classis. Frelinghuysen was chosen as their delegate to take the matter to the Netherlands. The opposition wrote quickly to the Classis of Amsterdam, which replied to the erstwhile *coetus* leaders: "How many are the wretched troubles and the soul-destroying discords which afflict unhappy New York! . . . Instead of the old quarrels being healed, new ones are continually arising."[14] In spite of the strong opposition from Amsterdam to both the idea of an American classis and the suggestion of a Dutch university in the colonies, Frelinghuysen sailed for the Netherlands in 1759, hoping to gain Dutch backing for the plan. So completely was he identified with the project that his opponents called it "Frelinghuysen's Academy." He was coolly received in the Netherlands and his efforts were to no avail. His death on the return voyage to New York foreclosed the possibility of his seeing the realization of his dream. In 1766, however, the American classis which he had done so much to create received a charter for Queen's College, now Rutgers University, in New Jersey. The Dutch could now have a college in which to train the young clergy the American classis was to ordain.

The division between the still-entitled *coetus* and *conferentie* factions continued until healed on paper in 1771 by the mediation of Dominie John H. Livingston, Dutch Reformed pastor and cousin of the eloquent lawyer and patriot politician William Livingston. In 1766, after completing college at Yale, John Livingston had sailed to the Netherlands, the last colonial American Dutch Reformed student to return to the mother country for further education and ordination. He attended lectures at the University of Utrecht and made numerous friends in the Dutch church. When he returned to New York in 1771, he brought with him a proposal from the Synod of North Holland for a plan of union between the factions, which now included thirty-four clergymen. General agreement was reached and the document was sent to the Netherlands for final approval. On June 16, 1772, the American classis reassembled to hear the letter of approval read. The American church of the Dutch Reformed was independent at last, tied to the homeland by the formality of sending back annual minutes of their general body. Though peace was welcomed in the church at large, embers of enduring antagonism remained, waiting only for the next wind to bring them to flame again. That wind was to come all too soon, this time in political guise—the Declaration of Independence and the seven years of revolution which followed.

When the war erupted in 1776, the clergy of the former *coetus* faction were solidly on the side of the Whigs; indeed, many became deeply involved in the day-to-day activities of the Revolution. The Whigs also drew strength from those pastors who had been neutral in the *coetus-conferentie* struggle, as well as those men who had come into the church since the Union of 1772. On the other hand, the four most committed Tory pastors had been leaders of the *conferentie* movement and at least three other former *conferentie* pastors were Tory-inclined neutrals.

Most of the *coetus* clergy had been trained by followers of old

Dominie Frelinghuysen. Pre-eminent among those teachers were John Henry Goetschius and Frelinghuysen's son John. John died in 1754 at the young age of twenty-seven, but not before training his successor, and later patriot leader, Jacob Rutsen Hardenbergh. Goetschius lived until 1774, having trained several young ministerial students and having shared actively with Hardenbergh in the movement to establish Queen's College. At its founding, Goetschius became one of its first trustees and Hardenbergh its first president.

Goetschius' pupils, foremost among them Dominies Dirck Romeyn and Johannes Leydt, were joined by Dominie Hardenbergh in providing leadership to the Whig pastors in the Dutch churches and in direct personal involvement in the Revolution itself. Hardenbergh had also been active in the Provincial Congress leading up to the Declaration of Independence. He helped draft the constitution of the state of New Jersey. Indeed Hardenbergh's involvement prompted the British to place a bounty of one hundred pounds on his head. Romeyn, too, dubbed "the Rebel Parson," had a price on his head. Among his many patriotic activities, Romeyn provided an indispensable chain of intelligence reports for Washington and other Revolutionary officers. Though much could be said about the individual exploits of the Dutch Whig pastors, and much too of their Whig parishioners, the essential point was best summed up by a member of the opposition, one of the Tory printers: "The people in the Jerseys . . . were quite tired of their democratic tyranny, and that he [believed] the people in general would embrace reconciliation but for the inflammatory exclamations and instigations of their preachers."[15] Troops were often raised in the course of a fiery sermon.

In the middle ground of New Jersey and New York, it was the Reformed clergy, Presbyterian and Dutch Reformed, who provided much of the commitment and the dynamism that were essential in holding the critical Hudson Valley from British control. Another Tory wrote to Lord Dartmouth: "The war is at the bottom a religious war." This view was attested to by Dominie John Livingston in a letter written at the war's end: "The common enemy to our religious liberties is now removed; and we have nothing to fear from the pride and domination of the Episcopal Hierarchy."[16] Calvinist theology, which had become the spring of personal regeneration in the hands of the rebirth theologians, became the theology of political freedom and liberation for the patriots of the Revolution. Typical is the fact that the sole surviving male Frelinghuysen, old Dominie Frelinghuysen's grandson Frederick, served before the war in the Provincial Congress, during the war in the Continental Congress and as an officer in the Revolutionary forces, and after the war as a senator in the United States Congress and a major general in the militia. Such were the heirs of awakening theology and of that Dutch Calvinism which brought war to the Netherlands in the sixteenth century and to America two hundred years later.

NOTES

1   Archibald Kennedy, *Serious Advice to the Inhabitants of the Northern-Colonies* (New York, 1755), p. 17.

2   *Ibid.*, p. 12.

3   Jonathan Mayhew, *A Sermon Preach'd in the Audience of His Excellency William Shirley* (Boston, 1754), pp. 34–35.

4   Aaron Burr, *A Discourse Delivered at New-Ark* (New York, 1755), pp. 8–9.

5   Samuel Davies, *Religion and Patriotism the Constituents of a Good Soldier* (Philadelphia, 1755), pp. 3, 9.

6   Francis Makemie, *A Narrative of a New and Unusual American Imprisonment* (New York, 1755). This pamphlet was edited by William Livingston, who is mentioned in detail later in this study.

7   Cornelius T. Demarest, *A Lamentation over the Rev. Solomon Froeligh* (New York, 1827), p. 61.

8   George Whitefield, *A Continuation of the . . . Journal* [no. 5] (2nd ed.; London, 1740), p. 41.

9   Theodorus Jacobus Frelinghuysen, *Sermons* (New York, 1856), p. 373.

10 *Ecclesiastical Records* [*of the*] *State of New York* (Albany, 1901–19), p. 2664.

11 Frelinghuysen, *Sermons*, p. 342.

12 *Ecclesiastical Records*, p. 3339.

13 *Ibid.*, p. 3367.

14 *Ibid.*, p. 3656.

15 Cited in Adrian C. Leiby, *The Revolutionary War in the Hackensack Valley: The Jersey Dutch and the Neutral Ground* (New Brunswick, N.J., 1962), p. 49.

16 Alexander Gunn, *Memoirs of the Rev. John H. Livingston* (New York, 1829), p. 258.

Exodus Netherlands, Promised Land America

Dutch Immigration and Settlement in the United States

· ᏮᎾᎽᎪᎿᏚᏚ ·

ROBERT P. SWIERENGA

Magnitude of Immigration

DUTCH settlement in North America antedates that of almost every other European nation, except the English; it spans three and a half centuries. Yet despite the lengthy time span, Dutch *non*-immigration rather than immigration is the salient fact.[1] For one of the most densely populated and land-starved nations of Europe, it is remarkable that less than 300,000 Netherlanders emigrated overseas from 1820 to 1920 (Table 1).[2] Dutch labor, as one scholar remarked, "showed little inclination toward long and adventurous voyages."[3] The proverbial Dutch attachment to family, faith, and fatherland outweighed the appeal of overseas utopias.

Among European nations, the Dutch ranked only tenth in the proportion of their population that emigrated overseas in the nineteenth century (Table 2), and in the United States in 1900 they ranked a lowly seventeenth among foreign-born groups. There are today an estimated 3 million persons of Dutch birth or ancestry in the States, or a little more than 1 percent of the population.[4] This proportion is considerably smaller than at the birth of the new nation, when Dutch Americans, 80,000 strong, numbered nearly 3.5 percent of the populace.

Unlike other Western European nations in the nineteenth century, the Dutch never contracted "America fever." While its influence was felt in a few villages, no mass migration emptied a third to a half of the countryside as happened in Ireland.[5] Few of the Dutch who emigrated were driven by a desperate struggle to survive. Most made a conscious calculation that their future in America promised more prosperity for them and their children than if they remained in their homeland. Religious and cultural motives were secondary, except among a few thousand Dutch Quakers and Mennonites in the seventeenth century and several thousand Seceders (*Afgeschiedenen*) from the Netherlands Reformed (*Hervormde*) Church in the 1840's. Nor did a failed revolution or political libertarian ideals impel the Dutch to America, as with the German "Forty-eighters."[6]

Characteristics of Immigration

Although the total Dutch immigration was relatively small, its impact on the United States was significant for several reasons. First, the Dutch who did depart had a strong "America-centeredness." Ninety percent of all Dutch overseas emigrants before the mid-1890's settled in the States; the remaining 10 percent went to Netherlands colonies in the East Indies and South America, or to South Africa.[7] Only Norwegians surpassed the Dutch in the desire for "destination—America." This funneling pattern, like a megaphone, amplified the Dutch visibility in America.

Netherlanders have also had a greater presence in the United States than their numbers warrant because of their clustered settle-

TABLE 1.

Annual Overseas Emigration per 100,000 Dutch Population, 1820–1920

Year	Population on Dec. 31 (1000s)	Overseas Emigration	Rate per 100,000
1820–29 av.	2,424	39*	2
1830–39 av.	2,737	96*	4
1840	2,894	107	4
41	2,931	103	4
42	2,957	127	4
43	2,989	296	10
44	3,020	321	11
45	3,053	874	29
46	3,061	2,831	92
47	3,050	8,090	265
48	3,055	3,103	102
49	3,057	3,143	103

TABLE 1. (continued)

Year	Population on Dec. 31 (1000s)	Overseas Emigration	Rate per 100,000
1850	3,031	1,299	43
51	3,080	1,771	57
52	3,128	1,951	62
53	3,163	2,653	84
54	3,195	5,074	159
55	3,216	3,087	96
56	3,252	3,050	94
57	3,282	2,844	87
58	3,303	1,363	41
59	3,309	713	22
1860	3,336	1,163	35
61	3,373	863	26
62	3,410	931	27
63	3,453	1,333	39
64	3,492	1,036	30
65	3,529	1,814	51
66	3,553	3,727	105
67	3,592	4,923	137
68	3,628	3,520	97
69	3,580	4,018	112
1870	3,618	2,288	63
71	3,637	2,520	69
72	3,675	4,447	121
73	3,716	5,576	150
74	3,767	1,719	46
75	3,810	1,245	33
76	3,865	875	23
77	3,925	603	15
78	3,982	832	21
79	4,013	1,553	39
1880	4,061	4,670	116
81	4,114	7,462	181
82	4,173	5,975	143
83	4,225	3,433	81
84	4,278	2,611	61
85	4,336	1,782	41
86	4,391	1,758	40
87	4,451	4,214	95
88	4,506	4,461	99
89	4,511	7,495	166
1890	4,565	3,143	69
91	4,622	3,825	83

TABLE 1. (continued)

Year	Population on Dec. 31 (1000s)	Overseas Emigration	Rate per 100,000
92	4,670	5,934	127
93	4,733	5,724	121
94	4,796	1,357	28
95	4,859	1,457	30
96	4,929	2,299	47
97	5,004	1,543	31
98	5,075	1,175	23
99	5,104	1,472	29
1900	5,179	1,548	30
01	5,263	2,886	55
02	5,347	3,603	67
03	5,431	5,296	98
04	5,510	4,030	73
05	5,591	3,927	70
06	5,672	4,958	87
07	5,747	7,221	126
08	5,825	4,680	80
09	5,858	6,769	116
1910	5,945	7,136	120
11	6,022	7,752	129
12	6,114	7,774	127
13	6,213	8,503	137
14	6,340	6,275	99
15	6,450	4,131	64
16	6,583	3,905	59
17	6,725	1,983	29
18	6,779	2,182	32
19	6,831	5,574	82
1920	6,926	11,924	172

TOTALS:			
1820–1920	380,104	272,882	72

* U.S. immigrants only: 1820–29 = 387, 1830–39 = 958

Sources: Emigration figures for 1820–80 are derived from the author's analysis of the *Landverhuizers* records and U.S. ship lists (see notes 10 and 19). Emigration data for 1881–1920 are in *Bijdragen tot de Statistiek van Nederland* and in *Bijdragen . . .* (Nieuwe Volgreeks), Central Bureau for Statistics, The Hague. Population data are from the *Jaarboekje over . . . , 1841–64*, and the *Bijdragen tot de Statistiek . . . , 1865–1920*.

TABLE 2. *Emigration from Different European Countries to North America*
(*mean annual emigration in per mille of the population, 1851–1910*)

	1851–60	1861–70	1871–80	1881–90	1891–1900	1901–10	Average
Ireland	—	14.7	10.2	14.9	10.1	11.1	12.2
Norway	2.4	5.8	4.7	9.6	4.5	8.3	5.9
Italy	—	—	1.0	3.2	4.9	10.8	5.0
Iceland	—	—	4.2	8.8	3.0	2.3	4.6
England	—	2.8	4.0	5.7	3.6	5.8	4.4
Sweden	0.4	2.3	2.3	7.0	4.2	4.2	3.4
Finland	—	—	0.2	1.2	2.4	5.5	2.3
Denmark	0.3	1.0	2.1	3.9	2.2	2.8	2.1
Germany	2.6	1.7	1.5	2.9	1.0	0.5	1.7
Netherlands	0.5	0.6	0.5	1.0	0.5	0.9	0.7
France	0.3	0.2	0.2	0.3	0.2	0.1	0.2

Sources: Hans Norman, "Emigration from the Nordic Countries: Some Aspects," in Rob Kroes, ed., *American Immigration: Its Variety and Lasting Imprint*, Table 1, p. 51 (European Contribution to American Studies, I, 1979). Based on Official Statistics of the Nordic Countries; and W. F. Wilcox, ed., *International Migrations*, Vols. I and II (New York, 1931). For the Netherlands, see Table 1.

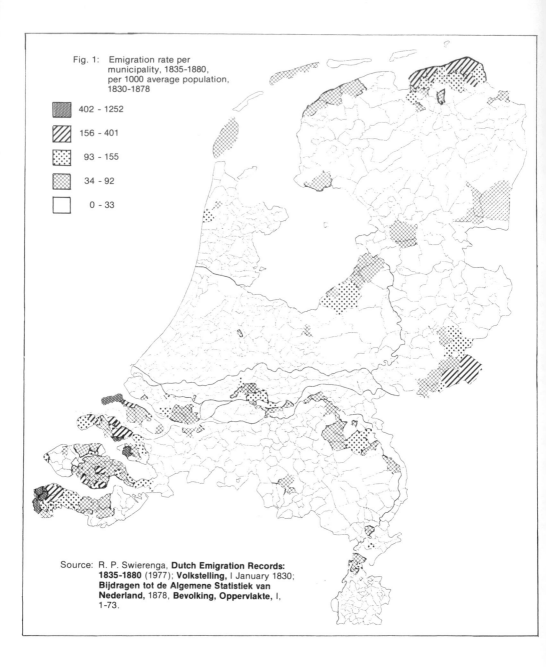

Fig. 1: Emigration rate per municipality, 1835-1880, per 1000 average population, 1830-1878

402 - 1252

156 - 401

93 - 155

34 - 92

0 - 33

Source: R. P. Swierenga, **Dutch Emigration Records: 1835-1880** (1977); **Volkstelling,** I January 1830; **Bijdragen tot de Algemene Statistiek van Nederland,** 1878, **Bevolking, Oppervlakte, I,** 1-73.

ments. In 1790, more than 125 years after the English seized New Netherlands, 80 percent of the Dutch Americans yet resided within a fifty-mile radius of New York City, where they comprised one-sixth of the population. Eighty years later, in 1870, after sixty to seventy thousand of the "new emigrants" had arrived, over 90 percent could be found in only eighteen counties or city wards in seven midwestern and mid-Atlantic seaboard states.[8]

The primary settlement field was within a fifty-mile radius of the southern Lake Michigan shoreline from Muskegon and Holland on the eastern side to Chicago, Milwaukee, and Green Bay on the western side. Secondary areas were in central Iowa and the New York City region including northern New Jersey. Subsequently, of course, the Dutch dispersed themselves over a wider area of the Great Plains and the Far West in search of cheap farmland. But few immigrant groups, if any, have clustered more than the Dutch. They chose precisely their intended destinations. Thus, in spite of a relatively weak volume of overseas migration, the Dutch single-mindedness for the United States and their clannish settlement behavior created a choice environment in which to nurture and sustain a strong sense of "Dutchness" for many generations.

At first the Dutchness was more apparent than real, given the fact that the Netherlands in the nineteenth century was a culturally diverse and locally oriented country, in which one's municipality or perhaps province often took pride of place over the nation. Indeed, in the 1870's Netherlands social scientists identified more than one hundred distinct subregions, based on variations in dialect, religion, soil types, and economic activity.[9] Only a few of these regions became significant "emigrant fields." These can be readily identified on an emigration density map (Fig. 1).[10] In the east, the Geldersche Achterhoek on the German border early became a prime field; in the north, it was the rich coastal farming regions (*bouwstreken*) of Groningen and Friesland; in the southwest, the Zuidholland island of Goeree-Overflakkee and the Zeeland islands of West Vlaanderen, Walcheren, Schouwen-Duiveland, and Zuid Beveland; and in the southeast, the Brabantse Peel centered in Uden.

The geographical origins of the Dutch emigrants, therefore, were as compact as the American settlement areas. Of the 1,156 Netherlands administrative units (*gemeenten*) in 1869—the equivalent of U.S. townships—only 134, or 12 percent, provided nearly three-quarters of all emigrants in the period from 1820 through 1880; 55 municipalities (5 percent) sent out one-half of all emigrants; and a mere 22 municipalities (2 percent) furnished one-third of all emigrants.[11] Thus within the Dutch immigrant funnel, there were actually many separate channels, like a clump of drinking straws, each carrying people from spe-

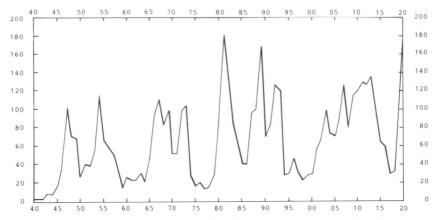

Fig. 2: Annual Dutch overseas emigration rates (per 100,000), 1840–1920

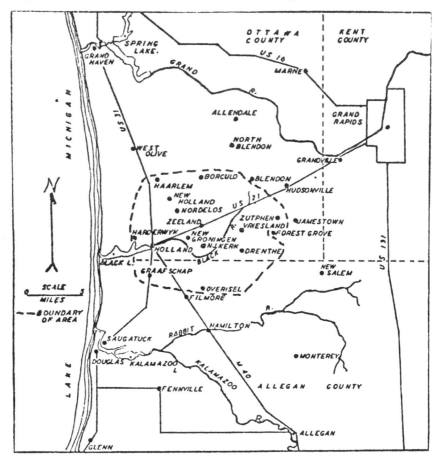

Fig. 3: Area of Dutch place names in Kent, Allegan,
and Ottawa Counties, Michigan

cific Dutch villages to specific American communities. The notorious "bacon letters" from earlier emigrants who had established themselves in the States provided the suction in the straws, so to speak, by appealing to and even compelling family and friends to come and join them in the bonanza. The fact that, over a period of six decades, three-fourths of the emigrants came from only 134 municipalities in the Netherlands, and in America three-fourths settled in only 55 townships and city wards by 1870, indicates the localized processes at work.[12] It was clearly a migration of transplanted communities and family chains: parents and children, siblings, grandparents, in-laws, and friends moving in an ever-widening circle from particular localities in the fatherland to particular communities in the States.[13]

Timing and Termini

Another feature of Dutch immigration in the last century is that "pull" forces in the States were more influential than "push" forces in the homeland. Theoretically, the moderate degree of emigration indicates that rational choices and pragmatic preferences, rather than dire want, led most of the Dutch to depart. They not only chose to leave, they also chose to come to the States, where cheap farmland or urban job opportunities among family and friends awaited them.

Both the timing of the Dutch transatlantic migration and its socioeconomic structure point to the greater influence of American forces. This is not to deny the importance of adverse conditions in the homeland; only to give them a subordinate place. Indeed, Dutch emigration began in earnest in the mid-1840's (Fig. 2), following a decade of religious strife and amid potato crop failures, cholera outbreaks, sharp price increases on basic foodstuffs, and lengthening relief rolls. But this was also a time, across the Atlantic, of the settling of the upper Midwest, after President Jackson's Indian removals and congressional liberalization of land policies. In 1841 Congress legalized squatting on surveyed public lands, and during the Mexican War, Congress offered soldiers millions of acres of land warrants to induce enlistments or reward those who served. This land paper quickly passed into the hands of land dealers and provided land buyers a substantial discount in the purchase of government land. In the initial Dutch colonies of Holland, Michigan, and Pella, Iowa, founded in 1847, the leaders stretched the groups' supply of Dutch Willempjes at the land office by entering thousands of acres of virgin land with land warrants purchased through dealers at discounts of up to 33 percent. Henry Peter Scholte, Pella's leader, entered nearly all of the colony's 16,000 initial acres of land with warrants.[14]

When the American land boom came to a sudden end in 1857,

due to a financial panic, prospective Dutch emigrants responded by postponing their move until conditions improved. Most waited for eight years until the Civil War ended, the major exception being a few hundred farm families, mainly from Zeeland Province, who decided rather than delay to go to Brazil in 1861–63.[15] From 1865 to the next American economic crisis of 1873, a second wave of Dutch emigrants crossed to the States, enticed largely by the Homestead Act of 1862. Yet a third wave, the greatest in Dutch history, except for the decade following the devastating World War II, began in 1878 when economic conditions improved and the farmer's last frontier was thrown open by Congress and the railroad companies. This phase was sustained by an agricultural crisis in the cash grain region of the northern Netherlands, resulting from a worldwide glut of grain.[16] This saturation phase of Dutch immigration continued until the American economy plunged into yet another economic depression in 1893, which was capped by war with Spain. In 1894, Dutch immigration dropped by 80 percent and continued at a low ebb until 1901, when it gradually began to rise, reaching its high point in 1913. World War I, of course, checked this fourth phase and again diverted Dutch emigrants away from the States. From 1915 through 1920, more than one-half of the reduced emigrant stream went to the Netherlands East Indies.

In the early twenties, the flow to the States increased sharply, but the quota limit, imposed first in 1921 and reduced in 1924, took its toll.[17] Never again, except by special congressional dispensation, could more than 3,100 Dutch annually enter the United States, even after World War II, when there was a lengthy waiting list of 40,000. This dismal prospect induced over 80 percent of the nearly one million post-1945 emigrants to settle in Canada, Australia, or elsewhere. In 1968 Congress replaced the national origins law with a quota based on needed skills; this has proven to be even more restrictive and only 1,500 Netherlanders per year have been admitted. Unprecedented prosperity at home in the 1970's also dampened the desire of many to emigrate, although in 1979 inquiries about emigration were up 100 percent over 1978 and 40 percent more people completed formal applications to emigrate.[18] This suggests that another emigration upcycle may be building.

The main point of this review of the timing and termini of Dutch overseas migration is that, at least until the quota system created artificial barriers, prospective Dutch emigrants favored the United States and they responded directly to American conditions. "Land booms" sparked each emigrant surge and economic panics and depressions dampened them. In the troughs of the cycle, most prospective immigrants waited at home, although the usual small numbers of white-collar types and the occasional farm family continued to go to the Dutch colonies or to developing countries elsewhere.

Structural Characteristics

The salience of American pull factors is also indicated by the social structural characteristics of the nineteenth-century migration, which can be determined from the *Landverhuizers* (Emigration) lists compiled by the Netherlands government and from the ship passenger lists collected by U.S. customs officials.[19] Of the more than 60,000 registered emigrants in the period 1835–80, only 12,000 (20 percent) lived in the Randstad cities, provincial capitals, or lesser urban municipalities. The remainder were from rural villages and the countryside. Farmers and farm laborers comprised 26 percent, day laborers—many of whom undoubtedly also worked in agriculture—made up another 39 percent, 21 percent were village craftsmen, and 4 percent worked in the industrial sector, mainly in textiles and small instruments. Only 10 percent were in the white-collar class—professionals, administrators, etc. (Table 3).[20] Farmland was the obvious objective of these largely rural, blue-collar emigrants.

Social class data likewise portray an exodus of lower-middle-class rural folk. Two-thirds were classified in the emigration documents as middling in economic status and a fifth were needy. Only one in eight was wealthy.[21] It is instructive that 96 percent of those in middling circumstances and 85 percent of the needy emigrants went to the States compared to only 60 percent of the well-to-do.[22]

Figures on age, sex, and family status for the years 1820–80 likewise indicate the exodus of young peasant families seeking upward mobility and trying to avoid a seeming inevitable decline in status.[23] The average age of all Dutch arrivals in the States was 22 years, adult males outnumbered females by a ratio of six to four, and more than three-fourths of all immigrants left with family members. This high degree of family involvement exceeds by fifteen to thirty points the German and Scandinavian migration and reveals the Dutch as a "folk" migration rather than a "labor-type" migration of solitary adult males, as with the British and Irish. Of the emigrating families, two-thirds were couples with children and half the remainder were single-parent families and half childless couples. The average age of husbands was 36 years, wives 33.5 years, and children of all ages 8.3 years. These were young, still growing families. The average family size at the time of immigration was only 4.3 persons. The fact that Dutch immigration was a family affair also increased the likelihood of newcomers settling near relatives and neighbors rather than striking out on their own.

TABLE 3. *Occupations by Industrial Sector, Dutch Emigrants, 1835–80**

Sector	1835–57		1858–68		1869–80		Total	
	Row N	Row %	Row N	Row %	Row N	Row %	Row N	Col. %
Primary								
Farmers	1,245	44	779	28	813	29	2,837	16
Farm Laborers	540	31	465	27	738	42	1,743	10
								26
Secondary								
Pre-industrial Crafts:								
Building trades	653	43	371	25	484	32	1,508	8
Food processors	261	33	295	37	235	30	791	4
Metal workers	162	49	76	23	93	28	331	2
Wood workers	487	49	234	23	273	23	994	5
Saddlers, tanners	148	40	113	30	112	30	373	2
								21
Industrial:								
Textiles	160	60	56	21	49	18	265	2
Iron and steel	6	35	5	29	6	35	17	0
Engineers	14	37	12	32	12	32	38	0
Watches, instruments	134	38	96	27	122	35	352	2
Printers	4	16	11	44	11	40	20	0
Misc.	14	25	17	30	26	46	57	0
								4
Laborers (unspecified)	2,176	31	2,256	32	2,673	38	7,105	39
Tertiary								
Clerical	24	19	41	32	64	50	129	1
Commercial	310	37	218	26	300	36	828	4
Officials, government	31	15	98	46	82	39	211	1
Professional	148	26	212	38	199	36	559	3
Gentlemen, students	44	44	25	25	31	31	100	1
Service	29	52	10	18	17	30	56	0
								10

* The categories are those employed by Charlotte Erickson, "Who Were English Emigrants of the 1820's and 1830's? A Preliminary Analysis" (unpublished paper, 1977). Excluded are 2,043 individuals with no occupation or trade or not employed.

Source: R. P. Swierenga, *Dutch Emigration Records, 1835–1880.*

Settlement Patterns

Dutch immigrants carried their familism and localism to America as part of their cultural baggage. Like other European peasants from areas generally isolated from the forces of the industrial revolution, the Dutch immigrants valued an ordered, traditional society based on kinship, village, and church. When these people emigrated, they sought to transplant their village cultures, churches, and kin networks. Most were not innovators seeking to break free of their identity group but conservatives intending to maintain their culture in a new environment. Group identity and the desire for religious and cultural maintenance dictated settlement in segregated communities on the frontier or in urban neighborhoods.[24] In-group marriage patterns resulted from these residential patterns and also perpetuated them. In 1850, only 4.8 percent of the Dutch in America had non-Dutch spouses, in 1860 the figure had risen to 11.1 percent, and in 1870 to 13.3 percent.[25]

Because Dutch from the same old-country villages preferred to settle together in the New World in order to lessen the emotional shock of leaving the homeland and to facilitate the adjustment to a new environment, provincial or local loyalties remained strong in most settlements in the States, at least until the first generation passed from the scene. In the classic example of this phenomenon, nearly every village and town in half a dozen townships surrounding the largest Dutch colony of Holland in Ottawa County, Michigan, boasted a Dutch place name derived from the province or town where most of the first settlers originated. The central city of Holland, called simply *de stad*, initially in 1847 consisted largely of people from Gelderland and Overijssel provinces. New arrivals soon founded villages within a ten-mile radius bearing the provincial names of Zeeland, Vriesland, Groningen, Overisel, New Holland, Drenthe, and the Geldersche Buurt (Fig. 3). The names of Dutch municipalities also appeared, such as Zutphen, Nordeloos, Haarlem, Hellendoorn, Harderwijk, and Staphorst. The majority of settlers in these villages originated in the place bearing the village name, they spoke the local dialect, and perpetuated dress and food customs. The entire settlement was known as *de Kolonie*, but it required the passing of the first generation before the colony became a community. Holland's sister colony of Pella, Iowa, also founded in 1847, similarly had its cultural divisions. The majority of the settlers were from the large cities of Utrecht and Amsterdam, but there was also a smaller group of rural Frisians who settled a mile north of Pella in the Vriesche Buurt. The entire colony consisted initially of religious Seceders from the Netherlands Reformed Church, yet their provincial differences caused friction for many years, despite a shared religious bond.[26]

In frontier settlements in the 1880's and 1890's, new Dutch immigrants continued to perpetuate such provincial distinctions. In Charles Mix County of South Dakota, for example, a group of Calvinist immigrants from Friesland and Overijssel in 1883 established separate communities five miles apart, bearing the names of their respective provinces. Each insisted on its own church congregation and edifice, although they belonged to the same denomination and shared a minister between them.[27]

In American cities and villages that predated Dutch occupancy, Holland settlers likewise clustered in neighborhoods with kin and friends. In Chicago, immigrants from the province of Zuidholland located their community in the Calumet district of south Chicago, calling their village Lage (Low) Prairie and later South Holland. Meanwhile, other immigrants from the province of Noordholland planted their settlement six miles north in Hooge (High) Prairie (later called Roseland), while yet another group from Groningen Province established themselves a mile west of the center of Chicago in a neighborhood popularly known as the Groningsche Hoek (Groningen Quarter). Milwaukee's "Dutch Hill" and Rochester's "Holland Settlement" were populated with Gelderlanders. Zeelanders founded the oyster-fishing village of West Sayville, Long Island, and the New York farm communities of Pultneyville and East Williamson on Lake Ontario. Other Zeelanders found work in the New Jersey manufacturing cities of Paterson, Passaic, and Lodi. Gelderlanders predominated in Clymer and Frisians in Lancaster, both farm settlements near Buffalo, in western New York. Dutch Jews, nearly a thousand in number, emigrated in an axis from Amsterdam to New York City, with a few proceeding to the inland commercial centers of Cincinnati, St. Louis, and Chicago. In Wisconsin the pattern is similar: Frisians founded the town of Friesland in Columbia County and New Amsterdam in La Crosse County. Zeelanders dominated the cities of Sheboygan and Oostburg, Gelderlanders in Alto, Groningers in Gibbsville, and Catholic Brabanters in the Fox River valley south of Green Bay centered at Little Chute. Lesser Dutch Catholic settlements were in Michigan's Saginaw Valley near Lake Huron, in Ohio's major cities of Cleveland and Cincinnati, and in Chicago.

Geographical Mobility

Even within the United States, internal Dutch migration was generally from one Dutch settlement to another, although patterns varied in rural and urban communities. In rural colonies, Dutch farmers first expanded locally by buying for their sons adjoining farms of non-Dutch neighbors, as these came on the market. Like a giant oil slick, the Dutch gradually expanded outward until land prices were driven up prohibitively within the perimeter area of the core community, which might have extended up to ten miles from the center. Thereafter, expansion was of the "mothering" type in which original colonies birthed daughter colonies up to 100 miles or more distant. The Holland, Michigan, colony in Ottawa County had within thirty years (1880) expanded into five adjacent counties and one small settlement 100 miles north. By 1900, its people even reached the Upper Peninsula. Pella, Iowa, within a generation was likewise a "beehive ready for swarming," according to a local resident. Farmland fetched $60 per acre and was scarce at that price. Consequently, in 1870 sixty families organized and founded a new settlement in Sioux County in the northwestern corner of the state, where free homestead land was yet available. The cheap land in the new colony, centered in Orange City, soon attracted settlers from other overpopulated Dutch colonies in Wisconsin and Michigan as well as new immigrants directly from the Netherlands. Again within a generation, by 1900, almost every township in Sioux County was filled with Hollanders and they spilled over into adjoining counties, and even across the border into the neighboring states of Minnesota and South Dakota. Subsequently, the Orange City settlement mothered a Dutch movement to the Pacific Northwest.

In rising metropolitan centers such as Chicago, Milwaukee, and Grand Rapids, the Dutch immigration pattern differed from the rural areas. It was both centripetal and centrifugal. The cities initially served as a magnet which attracted Dutch settlers from nearby rural villages and farms within a ten- to fifteen-mile radius. Several pioneer Dutch communities near Milwaukee, for example, lost virtually all of their families to the metropolis. Simultaneously, as the central cities became industrialized and densely populated, the Dutch tended to move outward in concentric circles. The more affluent moved into the better-class suburbs and those who preferred to continue truck gardening resettled beyond the suburban limits, moving repeatedly as the city encroached on them.

The Calvinist Dutch in Chicago and environs best exemplify this urban pattern.[28] Initially in the 1840's, Hollanders, as noted above, founded three core communities in the Chicago area: the near West Side Groningers, a lower-class group of teamsters, peddlers, and day laborers who worked in the central city; the Roseland Noordhollanders, a truck-gardening settlement fourteen miles directly south;

and the Zuidhollanders of South Holland, a general-farming settlement twenty miles southeast near Lake Michigan at the Indiana border. These communities grew slowly but steadily until the 1880's and 1890's, when a mass uprooting occurred under the combined forces of new affluence, urban sprawl, and a renewed wave of immigration from the Netherlands that created land scarcity in the two farming communities, and the press of other ethnic groups such as Italians and Greeks on the West Side settlement. Within a generation, the entire West Side Dutch community sold their homes, churches, and Christian day school building and moved two miles directly west to the Douglas Park–Lawndale district. A few West Siders went seven miles south to the vegetable farms of Englewood, where they were joined by new immigrants from Groningen and Friesland provinces, who had been victims of the agricultural crisis of the 1880's. Other West Siders opened truck farms at the city's western fringes. The Roseland vegetable gardeners were invaded in the 1880's by Chicago's major industrial firms, which attracted tens of thousands of Slavic and Latin laborers to the community. Most of the Dutch farmers who had bought their lands in 1849 for $5 per acre now sold them for $2,000 and more per acre. Many remained in Roseland, choosing to adapt to urban life, but others bought farms in South Holland or in northern Indiana. A few went north several miles to Englewood, where vegetable farming remained viable. Every location, of course, contained a Dutch Reformed community, complete with churches, a Christian day school, and Dutch-owned shops and services.

From the 1920's through the 1940's, the West Side community of Groningers, 2,000 in number, under the continuing pressure of the other ethnic groups, fled to the western suburbs of Cicero and Berwyn. Subsequently, after World War II, the inexorable "flight to the suburbs" continued, as the expanding black community pressed against the Dutch enclaves of Englewood, Roseland, and Cicero, all of whom within twenty years relocated beyond Chicago's city limits.

Thus, in the course of 130 years, the Protestant Hollanders of Chicago fanned out from three core areas by a series of community migrations, until they entirely abandoned first the inner city for the near suburbs and then the near suburbs for the far suburbs. Although they number only 30,000 to 40,000 out of a population of several million in Greater Chicago, their religious solidarity and in-group marriage pattern, plus their clustering tendency, have enabled them to retain their ethnic identity for five and six generations. Given the existence of Christian day schools and churches in each cluster area, the Chicago-area Dutch could virtually choose the way of life they preferred—urban, suburban, or rural—without jeopardizing their ethno-religious solidarity.

Economic Life

Immigrant Hollanders typically were farmers, laborers, and artisans, who brought to America an ethic of industrious work, practical farming methods, and a strong desire for agricultural land.[29] Prosperous Dutch settlements throughout the midwestern and northern plains states attest to their land hunger. Except for the Dutch Jews of New York City, and the Protestant enclaves in Paterson, Passaic, Cleveland, Detroit, Chicago, Grand Rapids, and Milwaukee, most Dutch pursued farming. They commonly had enough capital to open farms, or barring that, they rented before moving up the agricultural ladder to ownership. Having come from an area with advanced agricultural practices, they brought a knowledge of grain, livestock, and dairy farming that was readily adaptable to the American environment. Thus, the Dutch shared with other Northern Europeans a predilection for rural life. In 1880, less than 25 percent of the Dutch-born lived in the fifty largest American cities; in 1920, the proportion of Dutch-born farm operators was twice as large as their share of the total population.[30]

Farming patterns differed widely. The Dutch near metropolitan centers engaged in vegetable gardening, often after laboriously draining swampy mucklands that Americans had passed over. The Dutch supplied cauliflower, cabbage, onions, and especially celery to the urban farm wholesale markets. Dairying was another natural specialty for Hollanders, especially those in Wisconsin, Michigan, and New York. In Iowa, Minnesota, the Dakotas, and elsewhere on the plains, however, the Dutch adopted American methods of mixed grain and livestock farming on extensive acreages. Fishing and bulb growing, although traditional in the old country, attracted very few immigrants, except for the Zeelanders, who established a fishing settlement in West Sayville, Long Island, and Noordhollanders, who took up bulb growing in Grand Rapids, Michigan, Kankakee, Illinois, and Puget Sound, Washington.

The immigrant Dutch in the nineteenth century were artisans and rural laborers who understood simple mechanics but not a factory system with sophisticated machinery. Those who settled in Paterson, Grand Rapids, Chicago, and other cities, however, easily adjusted to industrial work, as did the sons of rural immigrants who gravitated from farm to cities. By 1880, the Grand Rapids furniture industry, largely Dutch-owned and manned by Dutch craftsmen, was nationally renowned. The Chicago Pullman Car Company in Roseland and Paterson textile mills also attracted an increasing number of Dutch workers in the late nineteenth century. In rural Michigan and Wisconsin, other Dutch young men took employment in the lumber mills.

Most urban Dutch preferred to remain independent. They opened small retail shops to cater to an almost exclusively Dutch clientele or they penetrated the service sector, becoming building contractors, general teamsters, and refuse haulers. Increasingly, as the third, fourth, and fifth generations attained higher educational levels, the Dutch moved upward into white-collar jobs in the professions, in the civil service, and in corporate management positions. A 1969 occupation survey of household heads in the most ethnically conscious Dutch-American denomination—the Christian Reformed Church—revealed that 41 percent held white-collar positions, compared to 33 percent blue-collar workers and 14 percent farmers.

Group Maintenance

This upward mobility, coupled with the virtual end of Dutch immigration to the United States, has threatened the survival of Dutch ethnic identity. Throughout the second half of the nineteenth century the Dutch strove for economic security and cultural space in a host society. They reached the high point of ethnic consciousness and pride in the period 1900–20, bracketed by the heroic Boer War and the chauvinistic World War I, when a hyperpatriotism took its toll on Dutch solidarity. Following the war, immigrant leaders encouraged the Americanization movement in their churches and schools. In the 1920's and 1930's Dutch-language preaching and teaching in the churches ceased, except in a few congregations, and most ethnic newspapers and periodicals likewise succumbed. Compared to other Northern European nationalities, however, even in the interwar years Dutch-American Protestants retained a relatively sharp sense of ethnic identity, although its decline was perceptible with each passing generation.

Viewed in this light, the great post-1945 Dutch immigration to Canada's Ontario Province directly across the U.S. border from Michigan and New York, and in lesser degree to the United States itself, was a most timely influx for renewing from within the lagging Dutch ethnic consciousness. This internal force was augmented by the rising sense of ethnicity among Americans generally, as reflected in the enthusiastic response to Alex Haley's book *Roots* and its television production.[31] Dutch-American institutions are presently thriving, many people are studying the Dutch language and culture, and the free flow of people and ideas across the Atlantic is greater than since the 1920's. As a result, the inevitable process of Americanization has slowed somewhat, thus providing at least a temporary reprieve for the survival of Dutch ethnic identity. It is a reprieve for which I am most appreciative.

NOTES

1 This point is analyzed in P. R. D. Stokvis, "Dutch Mid-Nineteenth Century Emigration in European Perspective" (unpublished paper). Stokvis notes (pp. 2–4) that W. S. Petersen was struck by the low emigration of the 1840's and F. D. Scott and F. Thistlethwaite were puzzled by the minimal outpouring of the 1880's and 1890's. See Petersen, *Planned Migration: The Social Determinants of the Dutch-Canadian Movement* (Berkeley, Calif., 1955), pp. 42, 58–60; Thistlethwaite, "Migration from Europe Overseas in the Nineteenth and Twentieth Centuries," *XIᵉ Congrès International des Sciences Historiques, Stockholm, 1960, Rapports, V; Histoire Contemporaine* (Göteborg, Stockholm, and Uppsala, 1960), p. 54; Scott, "The Study of the Effects of Emigration," *Scandinavian Economic Historical Review*, VIII (1960), 169.

2 For the latest estimates of the actual rate for 1820–80, see R. P. Swierenga, "Dutch International Migration Statistics 1820–1880: An Analysis of Linked Multinational Files," *International Migration Review*, XV (Fall 1981), 445–70.

3 J. Mokyr, "Industrialization and Poverty in Ireland and the Netherlands: Some Notes Toward a Comparative Study," unpublished paper presented to the American Historical Association meeting, San Francisco, 1978, p. 15.

4 R. P. Swierenga, "Dutch," in S. Thernstrom, A. Orlov, and O. Handlin, eds., *Harvard Encyclopedia of American Ethnic Groups* (Cambridge, Mass., 1980), 284–95.

5 Petersen, *Planned Migration*, pp. 7, 42–43, 60–64; II. S. Lucas, *Netherlanders in America: Dutch Immigration to the United States and Canada, 1789–1950* (Ann Arbor, Mich., 1955), pp. 44–58; J. van Hinte, *Nederlanders in Amerika: Een Studie over Landverhuizers en Volksplanters in de 19e en 20ste Eeuw in de Vereenigde Staaten van Amerika* (2 vols.; Groningen, 1928), I, 117–202; G. F. DeJong, *The Dutch in America, 1609–1974* (Boston, 1975), pp. 129–48.

6 The attribution of motivation is highly controversial. American scholars view religious factors as primary in the 1840's and economic forces thereafter; Dutch scholars stress the social and economic factors. Lucas, *Netherlanders in America*, pp. 42, 471–78; DeJong, *Dutch in America*, pp. 132–33; P. R. D. Stokvis, *De Nederlandse Trek Naar Amerika, 1846–1847* (Leiden, 1977), pp. 203–5; van Hinte, *Nederlanders in Amerika*, Ch. 4; G. B. van Dijk, "Geloofsvervolging of Broodnood: Hollanders Naar Michigan," *Spiegel Historiael*, V (1970), 31–36.

7 R. P. Swierenga, "Dutch International Labor Migration to North America in the Nineteenth Century," in M. Boekelman and H. Ganzevoort, eds., *Dutch Immigration to North America* (forthcoming, 1982), note 21.

8 Based on the author's compilation of Dutch-born persons in the U.S. manuscript population censuses of 1870; R. P. Swierenga, *Dutch Immigrants in U.S. Population Censuses, 1850, 1860, and 1870: An Alpha-*

betical Listing by Household Heads or Single Persons (Kent, Ohio, 1982).

9   Department of Binnenslandsche Zaken, *Verslag van den Landbouw in Nederland over 1871* (The Hague, 1871), pp. 22–31.

10 Derived from R. P. Swierenga, *Dutch Emigration Records: 1835–1880: A Computer Alphabetical Listing of Heads of Households and Independent Persons* (rev. ed.; Kent, Ohio, 1977).

11 Derived from a computer-accessible file, compiled by R. P. Swierenga, entitled "Netherlands Census, Labor, Land, and Migration Data, 1830–1878" (Kent, Ohio, 1979).

12 See note 8 for source.

13 Examples are in Y. Saueressig, "Catholic Emigration from the Southern Provinces of the Netherlands in the Nineteenth Century," paper presented at the Netherlands Interuniversity Demographic Institute, The Hague, May 1981; Irene Hecht, "Kinship and Migration: The Making of an Oregon Isolate Community," *Journal of Interdisciplinary History*, VIII (Summer 1977), 45–67; R. P. Swierenga, "The Anatomy of Migration: From Europe to the U.S. in the Nineteenth Century," in Val Greenwood and Frank Smith, eds., *Preserving our Heritage: Proceedings of the World Conference on Records* (12 vols.; Salt Lake City, Utah, 1980), IV, Series 357, 13–15.

14 R. P. Swierenga, *Pioneers and Profits: Land Speculation on the Iowa Frontier* (Ames, Iowa, 1968), p. 96.

15 M. C. Saris, *Emigratie naar Brazil, 1858–1862* (Paris, 1977); G. A. C. van Vooren, "Emigranten naar Brazilie uit West-Zeeuws-Vlaanderen, 1858–1862" (mimeograph, n.d.); "The Lost Dutch of Espirito Santo," New Westminster (B.C.) *Windmill Herald*, March 14, 1977, p. 10.

16 H. deVries, *Landbouw en Bevolking Tijdens de Agrarische Depressie in Friesland (1878–1895)* (Wageningen, 1971).

17 Philip Taylor, *The Distant Magnet: European Emigration to the USA* (New York, 1971), pp. 250–55.

18 "Dutch Alarmed at Soaring Emigration," Los Angeles *Times*, December 25, 1979, Part IX, p. 4.

19 R. P. Swierenga, *Dutch Immigrants in U.S. Ship Passenger Lists, 1820–1880: An Alphabetical Listing by Household Heads and Single Persons* (Kent, Ohio, 1981). See note 10 for the citation of the Dutch Emigration Records.

20 Compiled from Swierenga, *Dutch Emigration Records*.

21 R. P. Swierenga and H. S. Stout, "Dutch Immigration in the Nineteenth Century, 1820–1877: A Quantitative Overview," *Indiana Social Studies Quarterly*, XXVIII (Autumn 1975), 7–34.

22 For extensive statistical data on the demographic aspects, see R. P. Swierenga, "Dutch Immigrant Demography, 1820–1880," *Journal of Family History*, V (Winter 1980), 390–415.

23 Recent findings indicate that transplanted homogeneous communities were the norm rather than the exception among all European immigrant groups. See R. Ostergren, "A Community Transplanted: The Formative Experience of a Swedish Immigrant Community in the Upper

Middle West," *Journal of Historical Geography*, V (April 1979), 189–212; W. Kamphoefner, "Transplanted Westphalians: Persistence and Transformation of Socioeconomic and Cultural Patterns in the Northwest German Migration to Missouri" (Ph.D. dissertation, University of Missouri, 1978), Ch. 4; J. T. Cumbler, "Transplanted Working Class Institutions," *Journal of Historical Geography*, LXI (July 1980), 275–90.

24 Computed from Swierenga, *Dutch Immigrants in U.S. Population Censuses, 1850, 1860, and 1870.*

25 See, for example, the pamphlet published in the Netherlands written by the Pella pioneer Sjoerd Aukes Sipma. An English translation is R. P. Swierenga, ed., "A Dutch Immigrant's View of Frontier Iowa," *Annals of Iowa*, XXXVIII (Fall 1965), 81–118.

26 *75th Anniversary Booklet 1883–1953*, Platte Christian Reformed Church, Platte, S.D., pp. 7–9.

27 This section relies on A. Vanden Bosch, *The Dutch Communities of Chicago* (Chicago, 1928); Swierenga, "Dutch," pp. 288–89.

28 This section is a summary of Swierenga, "Dutch," p. 289.

29 *Compendium of the Tenth Census*, June 1, 1880 (2 vols.; Washington, D.C., 1883), I, 470; *Thirteenth Census of the United States, 1810*, Vol. I: *Population*, pp. 695, 794–95; Vol. V: *Agriculture*, p. 178.

30 R. P. Swierenga, "Ethnicity in Historical Perspective," *Social Science*, LII (1977), 31–44.

The Gilbert Stuart portrait of Isaac Roosevelt (1726–1794)
which hangs in the Roosevelt Home at Hyde Park, New York
(*Courtesy of the Franklin D. Roosevelt Library*)

The Dutchness of the Roosevelts

· COXXVO ·

FRANK FREIDEL

Two of the most notable of American Presidents in the twentieth century, Theodore Roosevelt and Franklin D. Roosevelt, took intense pride in their Dutch ancestry. It was the first topic that Theodore Roosevelt wrote about in the opening pages of his *Autobiography*. Franklin sketched the family line in a paper he wrote as a student at Harvard University, and at the beginning of each of his unprecedented four terms as President took his oath of office on the old Dutch family Bible.[1]

Yet both Roosevelts were Dutch more in name and in tradition than in origins. Theodore, a fifth cousin of Franklin, was less than a quarter Dutch; Franklin had only a trifling percentage of Dutch ancestry. Both Roosevelts, despite their name, were predominantly English in origin.

There were sound reasons, both political and social, for their pride in their Dutch name. Socially there was no more prestigious pedigree in New York than to be a member of one of the old Knickerbocker families, tracing descent from the founders of New Amsterdam. The Roosevelts enjoyed a secure position in New York society.

The political worth of a Dutch name was rather less tangible but nevertheless seemed consequential to both the Roosevelts. It was well to give the impression that one was somehow not an unadulterated blue blood of English colonial aristocracy, but rather a product of the American melting pot. Both Roosevelts had a tendency to claim as varied an ancestry as possible depending upon the ethnic origins of the group whose votes they were soliciting at a given moment. Both were prone to some exaggeration. There were those who joked that TR would have alleged any ancestry that would pull him a few additional votes, and that through citing it he sought to identify himself with almost any ethnic group he addressed. He could express his pride over not only his Holland but also his French Huguenot and English

[149]

Welsh Quaker ancestors, Scotch Covenanters, peace-loving Germans from the Palatinate, and "by no means altogether peaceful . . . Scotch-Irish." The historian Howard K. Beale, examining all of Roosevelt's lineage, found "forbears who had settled in seven of the thirteen colonies . . . and who religiously had included agnostics, members of the Dutch Reformed Church, French Protestants, Friends, Lutherans, Mennonites, Episcopalians, and Presbyterians." One of those who arrived in New Amsterdam in 1654 was Resolved Waldron, a wheelwright, from the group of Pilgrims who had remained in Holland when most of their number sailed to found Plymouth colony. Franklin D. Roosevelt had an equally diverse ancestry. On occasion he boasted of descent from a Finnish-Swedish saddle maker, Martinus Hoffman, who had come to New Netherland in the seventeenth century from the Hanseatic city of Riga on the Baltic (now a part of the Soviet Union).[2]

While the Roosevelts often talked about their non-Dutch forebears, their Dutchness was a matter of pride in all seasons, transcending social and political considerations. Theodore Roosevelt demonstrated that pride in the opening lines of his autobiography:

> My grandfather on my father's side was of almost purely Dutch blood. When he was young he still spoke some Dutch, and Dutch was last used in the services of the Dutch Reformed Church in New York while he was a small boy.
>
> About 1644 his ancestor Klaes Martensen van Roosevelt came to New Amsterdam as a "settler"—the euphemistic name for an immigrant who came over in the steerage of a sailing ship in the seventeenth century instead of the steerage of a steamer in the nineteenth century. From that time for the next seven generations from father to son every one of us was born on Manhattan Island.[3]

The direct Roosevelt line ran as follows: Nicholas Roosevelt (1658–1742), the son of Claes (d. 1659), was the common ancestor of both Theodore and Franklin Roosevelt. His second son, Johannes 1689–?), was head of Theodore's line, which ran: Jacobus (1724–ante 1774), Jacobus (James) (1759–1840), Cornelius Van Schaack (1794–1871), and Theodore (1831–78), father of the President.[4]

In addition, Theodore Roosevelt was descended from a considerable number of Dutch families in America. Howard K. Beale has enumerated them:

> Jean de la Montagne and Rachel de Forest landed in New Amsterdam from Leyden in the *Rensselaerwyck* on March 5, 1637. Abraham Isaacse Ver Planck and his wife, Maria Vinje, had a son born in New Amsterdam

January 1, 1637, and Cornelis Jacobsen Stille leased a farm on Manhattan Island Aug. 15, 1639. Hendrick Van Dyck and his wife Divertje Cornelise first came from Utrecht, Holland, in 1640 when he was an ensign of militia in New Netherland. They returned more permanently in 1645 when he was sent out as *schout fiscal.* . . . Cornelius Jansen Clopper had a business in New Amsterdam in 1652. Resolved Waldron and his wife Rebecca Hendricks, daughter of Hendrick Koch, came to New Amsterdam in 1654. Jan Peek sold two houses in Albany on April 14, 1655, and Volckjie Jurrianese, who signed with her mark, was living there in 1657. Also, the marriage of David Pieterse Schuyler was recorded on October 13th of the latter year. Jan Barentsen Kunst sailed to New Amsterdam on the *Gilded Beaver* in 1658, and Jan Louwe Bogert and Cornelia Evertse, arriving on the *Spotted Cow*, settled in Bedford (now a part of Brooklyn) in 1663. In 1674, Wynant Gerritse Van der Poel, husband of Tryntje Melgers, was trading real estate and running a business in Albany.[5]

From all this array of ancestors, some traces of Dutchness persisted into the nineteenth century. From his grandfather, Cornelius Van Schaack Roosevelt, came one memorable tale. Cornelius when a small boy, on a summer afternoon after listening to a second long Dutch Reformed sermon, came out of the church ready for excitement. He encountered a herd of pigs and jumped onto a big boar that immediately carried him back through the middle of the dispersing congregation.

A bit of Dutchness even formed one of Theodore Roosevelt's own memories. When he was tiny, his grandmother, Cornelius' wife, although she was not herself Dutch, taught him the only Dutch words he ever learned, "a baby song of which the first line ran, '*Trippe troppa tronjes.*'" In 1909 when Roosevelt was hunting big game and leading a scientific expedition in East Africa, he tried the words on Boer settlers he encountered, and found that although they had difficulty in understanding his pronunciation, they too knew the song, and it formed a bond of union between them and Roosevelt.

"It was interesting to meet these men whose ancestors had gone to the Cape about the time that mine went to America two centuries and a half previously, and to find that the descendants of the two streams of emigrants still crooned to their children some at least of the same nursery songs."

Part of the Boers' difficulty in understanding Roosevelt may have come from his imperfect memory of the song. A recent biographer, Edmund Morris, has found the song at the Theodore Roosevelt birthplace, and noted down the words as

> *Trippel trippel toontjes,*
> *Kippen in de boontjes . . .*[6]

It was Franklin Roosevelt with his lesser degree of Dutchness who seemed to take the greater interest in his Dutch forebears, not only in the paper he wrote at Harvard but even during his years as President. Perhaps it was because he was a collector, not only of stamps, small books, naval history, ship models, naval prints, and Dutch tiles, but also of ancestors. Genealogy interested him as it had his mother, Sara Delano Roosevelt, who relished reciting lineages. Eleanor Roosevelt, a niece of Theodore, was also descended from several other prominent families, including the Livingstons. Once when as First Lady she was queried about her Livingston ancestry, she did not try directly to answer but obtained the information from her husband. She has reminisced that Franklin knew her ancestry better than she did herself.[7]

The interest in his Dutch ancestry began early for Franklin D. Roosevelt. When he was nineteen years old, in his second year at Harvard University, he decided to write a college paper on "The Roosevelt Family in New Amsterdam before the Revolution." He asked his mother to copy for him "all the extracts in our old Dutch Bible," and consulted a genealogical document one of the Roosevelts had compiled in 1831. From documentary histories he obtained some additional data. In all, he turned out a sixty-page handwritten paper, upon which his professor noted: "Material good. Form fair." It was a correct estimate.[8]

Franklin D. Roosevelt began his account with the first Roosevelt in New Netherland, Claes Martensen van Rosenvelt. Franklin was not aware of the spelling "Rosenvelt," but did note that Claes almost immediately dropped the "van" and that there were numerous variations in early spelling. It was spelled, he explained, in almost a dozen ways, "due to the illiteracy not only of the members of the family but of the clerks of public offices." Most of the family, and those best known, he explained, spelled the name with two o's but pronounced it as in the original Dutch, as though it were a single vowel—like "rose." A bit of evidence that he introduced on the strange spelling of the name was a "Claes Roosinffelt" he found in a list of those in Ulster County, New York, who in 1689, after the English conquest of New Netherland, took an oath of allegiance to the King. Franklin thought this was the original Claes, but it was his son, who came to be known as Nicholas Roosevelt.[9]

The spelling "Rosenvelt" gave ammunition in the 1930's to anti-Semites hostile to Roosevelt, who used the name to try to prove him Jewish. Some Jews were eager to claim him as one of their own. In response to a query, Roosevelt wrote concerning the Roosevelts: "In the dim past they may have been Jews or Catholics or Protestants—what I am more interested in is whether they were good citizens and believers in God—I hope they were both."[10]

In the early 1900's neither Theodore nor Franklin D. Roosevelt tried to pinpoint the location in Holland from which the Roosevelts had come. In later years, Franklin came to believe, as he wrote a Michigan Dutchman in 1932, that they were undoubtedly from the island of Tholen, which is near the mouth of the Rhine in Zeeland.[11] Americans interested in Roosevelt's genealogy wrote the head of the General Netherland Tourist Association, W. P. F. van Deventer, who undertook an inquiry. It led to the small Zeeland village of Oud-Vossemeer on Tholen, where the name Roosevelt (spelled with one *o*) was relatively common. There were still three homesteads there which had belonged to the Roosevelts, and in the church was a large brass chandelier bearing an inscription stating that it was the gift of Johannis van Rosevelt. In the one-room town hall, the mantelpiece bore the coats of arms of local families; a portion of one of these bore a chevron with three roses. The villagers were ready enough to claim President Roosevelt, but one of them complained: "He does not care. When the Church, in which 'his' chandelier is hanging had to be repaired, a request was made, asking him to contribute, but nothing has come of it."[12]

The fact was, as Franklin D. Roosevelt pointed out when this information came to his attention, that the crucial evidence in the form of a record of Claes Martensen van Rosenvelt had not as yet been found. The Minister to the Netherlands, Grenville T. Emmet, in 1936 sent him a translated article about Oud-Vossemeer and a photograph of the Roosevelt coat of arms. Roosevelt was interested but cautious: ""Undoubtedly the Roosevelts of that place were kinsmen but, of course, the key of the Vossemeer connection would lie in discovering any definite record of the first Roosevelt who came to this country and from whom all the Roosevelts in America are descended." No such record subsequently came to Roosevelt's attention, but Allen Churchill in his collective biography, *The Roosevelts*, places the family firmly in Oud-Vossemer.[13]

The first Roosevelt was a farmer, who came with sufficient cash to purchase for one hundred guilders a forty-eight-acre *bouwerie* in mid-Manhattan, beginning at about Twenty-ninth Street. It came to be known as Rose Hill. When Claes's son, also called Claes, was nine years old, the British captured the colony, renaming it and the city New York. The younger Claes allowed his name to become anglicized; he became Nicholas Roosevelt. For a time he lived at Esopus (present-day Kingston), ninety miles up the Hudson, but then returned to New York City, where the two presidential lines of the family lived generation after generation. In the city, Nicholas was "a burgher of the major right," according to city records, a miller who became an alderman. He lived to be a patriarch of eighty-four, leaving some forty-

Franklin D. Roosevelt taking his oath of office as
Governor of New York, January 1, 1929, with his
hand placed on the old Dutch family Bible
(*Keystone Press Agency*)

five children and grandchildren, and was the progenitor of two Presidents.[14]

From this time on the Roosevelts were a family of civic-minded, prosperous businessmen. By the 1730's they were beginning to speak English as their first language although into the nineteenth century many spoke Dutch at Sunday dinner. Jacobus and Johannes Roosevelt became James and John. One of the Johannes Roosevelts was graduated from Yale in 1735. For five generations until 1821, the males in Theodore Roosevelt's branch of the family married women with Dutch names. After only three generations, in 1752, Franklin D. Roosevelt's branch broke away.

In his college thesis, Franklin D. Roosevelt wrote, betraying the sense of social status with which he had been reared: "As regards the marriages of the Roosevelts, the first three were, as was natural in a Dutch colony, with Dutch-descended women. After the third generation the marriages were for the most part with those of English descent, but Dutch marriages occurred even then, as the best New York families were still Dutch. Thus the stock kept virile and abreast of the times."

The ancestors of Theodore Roosevelt became successful as hardware merchants, a business which ultimately his father inherited. Franklin's ancestor Isaac Roosevelt built a comfortable family fortune as a sugar refiner and merchant from the 1740's through the American Revolution. During the conflict, most of the Roosevelts were conspicuous patriots. Franklin D. Roosevelt was particularly proud of Isaac Roosevelt, who was a member of the New York constitutional convention and one of the first members of the state senate. Gilbert Stuart's portrait of Isaac hangs in the living room at Hyde Park.[15]

The legacy of both Theodore and Franklin D. Roosevelt was one of generations of affluence—not enormous fortunes by the standards of their day and ours, but despite their modesty in protesting their limited means, substantial wealth. The $200,000 Theodore Roosevelt received as a legacy from his father would be the equivalent of perhaps a million and a half dollars in the 1980's.

Equally important was the legacy of public service. Already at nineteen, Franklin D. Roosevelt had had that firmly impressed upon him through the example of his parents, functioning like a family of benevolent country squires in Hyde Park, and by the energetic example of Theodore Roosevelt, who had just succeeded to the presidency that fall. He concluded the study of his ancestors ringingly:

Some of the famous Dutch families in New York have today nothing left but their name—they are few in numbers, they lack progressiveness and a true democratic spirit. One reason—perhaps the chief—of the virility of the Roosevelts is this very democratic spirit. They have never felt that because they were born in a good position they could put their hands in their pockets and succeed. They have felt, rather, that, being born in a good position, there was no excuse for them if they did not do their duty by the community, and it is because this idea was instilled into them from their birth that they have in nearly every case proved good citizens.[16]

Pride in their Dutch lineage and in the Dutch tradition was obviously important to both the Roosevelts. The Dutch image was a prestigious one, embodying good citizenship, stubborn courage, industry, resourcefulness, and cleanliness. It was in part compounded of the paintings of the Dutch masters—the bright, clean, affluent household scenes of Vermeer and the solidity of the burghers and their wives who sat for Rembrandt. The popular image of cleanliness and brightness came to be promulgated in two widely sold commercial products, Dutch Boy paint and Old Dutch Cleanser, which portrayed a Dutch housewife, stick in hand, energetically chasing dirt.

In part, the image in New York grew out of the frolicsome mock epic of Washington Irving's *History of New York*, first published in 1809 as the purported work of one Diedrich Knickerbocker. Irving's New Netherland, with its stolid, provincial Dutch settlers, formidable as trenchermen, bore some resemblance to Rabelais's Touraine and the book thinly disguised the foibles of some of Irving's contemporaries. Yet overall it created an appealing legend of a sturdy innocence soon swamped by an alien Yankee culture. Knickerbocker became the prized appellation of everything of Dutch descent; the cartoon symbol for New York City became "Father Knickerbocker" in his old-fashioned Dutch apparel.[17]

Dutchness implied democracy not only to the Roosevelts but to all educated Americans of the late nineteenth century. John Lothrop Motley augmented the image in his *Rise of the Dutch Republic* (1856), which presented the sixteenth-century revolt against Spanish rule as the cause of democratic, tolerant Protestantism. Mary Mapes Dodge in turn drew upon Motley's history for her *Hans Brinker, or, The Silver Skates* (1865), which introduced the virtues of the Dutch to generations of American children. Further, there was the admiration of William of Orange, who in 1689 had come to England with his wife Mary II to make secure for the English the rights gained in the Glorious Revolution.

Dutchness also symbolized economic enterprise, the resourcefulness of merchants sending their fleets throughout the world and of the millers and refiners like the Roosevelts in New York. These were also characteristics of the British and the French, but on one occasion Franklin D. Roosevelt found it useful to give them at least by implication a Dutch emphasis. In the neutrality period of 1939 when an American newspaperman quite correctly enumerated the Roosevelts' connections for several generations with the British and French, Roosevelt sought to refute him by citing Isaac Roosevelt's sugar trade: "If he would look into the question of 'family ties,' he would realize that the Roosevelt family, in the West Indian sugar business, was compelled to contend many years against the British and French interests in those Islands—and that is what made them revolutionists rather than tories in 1776."[18] (The greater likelihood is that Isaac Roosevelt had profited through illegal trade with the French.)

Both Roosevelts were members of organizations formed by those claiming Dutch descent. Theodore, like his father, belonged to the St. Nicholas Society of the City of New York, which in 1905 published a brief genealogical record of its members. Franklin D. Roosevelt was active in the Holland Society, and through it furthered his interest in colonial Dutch architecture. In 1923, he urged in its publication, *De Halve Maen*, that the society sponsor a book of photographs of old Dutch houses, and then as chairman of its Publication Committee, raised $7,000 for its undertaking.[19] It resulted in the attractive *Dutch Houses in the Hudson River Valley before 1776* (1929) by the historian Helen W. Reynolds. In the introduction, Roosevelt wrote: "The genesis of my interest . . . lies in the destruction of a delightful old house in Dutchess County, New York, when I was a small boy; for, many years later, in searching vainly for some photograph or drawing of that house, I came to realize that such dwellings of the colonial period in New York as had stood until the twentieth century were fast disappearing before the march of modern civilization and that soon most of them would be gone."[20]

Throughout the remainder of his life, Roosevelt continued through Miss Reynolds his interest in Dutch colonial houses and history. The style of architecture and the construction material of fieldstone so greatly appealed to him that he saw that they were incorporated into the post offices at Hyde Park and in neighboring Poughkeepsie and Rhinebeck during his years as President. It became the architectural style, too, that he used in building a small house for himself on a hilltop on the eastern bounds of his estate, and most notably in the Franklin D. Roosevelt Library, where his papers and mementos are to be found. Thanks largely to Roosevelt there was a renaissance of Dutch colonial architecture in Hyde Park and its vicinity.[21]

During the 1920's, Roosevelt was also active in the Netherlands-America Foundation, which sought to promote better relations between the two countries. He was a prime mover in 1922 to form a single organization with the Netherlands Chamber of Commerce in

New York to avoid overlapping activities and to make a stronger and wider appeal for support. Representatives of the two groups met at his home at 49 East Sixty-fifth Street, and typically Roosevelt presented them with a comprehensive scheme. He enjoyed planning of that sort:

> Mr. Roosevelt suggested that there be organized a Netherlands-America Federation to act as a sort of clearing house, and to include as many as possible of the societies working toward better relations between the Netherlands and the United States. He suggested that each society might keep its own identity but work with the others in joint enterprises, and share in a general publicity; and that if one organization undertook a piece of work the others would be invited to cooperate if they saw fit. Such a plan would limit duplication of interest. . . . He thought that there should be frequent meetings for joint conference between the heads of the separate branches, so that each might understand and support the enterprises of the other. If such a Federation were achieved, Mr. Roosevelt thought that the magazine, 'Holland and Her Colonies,' now published by the Chamber of Commerce, might be developed into a true Netherland-American magazine to serve the interests not only of commerce but of the arts, literature, and social activities, and of the West as well as of the East.[22]

The conference went well, but thereafter Roosevelt, who had a multiplicity of similar interests, does not seem to have played any role in the enterprise. He continued his association with the Holland Society and upon its fiftieth anniversary, January 17, 1935, telephoned his greetings from the White House to the assembled celebrants:

> Our early forebears brought from the Netherlands a quality of endurance against great odds—a quality of quiet determination to conquer obstacles of nature and obstacles of man. That is why for many years I have been so deeply interested in the preservation of the records and monuments left in New York City and the Hudson River Valley by the Dutch pioneers. The influence of New Netherland on the whole Colonial period of our history, which culminated in the War for Independence, has not as yet been fully recognized. . . . It is an influence which manifests itself today in almost every part of our Union of States.[23]

Both Roosevelts as public figures had some interest in the modern Netherlands, but were ordinarily preoccupied with the great powers. For Theodore Roosevelt, Dutchness seems to have been a matter of inheritance, not presidential action.

Theodore Roosevelt's view of the Netherlands was that the country, like Sweden, had long since lost its standing as a power but nonetheless was in a healthy state. To his friend Cecil Arthur Spring-Rice, who feared the decline of Great Britain, he wrote consolingly in 1901 that those two nations "have had a couple of centuries of perfectly healthy life since their greatness vanished. The loss of greatness was a real and terrible loss, but yet a good deal remained."[24]

A decade later, when Roosevelt visited the Netherlands while on a European tour, he became decidedly more positive about it. In part that might have been because he received such a warm reception. "Late in the evening we crossed into Holland," he wrote, "and at the first place we stopped there was a wildly enthusiastic mob of ten thousand people cheering and calling." He suspected that the Dutch, like the people of other countries he visited, took "a quite unwarranted feeling of interest in and liking for me, because to them I symbolized my country, and my country symbolized something that stirred them."

The warmth of the Dutch, whether warranted or not, stimulated a reciprocal warmth in Roosevelt. He formed a high opinion of the Dutch people—except for Queen Wilhelmina and her consort, whom he heartily disliked. "It was Wilhelmina's pretentiousness that made her ridiculous," TR observed in a patronizing critique. Holland in his eyes was a small country less important than some of the states in the federal Union, and the sovereign less important than the governors of those states. For her to behave "as if she belonged to the God-given-ruler class . . . was absurd." The comments reflected upon Roosevelt as much as upon the Queen. Perhaps he felt that she was not as deferential as she might be toward him since he was an ex-President, not an actual head of state. Roosevelt may have been a bit touchy about being a former rather than present President. Later he mentioned how in Denmark the Russian envoy had complained to the American minister because Roosevelt, not even an Excellency, was being entertained in the royal palace in the same rooms the Czar had occupied the previous summer. Perhaps one of the reasons why Roosevelt found the Dutch people quite charming was that "the crowd behaved exactly as if I were still President and home in America."

In total, Roosevelt's estimate of the Netherlands was quite positive, more so than before his visit:

> There was one thing I found really consoling about Holland. After the beginning of the eighteenth century it had gone steadily downhill, and was very low indeed at the close of the Napoleonic wars. Since then it has steadily risen, and though the nation itself is small I was struck by the power and alertness and live spirit of the people as individuals and collectively. They had completely recovered themselves. When I feel melancholy about some of the tendencies in England and the United States, I like to think that they probably only represent temporary maladies, and

that ultimately our people will recover themselves and achieve more than they have ever achieved; and Holland shows that national recovery can really take place.[25]

During World War I, when Roosevelt was distributing money from the fund he had established with the Nobel Peace Prize, he allotted $1,000 for the care of Belgian refugees in the Netherlands. "In Holland," he noted, "the burden of caring for the Belgian victims of the German horror has been very heavy."[26]

In those same war years, young Franklin D. Roosevelt, who was serving as Assistant Secretary of the Navy in the Woodrow Wilson administration, first became indirectly involved with the Dutch government. In March 1918 he sent an unofficial feeler through a submarine expert, Marley F. Hay, who was departing for the Netherlands, to find out if the government would be willing to sell the island of Curaçao off the coast of South America. Roosevelt may well have been acting on his own, since Secretary of the Navy Josephus Daniels asked Hay an hour later if Roosevelt had spoken to him. When Hay said he had, Daniels told him not to sound out the Dutch, that Daniels had taken up the matter with President Wilson, who had declared the United States already had trouble enough with South American countries. Shortly afterward, Roosevelt, who had heard of Daniels' conversation, asked Hay to query the Dutch nonetheless. When Hay arrived in the Netherlands he conveyed Roosevelt's message to the Foreign Minister, who replied that the government could not consider selling the island for fear Germany would regard it as an unneutral act.[27]

During World War II, when the Netherlands was again in the uncomfortable position of being a small neutral nation next to its powerful German neighbor, Franklin D. Roosevelt was a friend in the White House. When the threat of a Nazi invasion first became acute, he could not guarantee armed assistance but at least could offer a refuge. During the first few weeks of the war in September and October 1939, Hitler's forces wiped out opposition in Poland, then turned toward the west and paused. The Belgian and Dutch governments received reports that Germany might invade the Netherlands on November 9. Roosevelt sent personal and unofficial messages to both King Leopold and Queen Wilhelmina, offering to give refuge to their families. "In view of the fact that Leopold is an old friend of mine and that I have ancestral Dutch connections it would be a decent thing to do," he explained to Secretary of State Cordell Hull, adding: "in addition whether they accepted or declined, if war comes to them it might be a helpful political gesture for the future."[28] He sent a warm note to Queen Wilhelmina, whom he had never met:

"I am thinking much of you and the House of Orange in these

critical days, and it occurs to me that in the event of the invasion of Holland you may care to have the Crown Princess and the children come to the United States temporarily to be completely safe against airplane raids. It would give Mrs. Roosevelt and me very great happiness to care for them over here as if they were members of our own family and they could come to us either in Washington or at our country place at Hyde Park. . . ."[29]

The first threat of invasion did not materialize, but in December, Roosevelt renewed his offer in a lengthy letter. He assured Queen Wilhelmina that he would at a moment's notice send a cruiser to a safe point to carry her grandchildren, and Princess Juliana, should she want to come, to stay with him at the White House or with his eighty-five-year-old mother at Hyde Park:

"You, my good friend, I know will want to stick by the ship. . . .

"Some day I shall hope to have the great privilege of meeting you. You do not know it but the only time I have seen you was when we were both children—and you were driving in one of the parks at The Hague."[30]

Roosevelt was two years younger than Queen Wilhelmina.

At Roosevelt's direction, the minister to the Netherlands, George A. Gordon, had audiences with the Queen in November 1939 and again in January 1940, when there were fresh indications that Nazi troops were about to cross the Dutch frontier. Each time the Germans stopped short of action, leading Gordon to think that the audiences had had a salutary effect.

In the spring of 1940, there were incessant reports that the Germans were planning a major attack to the west, and on April 9 they dashed into Denmark and Norway. Four days later, Gordon cabled that the Netherlands was being threatened even more seriously than before, and asked Roosevelt to send a fresh message to the Queen. Roosevelt decided not to do so; it would have been pointless, since nothing he could do would prevent the Germans from acting.[31]

Finally, as had been so long threatened, the Nazis on May 10 opened their blitz of the Netherlands, Belgium, and Luxembourg. Within four days the Netherlands was overrun and Queen Wilhelmina had to move her government to London and to continue resistance from there.

While Roosevelt had not been able to help fend against the German sweep, he reiterated on May 18, 1940, by secret cable through Ambassador Joseph Kennedy in London, his offer to help the Dutch royal family if the "inhuman bombing of England" made it advisable. He would send a cruiser or a merchant ship with convoy to an Irish port, if Queen Wilhelmina wished.[32]

Instead Queen Wilhelmina stayed in London with the government-in-exile, distinguishing herself with her broadcasts to bolster the morale of the Dutch people. Juliana and her daughters departed in June for Canada, rather than the United States, since only in an allied country could she with certainty resume royal powers in the event of Wilhelmina's death.

In the summer of 1942, with the United States in the war, there were no longer, as Queen Wilhelmina has written, "the theoretical problems that could have been created by a visit from me, as a belligerent, to a 'neutral' country." She accepted President Roosevelt's invitation, flying to Canada, then taking a train to Lee, Massachusetts, in the Berkshires, not far from Hyde Park. Juliana had rented a house there so that her mother could rest for several weeks. Roosevelt came up to pay his respects to Queen Wilhelmina, bringing with him Princess Martha of Norway. Juliana had already visited the Roosevelts twice, and went with her mother to Hyde Park. In her memoirs, Queen Wilhelmina has written:

"To me everything was new, and meeting the President and Mrs. Roosevelt was an experience, although even at the first meeting with him I felt as if I was addressing an old friend, so cordial were his feelings for the Netherlands and for Juliana, Bernhard, the children and me.

"My respect and admiration had not only been aroused by my correspondence with him and the messages he had sent me; even more, perhaps, had I been impressed by his 'fireside chats' (to which I could listen regularly at Stubbings [in England] at 3 a.m.) and his statesmanship, first as a sympathizing neutral, then as an ally in the war. Meeting him, one was impressed by his strong personality, his willpower and perseverance, which had been steeled by his courage in dealing with the consequences of the poliomyelitis which had struck him years before. One felt certain that he would never yield and never abandon a cause he considered just, but would persevere in battle until he had attained his goal."[33]

Roosevelt had already formed a warm, informal relationship with Princess Juliana, as he had with other royalty in exile during the war, but was apprehensive about the Queen. The President rather dreaded her visit "because of stories of her stiff and stern ways which have preceded her," one of Roosevelt's secretaries, William Hassett, noted in his diary. "From the members of her entourage come stories of their . . . fear of her arbitrary ways." But the President's closest adviser, Harry Hopkins, reported that she had been pleasant and gracious to him in London, and so she was with Roosevelt. First they had tea in Lee, then she came to Hyde Park. "The Boss said he liked her," wrote Hassett, ". . . and that the picnic was very enjoyable."[34]

In August 1942, Queen Wilhelmina visited President Roosevelt in Washington, and accepted a 173-foot submarine chaser bearing her name upon behalf of the Netherlands navy. It was a felicitous ceremony. Roosevelt declared:

"From the earliest days of history, the people of The Netherlands—your people—have been willing to fight for their freedom and independence. They have won out in the face of great odds.

"Once more they are fighting for that independence. Once more they will win and maintain it."

Queen Wilhelmina in her response to Roosevelt remarked, "May your love of the sea and of seamanship pervade this vessel and inspire those on board."

While she was in Washington, the Queen also appeared and spoke briefly at one of Roosevelt's press conferences and addressed a joint session of Congress. Her visit was so successful that a year later she returned to the United States and again was a guest of the President.[35]

Roosevelt continued to write to Wilhelmina as to a dear friend, and acted as a warm patron to Princess Juliana and her husband. When, in January 1943, a third daughter, Margriet, was born to them, they asked Roosevelt to be the godfather. That fall Roosevelt wrote Prince Bernhard: "Juliana and the children were at Hyde Park for three days and I have completely fallen in love with my Godchild— the very best behaved baby I have ever seen. She took to me at once and she was brought to my room in the mornings when I was having my breakfast, and she was perfectly happy playing with a spoon."[36]

Even in the spring of 1944, with his health declining, and planning for the imminent landing in France heavily occupying him, Roosevelt found time to write Juliana to offer her the use of his summer place at Campobello Island, New Brunswick. He described the main house and the simpler one next door with care, then like a benign older relative noted: "We are not using either of the houses this Summer and it is the kind of a location, with very few neighbors, where it would be really impossible to rent the houses. Therefore, they are yours to occupy, and, because we are both Dutch, the terms would be extremely simple—no rent."[37]

As for Queen Wilhelmina, Roosevelt continued to correspond with her, despite his failing physical condition. In late March 1945, with the war winding to an end in Europe and the liberation of the Netherlands underway, Roosevelt expressed his delight over her "flying visit to a little piece of the Netherlands." Food for Europe was in short supply, he warned her, but he had instructed General Eisenhower to channel as much as possible to Amsterdam. "You can be very certain that I shall not forget the country of my origin," he assured her.[38]

Three weeks later, Roosevelt died at Warm Springs, Georgia. It was not unexpected, Queen Wilhelmina has written. Juliana had

(TOP) The Roosevelts welcome Queen Wilhelmina to
Washington, August 5, 1942

(BOTTOM) The Roosevelts entertain Princess Juliana at a
picnic lunch at Mrs. Roosevelt's Val-Kill cottage,
Hyde Park, New York, October 9, 1943
(*Courtesy of the Franklin D. Roosevelt Library*)

seen him that March and had been shocked at the change in his appearance. Wilhelmina remembered her last long weekend with him at Hyde Park in the summer of 1943. Her recollections are a poignant memorial to the personal relationship, and to the Dutchness of Franklin D. Roosevelt:

"How well I remember Roosevelt taking me round his estate in a car with exclusively hand-operated controls, and how visibly he enjoyed driving his own car. He also took me to the station in it; I can still see him waving to me from his car as the train moved out. His last words contained good wishes for the resurrection of the Netherlands who held such a special place in his heart and for us all."[39]

NOTES

1 The lineage of both Roosevelts is traced in Hugh Montgomery-Massingberd, ed., *Burke's Presidential Families of the United States of America* (London, 1975), pp. 421, 503. Howard K. Beale, "T.R.'s Ancestry: A Study in Heredity," *New York Genealogical and Biographical Record*, October 1954, pp. 196–205, is indispensable, since it examines all of TR's ancestors, not merely the male line as in Burke. Franklin D. Roosevelt, "The Roosevelt Family in New Amsterdam before the Revolution," Roosevelt mss., Franklin D. Roosevelt Library, Hyde Park, New York. All manuscripts hereafter cited are from the Roosevelt Library. The writer wishes to express his appreciation to Dr. William Emerson, director of the Roosevelt Library, Mark Renovitch of the Roosevelt Library staff, and Ms. Jean Coberly, History Department head, Seattle Public Library, for their invaluable aid in his research.

2 Theodore Roosevelt, *An Autobiography* (Vol. XXII of *The Works of Theodore Roosevelt*, New York, 1925), pp. 3–5; Beale, "T.R.'s Ancestry," pp. 197, 204.

3 T. Roosevelt, *Autobiography*, p. 3.

4 Burke, *Presidential Families*, p. 421.

5 Beale, "T.R.'s Ancestry," p. 197.

6 T. Roosevelt, *Autobiography*, pp. 4–5; Edmund Morris, *The Rise of Theodore Roosevelt*, New York, 1979), p. 37.

7. Frank Freidel, *Franklin D. Roosevelt: The Apprenticeship* (Boston, 1952), p. 5.

8 F. D. Roosevelt, "The Roosevelt Family in New Amsterdam before the Revolution"; Elliott Roosevelt, ed., *F.D.R.: His Personal Letters, Early Years* (New York, 1947), p. 464 (hereafter cited as PL). FDR wrote the thesis in a course in American History to 1783 taught by Professor Edward Channing. He wrote his mother: "I have been in the library constantly looking up old records, but nothing much is to be found. Do please copy for me all the extracts in our old Dutch Bible & send them to me. Also the old brown genealogy which you have, a pamphlet, & any other records you have."

9 F. D. Roosevelt, "Roosevelt Family"; Allen Churchill, *The Roosevelts of New York: American Aristocrats* (New York, 1965), pp. 30–31. Other useful studies of the Roosevelts are Bellamy Partridge, *The Roosevelt Family in America* (New York, 1936), and Karl Schriftgiesser, *The Amazing Roosevelt Family, 1613–1942* (New York, 1942). For a brief account of FDR's ancestors, see Freidel, *Roosevelt,* pp. 6–15.

10 FDR to Philip Slomowitz, March 7, 1935, cited in Freidel, *Roosevelt,* p. 6.

11 FDR to C. Heÿstek, June 7, 1932, Family, Business, and Personal File, #115. Hereafter cited as FBP File.

12 "In the Cradle of the Roosevelts," President's Secretary's File, #62. Hereafter cited as PSF.

13 FDR to Grenville T. Emmet, March 7, 1936, PSF #19, cited in *F.D.R.: His Personal Letters, 1928–1945* (New York, 1950), II, 1567–68. Hereafter cited as *PL. 1928–1945.* Churchill, *Roosevelts of New York,* p. 2.

14 Churchill, *Roosevelts of New York,* pp. 30–47.

15 Freidel, *Roosevelt,* pp. 6–7; Churchill, *Roosevelts of New York,* pp. 48–61; F. D. Rosevelt, "Roosevelt Family."

16 F. D. Roosevelt, "Roosevelt Family."

17 Washington Irving, *A History of New York from the Beginning of the World to the End of the Dutch Dynasty, by Diedrich Knickerbocker* (Vol. I of *The Works of Washington Irving,* New York, 1860); Martin Roth, *Comedy and America: The Lost World of Washington Irving* (Port Washington, N.Y., 1976), pp. 114–54.

18 FDR to Stephen Early, October 19, 1939, *PL, 1928–1945,* II, 942.

19 St. Nicholas Society of the City of New York, *Genealogical Record* (New York, 1905); FDR, "Preserve the Pictures of Old Landmarks," *De Halve Maen,* April 1923; Holland Society correspondence, Group 14.

20 Helen Wilkinson Reynolds, *Dutch Houses in the Hudson River Valley before 1776* (New York, 1929), introductory pages not numbered.

21 Not everyone shared FDR's enthusiasm for construction in Dutch colonial fieldstone. Roosevelt at the dedication of the Rhinebeck post office in 1939 said: "We are seeking to follow the type of architecture which is good in the sense that it does not of necessity follow the whims of the moment but seeks an artistry that ought to be good, as far as we can tell, for all time to come." But during World War II when FDR drove Princess Juliana to see the site at which a Rhinebeck high school was to be built, he impeded construction of the building. Rhinebeck residents, staunchly Republican, circulated the rumor that he was insisting upon another fieldstone building. His friend Olin Dows writes: "This gossip added materially to the difficulties in getting the community to vote for a much needed building." Olin Dows, *Franklin Roosevelt at Hyde Park* (New York, 1949), pp. 111–12.

22 Hannah W. Catlin to FDR, May 24, 1922, enclosing memorandum, FBP File, #59.

23 Franklin D. Roosevelt, *The Public Papers and Addresses of Franklin D. Roosevelt* (13 vols.; New York, 1938–50), IV, 41–42.

24 Elting E. Morison et al., eds., *The Letters of Theodore Roosevelt* (8 vols.; Cambridge, Mass., 1951–54), III, 16.

25 TR to George Otto Trevelyan, October 1, 1911, in Morison, *Letters*, III, 383–84, 391.

26 Morison, *Letters*, VIII, 135.

27 Interview with Marley F. Hay, April 1950, Oral History Project, Columbia University, cited in Frank Freidel, *Franklin D. Roosevelt: The Ordeal* (Boston, 1954), p. 135.

28 FDR to Cordell Hull, November 11, 1939, *PL, 1928–1945*, II, 952; Cordell Hull, *The Memoirs of Cordell Hull* (2 vols.; New York, 1948), pp. 712–13.

29 FDR to Cordell Hull, November 11, 1939, *PL, 1928–1945*, II, 952–53.

30 FDR to Queen Wilhelmina, December 19, 1939, *PL, 1928–1945*, II, 971.

31 Hull, *Memoirs*, pp. 762–63.

32 FDR to Queen Wilhelmina, May 18, 1940, *PL, 1928–1945*, II, 1027.

33 Wilhelmina, *Lonely But Not Alone* (English translation of *Eenzaam maar niet Alleen*) (New York, 1960), pp. 149–80; L. de Jong, *Konigin Wilhelmina in Londen, 1940–1945 (Mededelingen der Koninklijke Nederlandse Ahademie van Wetenschappen, Nieuwe Reeks, Deel 29, Afdeling Letterkunde, No. 2* (Amsterdam, 1966); Werner Warmbrunn, *The Dutch under Geman Occupation, 1940–1945* (Stanford, Calif., 1963), pp. 278 *et passim*.

34 Wilhelmina, *Lonely*, pp. 180–81; William D. Hassett, *Off the Record with FDR, 1942–1945* (New Brunswick, N.J., 1958), pp. 87, 91.

35 Roosevelt, *Public Papers and Addresses*, 1942, pp. 322–23.

36 FDR to Prince Bernhard, October 12, 1943, *PL, 1928–1945*, II, 1452.

37 FDR to Princess Juliana, May 20, 1944, PSF, #62.

38 FDR to Queen Wilhelmina, March 21, 1945, PSF, #62, cited in *PL, 1928–1945*, II, 1576–77.

39 Wilhelmina, *Lonely*, p. 189.

Part Three

·⚜·

BILATERAL
PERCEPTION

John Lothrop Motley and
the Netherlands

· ⊕⊗⊗⊗⊕ ·

D. D. EDWARDS

IT is fitting—indeed, supremely fitting—that a study of John Lothrop Motley (1814–77) should begin with a superlative: his admirers and adversaries would be largely at one on that. Here it is: The case of Hotley's historical writing on the Netherlands would seem to be unique in the force and nature of its initial impact in international cultural relations. There are, happily, innumerable examples of historians of one country making the history of another their professional life's work. Often the result of their work will be to awaken readers limited to the language in which they write to interest and excitement respecting the country under investigation where hitherto ignorance and indifference were the only reactions. But seldom if ever can the thing have been as violent as it was in Motley's case. When *The Rise of the Dutch Republic* was published in 1856, the Dutch historical profession possessed a science and a sophistication superior to historical scholarship in the English-speaking countries, but its achievements were virtually unknown to them. The *Edinburgh Review*, in a lengthy article for January on Motley's book and Prescott's *Philip II*, alluded with assurance, knowledge, and respect to the archival publication, editing, and commentary of Groen van Prinsterer, but the anonymous review was the work of Guizot, who was to translate and introduce Motley for a French audience. Robert Jacobus Fruin, who has been termed the Ranke of the Netherlands, had to wait until the twentieth century for even fragmentary translation into English, and his lengthy, kindly, and devastating commentaries on Motley never reached an English-speaking readership at all. A few readers in the British Isles and North America would have seen the translation of Schiller's unfinished *Revolt of the Netherlands*, led to it perhaps by the characteristic vehemence with which it is trumpeted in Carlyle's *Life of Schiller*; fewer would have looked at Watson's eighteenth-century work which provided the chief source for

[171]

John Lothrop Motley (1814–1877)—after an engraving
in the Dutch magazine *Eigen Haard*, 1877

Schiller (who, in common with Watson, and the present writer, knew no Dutch). So little was a market assumed to exist that Motley had to pay the expenses of his work's publication by John Chapman of London: it then sold 15,000 copies (each containing about 600,000 words) in a single year. It remained a best seller for decades in both the British Isles and the United States; it was adapted into school editions, illustrated editions, text editions, de luxe editions, cheap editions, popular editions, and was still reaching a wide public one hundred years later. It was a prime favorite at (Protestant) school prize-givings, decked out with engravings of Dutch landscapes considerably inferior to the work of the artists of that country, and sometimes concluding with a view of an assassinated William the Silent keeling over with an expression of acute dyspepsia, in which presumably piety, statesmanship, and martyrdom were felt to be nicely blended. As a general rule it was also distinguished by a total absence of maps, save occasionally for a general representation of the possessions of Charles V, a point which, however irritating to the conscientious reader, did at least symbolize that lack of local geographical understanding which was the foremost point in the future indictment of Motley by the scholar who ultimately supplanted him, even in the parochial hearts of the English-speakers, Professor Pieter Geyl. But although it was on Motley's own launching pad, London, that Geyl and his lieutenants in England such as G. J. Renier and S. T. Bindoff commenced the campaign which so utterly called into question the conclusions of the American writer, their work only began to reach a wide audience by the 1930's. For about three quarters of a century, when British or American readers thought about the Netherlands, it was the prose of Motley's *Dutch Republic* they had in mind.

This last fact alone merits a fresh look at Motley and his place in American cultural history. He and he alone had created a Dutch awareness on a wide scale: before his advent, when the great American reading public had thought of the Dutch, it did so in the comic if affectionate terms associated with Father Knickerbocker, Rip Van Winkle, and, presumably in less comic terms, Vanderdecken of the *Flying Dutchman:* the editor of Motley's *Correspondence*, George William Curtis of *Harper's*, was to declare that Motley's work was an act of atonement for the belittlement of the Dutch in American eyes by Washington Irving. Certainly nobody could suggest that Motley's Sunday-school hero portrayal of William the Silent had the slightest intention of being anything but an essay in the utmost reverence: indeed William became the first competitor George Washington had to date received in the United States, in edification of character, profundity of statesmanship, and nobility of intellect. However, despite the significance of competition in Dutch and American history, William and Washington were not in competition really, any more than Moses and Elijah had been. In any case, Irving himself heartily welcomed the new evangel and wrote Motley on July 17, 1857: "The minute and unwearied research, the scrupulous fidelity and impartial justice with which you execute your task, prove to me that you are properly sensible of the high calling of the American press—that rising tribunal before which the whole world is to be summoned, its history to be revised and rewritten, and the judgment of past ages to be cancelled or confirmed." Here was the imperialism of historiography with a vengeance!

And indeed, for all of Motley's fulmination against Philip II and his alien invasion of the Netherlands, the hard-working Dutch historians of his day might well be forgiven for seeing him as almost as alien an invasion himself. Irving's bombast was not prompted by similar tones in Motley's preface: he was gentlemanly, and civil, by nature, where his temper was not aroused—he was, in fact, a very likable and kindly person—and he knew his manners in thanking librarians and archivists. His sense of obligation to Dutch historiography, one might say his sense of its existence and achievements, is less evident in the *Dutch Republic* than in his later work; the successor volumes to it, *The History of the United Netherlands*, contain references to Fruin of an almost embarrassed respect, as though Motley had become sensible that his best seller might seem a jay in eagle's feathers, or, at best, the moon to a sunless audience benighted in their Anglophone ignorance. It was his tragedy that at his historiographical christening the bad fairy might have been thought to declare that he would only succeed by failing, and fail by succeeding. For *The Rise of the Dutch Republic* is far and away the worst as well as the most popular of Motley's three works on Dutch history. Superficially, it possesses more artistic cohesion, taking its readers from the grand spectacle of Charles V's abdication (after a lengthy introduction opening with Caesar's Gallic wars) and concluding with the high drama of the murder of William the Silent; the *United Netherlands* merely spanned the period from that murder to the synod of Dort, hardly a comparable end game in American eyes, and *The Life and Death of John of Barneveld* was, as even its dimmest critics realized, no biography but rather a view of the last ten years of Oldenbarneveldt's life ranging loosely through the European diplomacy observed in his correspondence and the circumstances of his fall and death. Yet as history the progress in quality moved inversely to the decline in popularity: by the last book, Motley was operating almost entirely from archives, much of it manuscript material unused by any scholars, where in the first his dependence had been very largely on published sources. Likes and dislikes he could never refrain from asserting and reiterating, but by *Barneveld* he was showing capacity for drawing complex and even somewhat subtle portraits, in which darkness and light were impressively mixed, whereas the *Dutch Republic* is famous or infamous for its obsessiveness about the utter goodness of William the Silent and the utter badness of Philip II. Henry IV of France, in particular, is drawn with skill, appreciation, and real humor in both the *United Netherlands* and *Barneveld*, followed by the writer with evident equal zest whether in the skill and foresight of his diplomacy or in the absurdity of his passion for the Princesse de Condé, with all of its far-flung political repercussions. Sir George Clark, in his lecture to the British Academy in 1946 on the revolt of the Netherlands, remarked that even then neither English nor Dutch historians seemed fully to realize how much the English owed the defeat of the Spanish Armada to the Dutch immobilization of Parma's forces; that was no fault of Motley, who harangued his English-reading audience on the point at great length in the *United Netherlands* over eighty-five years before Sir George's paper. The recent work of Professor Charles Wilson has reaffirmed Motley's indictment against Elizabeth's failure to give sufficient support to the Netherlands, and its decisive role in the loss of Antwerp, despite the anger that Motley's strictures aroused in admirers of the Tudor Queen ever since he wrote, and it is arguable that the vociferous American maintained a perspective on the reality of Elizabethan Dutch policy which the neo-Elizabethan votaries of supposedly more scientific historical days have lost. Greater depth in research and greater confidence revealed Motley's gifts for comedy, even for Gibbonian satire, in place of the stark moralism of the *Dutch Republic;* the comedy, like the moralism, readily strayed into caricature, but caricature of a much more suggestive and intellectual kind. And, most of all, Motley's struggle to defend and vindicate Oldenbarneveldt really was a superb service to historians, and commenced the modern re-evaluation of a European statesman whose achievement had been unjustly obscured and traduced for two and a half centuries. Geyl deplored the vehemence of Motley's partisanship on this as on so much else, but he threw the weight of his judgment on the side of Motley rather than on that of his opponent and great defender of Maurice of Nassau, Groen van Prinsterer.

The fact remained that the *United Netherlands* and *John of Barneveld* scarcely survived into the twentieth century on the general market, and neither of them joined the *Dutch Republic* in cheap mass popular reprint. Motley was in any case by now respected more than read, one of the few points on which Woodrow Wilson and Henry Cabot Lodge agreed with one another (fortunately they were unaware of it), but where he was read after World War I, it was the *Dutch Republic.* The growing preference for publishing extracts from authors favored the earlier book; the subtleties of the later two, and they contained many, offered less opportunities to the anthologizer than the simplistic purple passages of the *Dutch Republic*. Its name was identified with him. His American audience—although, as we shall see, not so much himself—readily identified the rise of the earlier republic as precursor to the rise of their own (William the Silent's Mosaic qualities thus extending to failure to inhabit the Promised Land). In the late 1920's Samuel Eliot Morison chose to call the enormously successful textbook he was writing with Henry Steele Commager *The Growth of the American Republic* and might indeed have said "Rise" instead of "Growth" had the term not been preempted a few years previously by his great historiographical opponents Charles and Mary Beard for their *Rise of American Civilization*; Morison was born almost exactly ten years after his father had written the obituary of Motley for the *Unitarian Review*, the intellectual journal of Motley's religious sect.

The *Rise of the Dutch Republic* thus became Motley's Nemesis as well as his triumph, and when in the twentieth century Geyl did his work, the consequences for its reputation and Motley's were disastrous. Geyl's insistence that the division of the Netherlands had been dictated by geography, specifically by waterways, made Motley not merely wrong but irrelevant. His insistence on ending with William the Silent's death had created a wholly unhistorical view of the outcome; despite Motley's later work, despite his unstinted admiration for the services of Oldenbarneveldt during the war as well as the subsequent truce, he left firmly in his readers' minds the sense that the future partition of the Netherlands in the form it would take was inevitable, give or take the inadequacies of Elizabeth and Leicester with respect to Antwerp. (In some ways the *United Netherlands* seems to question the earlier assertion of inevitability, but for the mass of Motley's readers, who never got beyond the *Dutch Republic* into its much larger and more unwieldy sequel, the damage had been done.) Geyl indeed remarked sarcastically that none of William the Silent's enemies had charged him with anything quite as inept as his greatest admirer Motley had unintentionally done, in that to end the story with William's death was, given Motley's terms, to indict William for the irreparable losses of Flanders and Brabant, in reality anything but inevitably lost at the time of his assassination. And as Geyl acknowledged, he was not the first to make that criticism: Fruin had already done so, in gentler terms. Fruin's essays, however much a product of the religious-dominated historiography of the nineteenth century, had made it all too clear that Motley virtually lacked a Dutch sense. His lack of geographical awareness was perhaps the main thing; but the reader of Fruin was led to realize that Motley's great sweep took him from history into polemic where Fruin showed the real points of detail which added up to a very different and far more real picture. In that sense the symbol of Motley's downfall was exhibited when G. M. Trevelyan, an obvious English heir to the historical attitudes associated with Motley, introduced to an English audience in 1924 Fruin's account of the siege of Leyden, ruefully admitting the appalling crudity of the American writer once compared with the Dutch master. Fruin held much in common with Motley, notably in his liberalism, his hostility to Catholicism, and his reliance on both to account for the independence of the north and reconquest of the south: Geyl and his disciples were to stress how Motley was but the most extreme of the Protestant historians of the nineteenth century in failing to see the tremendous significance of the Catholic revolt against Philip II. But the violence of Motley's anti-Catholicism worried historians much more ferociously Protestant than Fruin. James Anthony Froude, the disciple of Carlyle, himself then coming before an admiring public with his paean in praise of Henry VIII, otherwise his *History of England*, actually declared that "the fault throughout Mr. Motley's book is the want, absolute and entire, of all sympathy with Catholicism, in its vigour as well as in its degeneracy," in his famous notice in the *Westminster Review* for April 1856 which described *The Rise of the Dutch Republic* as "the result of many years of silent, thoughtful, unobtrusive labour, and unless we are strangely mistaken, unless we are ourselves altogether unfit for this office of criticizing which we have undertaken, the book is one which will take its place among the finest histories in this or any other language."

Froude also asserted: "Mr. Motley uses no sweeping colours, no rhetorical invectives; there is scarcely a superlative or a needless expletive in the book," which would qualify as the most staggering comment on Motley penned by anyone were it not for the light it throws on the yardsticks employed by Froude. In fact, Motley's sweeping colors and rhetorical invective, superlatives and expletives, easily rode their way into the welcome of audiences wallowing in the North Atlantic high-flown romanticism of the 1840's and 1850's. Despite the publishers' failure to recognize the fact, a public nurtured on Carlyle's *French Revolution* and Macaulay's *History of England*, was joyfully ready to lap up another installment in a fresh world as newly opened for literary conquest as the lands of the American interior. Carlyle had taught them to seek for heroes; Motley obliged with William the Silent. Macaulay had broken from his normally critical portraiture of personalities to make an icon of William of Orange; Motley provided an earlier William of Orange. If his style was scarcely the equal of either, especially given the signs it exhibited of excessive emulation of both, he was not wholly inferior to either.

He connected the progress of events with a logic foreign to Carlyle; his William of Orange, if unreal, seems slightly less unreal than that of Macaulay. The difference was, in part, that Motley showed some sense of perspective in keeping his hero and his narrative in some suitable proportion to one another, which Carlyle never really succeeded in doing, while Macaulay, unlike Motley, was not so much canonizing a prince as the embodiment of a presumed constitutional principle. If Motley's William was basically an embodiment also—of worship of freedom, defiance of tyranny, hostility to superstition, and belief in toleration—it was the embodiment of ideas, albeit largely eighteenth- and nineteenth-century ideas, which are more easily assimilable into the likeness of a hero than is a constitutional principle.

But Motley's excesses stood naked before his audience, however much they admired him. Carlyle's speed of movement, Macaulay's judicious argument, were both outside his scope. Again, Motley, especially in the *Dutch Republic*, weakened himself dangerously by his want of interest in social and economic questions, his impatience with religious complexity, and his apparent indifference to cultural achievement. This was a retrograde attitude: Macaulay and Froude had won romantic responses, but they had been responses conditioned by the historians to demand accounts of human life and economic movement as well as of battles, sieges, and personalities. William Dean Howells in his *Literary Friends and Acquaintances* records meeting Motley before reading his work, liking him enormously and yet being disappointed when coming to his books by their curiously old-fashioned quality. The recent biography of Motley by J. Guberman (The Hague, 1973) comments in general that "Motley was, in fact, an anachronism," and more general critics at the time noted that his work stood strangely between pre-scientific partisanship and archivally dominated modernity of approach. Even in America, where Motley's old schoolteacher George Bancroft had thoroughly saturated the public with chauvinistic bias in his volumes on the birth of the United States, such figures as William H. Prescott had shown that obvious prejudices on the part of the historian did not need to be urged with vehemence of tone. Yet Motley was supposed to be almost the lineal successor of Prescott; the historian of seventeenth-century Spain and its empire had fortunately insisted on his continuing his work on the Dutch revolt against Philip despite being engaged himself in a large general account of Philip, had more fortunately welcomed the forthcoming appearance of Motley's work in a footnote to the preface to his own work, and had most fortunately of all died three years after the publication of the *Dutch Republic*, thus leaving Motley the foremost American historian in active practice.

And Motley's crudity was to have its repercussions. He would have agreed with much of the savagery of the exposure of British (and American) society in the Gilded Age which Anthony Trollope revealed in its corruption and greed in *The Way We Live Now*— after all, his successor as minister to the Court of St. James's, whence he had been so humiliatingly ousted in 1870 by the Grant administration became involved in drawing his hosts into questionable speculation of the kind so well described in that novel—yet the first lines of *The Way We Live Now* are a ruthless exposure of what nonsense had been made of popular history once moral judgment was opened up to any literary hack employing rhetoric to conceal poverty of scholarship. The comments of Lady Carbury in quest of a puff for her ludicrous *Criminal Queens* are the product of worthless quilting from hastily grabbed and ill-assorted patches: "I am afraid that I have been tempted into too great length about the Italian Catherine; but in truth she has been my favourite. What a woman! What a devil! Pity that a second Dante could not have constructed for her a special hell. How one traces the effect of her training in the life of our Scotch Mary. I trust you will go with me in my view as to the Queen of Scots. Guilty! guilty always! Adultery, murder, treason, and all the rest of it. But recommended to mercy because she was royal. A queen bred, born and married, and with such other queens around her, how could she have escaped to be guilty? Marie Antoinette I have not quite acquitted. It would be uninteresting—perhaps untrue. I have accused her lovingly, and have kissed when I scourged." All of this may seem far from Motley, in whose views of Alva or Philip II no reader could detect surreptitious osculation, and in whose formation of those views hard work (if not as hard as for later volumes) had provided the basis, yet the insistence on the repetition of reprehension inevitably bred its inadequate imitators. And if (like Lady Carbury's Scotch Mary) he could be little else given his training, in a world where Carlyles, Macaulays, and Froudes hurled their judgments with such freedom, he stood below them, and invited lower descent still, by the substitution of his sloganeering in place of their appeal to intellect.

Motley's intentions were taken to be those of providing a landmark in the development of the future United States of America; admirers and critics have assumed that he saw the Dutch Republic along the lines of what he took the United States to be, a republic conceived in liberty and rooted in a Puritan heritage, he being the child of Massachusetts. There is a natural readiness on the part of commentators, including the perceptive David Levin, in his *History as Romantic Art*, to see the unity of thought in Prescott, Motley, Bancroft, and Francis Parkman, and certainly there is much unity to see. But Motley was in many respects different from the rest, and nowhere more than in his choice of subject. Prescott's field was that of the origin and development of the territories an expanding United States might draw under its flag or its powerful influence, in place of the base Iberian antecedents he recorded. Parkman concerned himself with conquests of British over French North America which might ultimately end in American supremacy over British. Bancroft dealt directly with his own republic. Motley seems to have been drawn to the Dutch by a very different route. If anything, his emphasis is to fight the parochialism of his fellow countrymen. In discussing the sufferings of the Netherland heretics under the Inquisition, he goes to some lengths to remind votaries of the so-called persecuted Puritan exiles of England how much milder their experience had been. "The reader will judge," he declares at the close of Book II, Chapter I, of the *Dutch Republic,* "whether the wrongs inflicted by Laud and Charles upon his Protestant ancestors were the severest that a people has had to undergo, and whether the Dutch Republic does not track its source to the same high origin as that of our own civil and religious liberty. . . . The Puritan fathers of the Dutch Republic had to struggle against a darker doom." The whole thrust of all of his work is in protest against the parochialism of the English-speaking peoples, that parochialism which ironically gave him a reputation he could not have sustained had contemporary Dutch scholarship been open to his readers. If he did not understand the Netherlands well, at least he understood it was worth study and that such study should not be limited to forerunner status for the Republic, or to American roots, or to labored comparisons. Hence his insistence on doing justice to the Dutch contribution to the defeat of the Armada—where an English-speaking readership in the United States or in Britain would have thought of a single achievement by their own putative ancestors. Hence his demand for recognition of the genius of a statesman like Oldenbarneveldt, whose hold on American self-interest must be limited to his general contribution to the cause of international Protestantism, liberty, and hostility to intolerance. Certainly in *John of Barneveld* Motley did sketch the origin of the Pilgrim Fathers' voyage, but in a curiously perfunctory way, rather in the manner of the references to the insanity of the English included in *Hamlet* to get a laugh from the pit; he makes little connection of them to his larger story. His intention seems to have been to cultivate in Americans an enthusiasm for non-American history. In this he failed. His general arguments were accepted, bar some minor Catholic objections (of which the most interesting, led by Orestes Brownson, absolutely refused to identify Philip II with the Catholic cause—in fact Brownson, and later the *Dublin Review* of April and October 1878, show signs of awareness of the case against Motley, Fruin, and the Protestant historians put forward by Catholic critics in the Netherlands). The official historical seal of approval on his overall picture was placed by John Fiske, in his "Spain and the Netherlands" (an essay of 1868–69, reprinted in Fiske's *The Unseen World* (Boston, 1876). Yet Fiske himself would be given the credit by Charles M. Andrews in his Presidential Address to the American Historical Association, "These Forty Years" (*American Historical Review*, XXX, January 1925), with bringing American history "out of its isolation into touch with the forces of world history . . . he turned the American people from Prescott, Irving, Parkman, and Motley, and others, whose subjects lay chiefly outside the limits of the present United States, and caused them to read with enjoyment books that dealt with their own origin and growth." That such a claim could be made in such a way is a tragic indication of how far Motley had failed. His history had been pragmatic, in that it sought to teach lessons about liberty and intolerance he regarded as essential to Americans, but his pragmatism had been one of idealism rather than the additionally chauvinistic motivations of his contemporaries. Now, in his wake, he was assumed by Fiske to have settled Netherlands history, and by Andrews to have been a stage in a historiographical digression whence the country was rescued by Fiske. And Motley in his evangelization of the significance of Dutch history had few disciples, even if the lengthy magazine essays on his work produced a plethora of regurgitations. His only notable American successor was Ruth Putnam, of the publishing family, who produced a life of William the Silent which appropriately appeared in the "Heroes of the Nations" series. Certainly he held sway where readers did turn to the revolt of the Netherlands; the chapter on William the Silent in the *Cambridge Modern History* by the Rev. G. Edmundson, the author of a monograph on Dutch history of a later period, was largely a paraphrase of Motley including the time limits of the *Dutch Republic* (hence moving a specific denunciation from Geyl, but in all probability the dates indicate the influence of Acton as planner of the enterprise). Motley had failed to make cosmopolitans of his fellow countrymen, and the British more or less remained as he had left them until the advent of Geyl.

To understand the significance of Motley's American antecedents in the shaping of his work, we must look back at his specific heritage. As Mr. Guberman reminds us, he was an anachronism; which means that he was a Federalist living in a world at best Whig and later Republican. This assumed an ideological inheritance of devotion to liberty, but an oligarchic and not a democratic outlook, albeit the oligarchy would be assumed to be a large and educated one. The Netherlands, then, attracted him because it was oligarchic, although for all of his difficulties in seeing the divergences in ideology over centuries, he admitted in *John of Barneveld* that the oligarchy with which he was dealing in the Netherlands was proportionately much smaller in relation to its mass of population. For mob rule in general he had the utmost revulsion. He would be criticized for his indulgence to mob excesses from time to time, provided the cause was libertarian and the mob seemingly Protestant; but behind his excuses there is evident distaste and fear. He avowedly shared much of the cultural outlook of his contemporary Hawthorne, whose "My Kinsman, Major Molineux," raises its doubts about mob cruelty in the cause of liberty. His remarks on the Anabaptists, even in the *Dutch Republic* with its firm identification of Protestantism and liberty, are the writing of a hater of democratic extremism, and the offspring of other haters. Part of the Federalist heritage was a historical sense. The future Federalists, most notably John Adams, had supplied a view of the causes of American revolt in their pamphlets at the time which was extraordinarily historical in approach. In its simplest form, Motley could readily identify the American with the Dutch insurgents: at the back of his elaborate if loosely constructed recital of ancient Netherlands liberties against new and alien despotism being introduced by an outside tyrant with a title of descent but the destruction of any right of rule by conduct, lie the arguments adduced in Massachusetts by John Adams and his associates against George III. But on a deeper level, the force of Adams' arguments lies in his conviction that he and his fellow actors are a part of a European historical process and a European heritage. Federalists by other names in the nineteenth century followed Federalists and their ancestors of the eighteenth in invoking that heritage, and in the internationalism of their outlook. They repudiated Paine, and Jefferson, and world revolution, yet more than either of them they would have held with Donne that no man was an island. This does not mean that Motley was seeking to Americanize the world, any more than he would have agreed with Froude's intended compliment that *The Rise of the Dutch Republic* proved that "in truth and reality the Americans are nearer to the English in heart, in sympathy, in their deepest and surest conviction, than to any other nation in the world"; admittedly, that does unkindly underline how far the origins of the Dutch Republic could become a crude ideological device with little reference to the contemporary Dutch themselves in the eyes of certain English-speaking readers, and if Motley had not asserted that, his book, with its distance from Dutch realities, inspired it. In fact, Motley approached the Dutch experience with a sense of the European dimension of his thought, but his affection seems at that stage to have been much more strongly directed toward Germany than to either Britain or the Dutch Netherlands.

For Motley had made his initial European landfall at a very young age, eighteen, when he went to study at the University of

Göttingen. There is a pleasing irony there, in that Göttingen has been singled out by students of historiography for a great place in the establishment of scientific historiography. "The dynamic ideas which helped to transform historical study may have arisen outside the universities; but in Göttingen we see them critically considered and carefully combined so as to form a system of historical scholarship. Whether we envisage the attitude adopted to this kind of scholarship, or the treatment of universal history, or the revision of national and regional studies, or the teaching of contemporary politics, or the development of historical method and the editing of texts, the school of Göttingen seems to bring us to the very brink of the modern world." Thus Sir Herbert Butterfield in his *Man on His Past* (Cambridge, 1955), but it has to be said that if Göttingen seems to bring us to that brink, it certainly did not bring Motley. Indeed it is clear that the process he describes was one Motley did not find, and probably did not anticipate, until he arrived in the Netherlands in 1851 with the intention of adding some local detail to a work already largely written. A remarkable dispatch to the *Athenaeum* from The Hague, by A. C. Loffelt, printed on June 9, 1877, points out that on his arrival with two volumes of the *Dutch Republic* in manuscript he found himself obliged to rewrite the entire thing; that is to say, when he discovered the advanced state of scientific history in the Netherlands, the achievements of Bakjuyzen van der Brink, who afterwards edited with notes his work in Dutch translation, and the archival work of Groen van Prinsterer; and, as I have stated, he clearly discovered after his initial success that he had even more to learn and deeper humility to discover the more he saw of the Dutch achievement. The fact that the Dutch were extraordinarily kind to him in hospitality, advice, and welcome for his egregious work (admittedly, it probably did much for Dutch tourism) only increased that sentiment. Yet he had established the framework of the *Dutch Republic*, however much he might rewrite it, by the time of his arrival. And while Motley said all the interesting scholars were too old or had died when he was in Göttingen (as Butterfield noted), it is clear that from there and from his subsequent residence at Berlin, in 1832–34, he encountered a very different influence. He became steeped in Goethe, Schiller, and the Romantic movement; he moved much in society; he got drunk, was briefly locked up, and embarked on a lifelong friendship, all with Otto von Bismarck.

Much too much can be made in biographies when the subject falls over a Great Man (even when he does so literally, as no doubt happened in the present case on late nights). In any case, Motley met his fair share of them: he grew up with the future abolitionist and greatest American orator of his time, Wendell Phillips; Longfellow so wanted to advance him as to propose to review his first novel if it proved good but apparently decided it was not; Charles Sumner was his friend and patron for forty years at least; he briefly found himself "in Abraham's bosom," as he irreverently phrased a presidential audience during the Civil War; Grant he learned first to admire and then to detest; to Henry Adams he foolishly confided admiration for London society, for which he was ultimately served up in a marvelously malicious and hilarious dissection in *The Education of Henry Adams*; the young Henry Cabot Lodge called him Uncle and seems to have been more deeply moved by compassion for him than for almost anyone in his malevolently patrician life; in his last days his daughter married Sir William Harcourt, afterward the Leader of the Opposition in the British Parliament. This formidable range of acquaintances and friends was of importance in his writing of history and helps to account for the touches of realism even in his most unrelieved portraiture—for instance, the variations of his theme of Philip II as monster of depravity by revealing him as an asinine and pedantic civil servant and, indeed, as a figure of indomitable courage in facing the incredible pain of his last illness. It is easy to see him as stereotyping his characters, but he knew enough of the many-sidedness of the great to respond to impulses which left him open to charges of inconsistency but not of lightlessness. For all of his rhetoric, he impliedly leaves it to the reader to cast up the sum of judgment in different forms than his hortatory conclusions suggest. He leaves Parma with a harsh word, yet more than one reviewer saw him as the hero of much of *The History of the United Netherlands*, as zeal for his skill of generalship stills the Rhadamanthine excoriations. All of this played its part in the making of the historian, sometimes for the better, sometimes for the worse. In *John of Barneveld* Aerssens is cast as the Iago who betrays Oldenbarneveldt, as Professor Levin has shrewdly pointed out; but Motley's own experience as the victim of malicious gossip led to at least one very sympathetic passage on the victimization of Aerssens during his French mission and the effect of the calumnies in circulation against him in giving him a grievance against his former patron. On the other hand, the account of Oldenbarneveldt's misfortunes at the hands of Maurice of Nassau clearly owes something of its passion to Motley's own dismissal as minister to London by another great general in civilian life, Grant. Yet the personal element does not wholly fault the wisdom of certain observations and their relevance to both situations: "all history shows that the brilliant soldier of a republic is apt to have the advantage, in a struggle for popular affection and popular applause, over the statesman, however consummate. The general imagination is more excited by the triumphs of the field than by those of the tribune, and the man who has passed many years of his life in commanding multitudes with necessarily despotic sway is often supposed to have gained in the process the attributes likely to render him most valuable as chief citizen of a free commonwealth. Yet national enthusiasm is so universally excited by splendid military service as to forbid a doubt that the sentiment is rooted deeply in our nature, while both in antiquity and in modern times there are noble although rare examples of the successful soldier converting himself into a valuable and exemplary magistrate." In any case, this is not wholly the product of his fate at the hands of Grant: his first real political disappointment must have been the rejection of John Quincy Adams by the electorate in 1828 in favor of General Andrew Jackson. No doubt Washington was one of his "noble although rare examples"; equally without doubt Jackson, Grant, and Maurice of Nassau were not.

Bismarck is so readily identified in the popular mind with militarism that it must come as a shock to realize that if he had any impact at all on the portraiture of *John of Barneveld* it would have been on that of Oldenbarneveldt himself: although the most obvious parallel was not effected until 1890, when Motley had been dead for thirteen years. Certainly the venerable Dutch statesman would have had little in common with the dueling, wenching blood-brother with whom Motley removed from Göttingen to share lodgings in Berlin. But the overwhelming affection between Bismarck and Motley survived years of separation and long gaps in correspondence until the final meeting, at Bismarck's silver wedding celebration in 1872, when Motley, at the insistence of Bismarck's daughter, proposed the toast of the Chancellor in a speech in German lasting twenty-five minutes. (Motley's command of languages was so good that when he presented his credentials as minister to the Court of Vienna, the Emperor Franz Josef took him for a German and was vastly relieved to discover his mistake.) He seems to have been one of the two or three men for whom Bismarck had utter trust and affection, not particularly mingled with respect for his political ideology. Together from student days upward they argued about liberalism, tolerance, democracy, and everything under the sun. It was the attraction of opposites, mental and physical: Bismarck seems from the first to have impressed Motley with his extraordinary ugliness of appearance, while the Prussian himself, dictating a brief sketch of Motley for use by his biographer Oliver Wendell Holmes the elder, remarked, "The most striking feature of his handsome and delicate appearance was uncommonly large and beautiful eyes." The pledging and swearing of eternal fellowship through which the students went persisted in their mode of address: Motley remained "Lieber Mot" to "Dein treuer Freund," while the American, less capable of finding an absolute intimacy of expression, compromised on "My dear old Bismarck." For all that, their correspondence took fairly significant turns at times; whatever the value of Motley as a minister in Vienna to Austro-American relations (and it is certain he occupied most of his time in archival research, having accepted the Austrian mission in lieu of The Hague, which he really wanted, for similar reasons), he certainly did the United States good service by succinct answers to Bismarck's personal inquiries as to the realities of the American Civil War. Less successfully, he pleaded, with much apology, for clemency in the treatment of France after Sedan; it would, he said, help to restore international confidence in Germany. *"Damn* confidence," scrawled Bismarck in the margin, which, said Theodore Roosevelt in a letter to George Otto Trevelyan on October 1, 1911, was what Motley ought to have expected. But it was clear while Bismarck had no intention of transplanting Motley's soft heart into his own ferrous bloodstream, he liked his idealistic friend to be himself. Apparently at their last meeting Motley did get some assurance that his dear old Bismarck cherished no sanguinary intentions at the expense of the Netherlands. The totality of their association in any case gave Motley a vision of this extraordinary administrator, controlling his own country, the complexity of its foreign policy and expansionist intentions, and the private and official correspondence throughout Europe his ambitions for mastership entailed. It is this which in part gives such strength to the portrait of Oldenbarneveldt as a European statesman, although the diffusion of Oldenbarneveldt's diplomatic correspondence so painstakingly deciphered by Motley justified the emphasis, however much he may have overvalued the strength and power enjoyed by the Advocate in other European courts. The deciphering was so daunting a task that Motley, for all his literally personal anguish at Oldenbarneveldt's execution, wrote to Lady William Russell on July 13, 1871: "If they had cut his head off on account of his abominable handwriting, no creature would have murmured at the decree who had ever tried to read his infinite mass of manuscripts.[4] But the labor involved had the advantage that it ensured Motley would keep his Oldenbarneveldt as much as possible within his own character as revealed in his writing. For the rest, Bismarck kept alive within him the magic of the administrator and enabled him to transmit much of that magic respecting a period in history when imaginations such as his own were more conspicuously fired by men of physical action. However suspicious of generals Motley had always been, he was not immune to the excitement of their achievements, as the case of Parma shows.

Oddly enough, given the cold-blooded realism of Bismarck's statesmanship, the main intellectual effect of those student years seems to have been a thorough immersion of Motley in German romanticism. It was not binding absolutely; he showed much more initial response to Goethe than to Schiller, and had indeed produced a graduation essay on Goethe at Harvard, but his cold delineation of Egmont's vanities and follies in the *Dutch Republic* has little echo of Goethe's conception even if the drama of his martyrdom catches an echo of Beethoven's music. But Schiller's fragment on the revolt of the Netherlands virtually dictated the contours of *The Rise of the Dutch Republic*. From Schiller he took the absolutes of William the Silent and Philip II as "freedom, democracy, integrity" against "despotism, feudalism, hierarchy, intolerance," as the Dutch critic Deric Regin has summed up the polarization in his study of Schiller whose title, *Freedom and Dignity* (The Hague, 1965), equally sums up what Motley found at the heart of his inquiry. Dr. Regin, indeed, reminds us that as early as 1859 Julian Schmidt, in his *Schiller und seine Zeitgenossen*, noted that Motley had incorporated many of Schiller's phrases verbatim into his recently published work. It launched Motley on his subject in an utterly unhistorical frame of mind, with his prejudices asserted before he commenced a line of research. His own assets of persistence and linguistic facility, both points decidedly lacking in Schiller, were placed at a discount in his intoxication with the grandeur of the gospel laid before him.

But Schiller's influence on Motley was not limited simply to enlisting him in the cause of freedom and dignity. From the German Romantics, and no doubt from Bismarck also, Motley emerged with the deepest of convictions as to German racial superiority. In the present context this meant that Motley followed Schiller's lead in opening his story by an airy survey of the spirit of resistance as seen among the inhabitants of the Low Countries accountable to their Germanic origin, with scant interest in alterations in their bloodstock over the vicissitudes of a millennium and a half. After all, as Pieter Geyl pointed out, the Netherlanders themselves after the struggle sought to symbolize their achievement by commissioning Rembrandt's "Conspiracy of Claudius Civilis": "The barbaric, the savage, the vigorous, the passionate—in the countenances and in the attitudes of the plotters who crowd about the table lighted up by torches in the vast dark room—it has all been grippingly evoked, and the effect is embodied in the mighty one-eyed figure, who, sturdily and fatefully seated, holds his sword aloft while the others touch it with theirs. That blunt presentation of the first Dutch warrior for freedom apparently offended the chastened convention . . . At any rate," concluded Geyl (in the last lines of his tragically unfinished "Shakespeare as a Historian"), "the burgomasters of Amsterdam refused Rembrandt's largest historical painting. Today only the central fragment survives—in the museum in Stockholm!" Motley's depiction of Civilis as the forerunner of William the Silent has rather more in common with the spirit of the burgomasters of Amsterdam than that of Rembrandt, but at least he did a service in reminding his audience how the sixteenth-century struggle was idealized even if he identified the idealization with his own views instead of those of the heirs of the Dutch insurgents. However, he went on from there to take the lessons of German racialism dangerously farther. Schiller left it as a historic and glorious tradition. Motley made it the key to the ultimate partition of the Netherlands. He drew heavy distinctions between Gauls and Germans: "In Gaul were two orders, the nobility and the priesthood, while the people, says Caesar, were all slaves. . . . With the Germans the sovereignty rested in the great assembly of the people. . . . The Gauls were an agricultural people. . . . The truculent German, Ger-mann, Heer-mann, War-mann, considered carnage the only useful occupation . . . The Gauls were a priest-ridden race. . . . The German, in his simplicity, had raised himself to a purer belief than that of the sensuous Roman or the superstitious Gaul. He believed in a single, supreme, almighty God, All-Vater or All-Father. . . . The Gaul was singularly unchaste. . . . The German was as loyal as the Celt was dissolute. . . . The funerals of the Gauls were pompous. . . . The German was not ambitious at the grave . . . The characteristics of the two great races of the land portrayed themselves in the Roman and the Spanish struggle with much the same colours. The Southrons, inflammable, petulant, audacious, were the first to assault and to defy the imperial power in both revolts, while the inhabitants of the northern provinces, slower to be aroused, but of more enduring wrath, were less ardent at the commencement, but alone steadfast at the close of the contest. . . . The Batavian republic took its rank among the leading powers of the earth; the Belgic provinces remained Roman, Spanish, Austrian property."

It says little for the intelligence of the scientific historians among the English-speaking peoples that this balderdash did duty as an explanation of the division of the Netherlands in the late sixteenth and early seventeenth centuries until Geyl's work, in translation, came to sweep it away like the flood waters on whose significance his interpretation relied. But in fact Motley's racism was one of the most fashionable legacies he transmitted to the professional historians in Britain and America. The emerging graduate schools at Johns Hopkins and Columbia drew in more of it with the historical methodology they sedulously copied from the German, and their English colleagues supported them. Edward Augustus Freeman, who was invited from Britain to launch the Johns Hopkins series in Historical and Political Science, was a devotee of the same type of approach, and Herbert Baxter Adams, his host at Johns Hopkins, sought to put it on a scientific basis by tracing the early Teutonic origins of American political institutions. The hero worship formed part of the package; Freeman, indeed, took Motley's excesses to the auction block by announcing at the commencement of his mighty *History of the Norman Conquest* that Alfred the Great was "the most perfect character in history," specifically pointing out his superiority to both Washington and William the Silent because of his writing ability. (Motley could hardly have cited William's *Apology*; it remains one of his points of common sense in the *Dutch Republic* that he does not base himself on the hysterical and indiscriminate accusations made in that document at his hero's darkest hour.) It is hardly surprising to recall, in the light of this, that Freeman stated what a grand country the United States would be if every Irishman killed a Negro and was hanged for it; it is a sad commentary on the whirlwind Motley was reaping on his racial wind, for he himself was a fervent enemy of slavery and advocate of the blacks, despite his belief in their innate inferiority. He might, however, have sympathized with the anger, if not with the final solution, implicit in Freeman's view of the Irish. His experience of Massachusetts politics during an ill-starred term in the legislature in 1849 would have done nothing to alleviate that sentiment, and his stress in the passage quoted above on the priest-ridden Gauls or Celts no doubt owed force to this. It was understandable that such a descendant of old New England on his mother's side (his great-great-great-grandfather was killed in an Indian raid on Haverhill and his great-great-grandmother spared by being hidden in a cellar) and great-grandson of an Ulster Protestant on his father's, would view with horror the advent of the barbarian invasion from Ireland in the wake of the great famine of the late 1840's, and view with rage the effects of the invasion on the political life of the state. *The Rise of the Dutch Republic* was planned and its initial draft written in the Massachusetts of those years, years which yielded their fruit in the bitter nativist movement of the mid-1850's. Motley had some reason to fear the slavish hordes of Rome, as he doubtless saw them, and this, too, is an obvious point of origin for the burning anti-Catholicism of the book. His sentiments were not, in theory, modified in later works, but in practice he made far less of them, and he alternated them in the *United Netherlands* with some nasty remarks about Elizabeth's persecution of Catholics and cruelty to Mary Queen of Scots (for which Schiller again may deserve some credit).

But on the basic question of the partition of the Netherlands there was a different point of origin. On December 17, 1844, Motley wrote a letter to his brother-in-law Park Benjamin which his biographer Oliver Wendell Holmes professed himself not venturing to quote in full a third of a century later; but Benjamin himself printed part of it in *Harper's* for September 1877, although it was omitted both from

Curtis' edition of the *Correspondence* and from the subsequent *John L. Motley and His Family*. Motley was in a state of rage over Polk's narrow victory at the expense of Henry Clay, a man whom he put second only to John Quincy Adams in experience. Polk, the unknown from Tennessee, succeeding Tyler of Virginia, was "the lowest of the low" whose administration "will be even worse and more low-lived than that of Tyler. . . . As to Texas, if it be annexed, the result will inevitably be a separation of the Free States from the Slave States—a dissolution of the Union, which will, I think, ensue much sooner than we have been accustomed to believe. This is, perhaps, a result not very much to be deprecated; so that, so far as we of the North are concerned, it does not matter much whether Texas is annexed or not. . . . There is no attachment to the Union, no loyalty any where. The sentiment of loyalty is impossible under our institutions. Loyalty implies both respect and love; and who can respect or love institutions of which the result is four years of Tyler followed by four years of Polk?"

If we take this into account with the overview of Gaul and German in the introduction to the *Dutch Republic*, the problem of its assumptions on the inevitability of partition becomes much clearer. Motley's overriding motivation was a concern to find European precursors less for the creation of the American union, than for its impending dissolution. Naturally Motley, like many another Northerner, rallied to Lincoln's call and vociferously supported war to maintain the Union. But in the mid-1850's the southern Democrats were effectively in control under nominal and acquiescent northern leadership, and Motley had no reason to think better of Pierce than of Polk. His Gauls, then, were no doubt Irish-Americans, but they were even more the future Confederates. His first point of description was to stress their being a society utterly dependent on slavery, his next to emphasize their agricultural character, his third their lack of chastity. The last point was a characteristic neo-Puritan view of the would-be Cavaliers below the Mason-Dixon line. Although Professor Levin does well to stress the racist character of the passage, along different if allied lines to my analysis, the relevance to the crisis of the Union seems to me a new and even more important feature of it. Particularly notable is the use of "Southron," by which term the devotees of Sir Walter Scott in southern literary society loved to style themselves. The final point that the Southerners were the first to rise took care of the pride of place of Patrick Henry and Thomas Jefferson—and even George Washington—in the coming of the American Revolution. New Englanders, led by John Adams, had jealously protested against the cult of Virginia patriots at the expense of the New England forerunners in the struggle against Britain. Motley, writing in disillusionment, is prepared to let them have their first cry in the field; it is the honest, chaste, freedom-loving North which would prove the more enduring. The slave mentality would be the mark of the slave society in the end.

Viewed from this perspective, *The Rise of the Dutch Republic* becomes a very different book, and the urgency and even hysteria of its writing acquires a new meaning. The retention of slavery in the South and the acceptance of "slavery" under the Spaniards acquire the same force, and render impossible the continuation of any union. Certainly the imagery is flickering from point to point in anger and fear. Motley brought a whole variety of personal anxieties into his writing. Even the hostility to his Unitarian faith in the Massachusetts of his youth, so urgent a motive for his sympathy for the Arminians (which would much have displeased them) in *John of Barneveld*, receives a side-flick of his lash in this passage: the Germans, it would appear, were the original Unitarians. But the most important point of all is the inevitability of disunion. The shrewdness of Fruin and Geyl pinpoints the matter with their consciousness of the oddness of Motley's assurance on it as exemplified by his conclusion at William's death. I do not know whether Geyl took the point farther—he wrote extensively in four languages and I have read him only in one—but he certainly picked up an aspect of it, without referring to Motley, in his "The American Civil War and the Problem of Inevitability," written about a century after Motley started work on the *Dutch Republic*. Examining the American crisis, Geyl noted the small numbers of abolitionists and compared the necessity for the Dutch dissidents to exaggerate the small number of Calvinists. Elsewhere, Geyl had remarked how deeply Motley in the *Dutch Republic* exaggerated the numbers of Calvinists: did not Motley, thinking about the desirability of a break with the slave power, find it necessary to tell himself that there were far more followers of his friends Wendell Phillips and Charles Sumner than was actually the case? Motley's stress on William the Silent's wisdom in delaying so long to declare for the new religion again echoes his own retention of status as Whig (and hence deliberate blindness to Henry Clay's Kentucky residence and slaveholding status). From this angle, Motley's defense of William's caution is not so much special pleading for his hero as rationalization of his own conduct. Here he, and perhaps his brother-in-law, constitute his sole audience to the inner meaning of his analysis. On the other hand, he would have expected an audience which had recently devoured *Uncle Tom's Cabin* to read his meaning from references to slavery, Southrons, agricultural pre-eminence of Gauls, and the like. In its way, *The Rise of the Dutch Republic* had work of a similar kind to that of *Uncle Tom* to do, and the gratifying response to it may have owed something to analogies evident to Motley's generation if not to ours. The very horrors listed and lingered on in his pages have their counterpart in the horrors of slavery so successfully ladled out by Harriet Beecher Stowe. The book, then, was a concealed party pamphlet. Motley had, in his earlier, unsuccessful work as a novelist, disguised concerns and anxieties of his own in fictional forms, as well as let himself go with such figures as Otto von Rabenmark in *Morton's Hope*, directly modeled on his closest German friend. But, as more than one commentator has tactlessly observed, he was bad at plotting, and history offered him a plot already written. It was for history to provide the concealment hitherto offered by fiction for the cause of inevitability of disunion he wished to preach. Unlike Harriet Beecher Stowe, it was not a door he had the slightest intention of opening with a *Key*. In their way, the speeches of Wendell Phillips and Charles Sumner were giving the same covert message at the same time.

The election of Lincoln changed all that. Disunion was inevitable, but now in the eyes of the white Southerners. The opponents of slavery, apart from brief waverers, insisted on the integrity of the Union. Ironically, Geyl's essay on the American Civil War picked up an analogy which Motley, having killed off William, could no longer make in his time. To Geyl, Lincoln's insistence that the cause was the Union and not abolition of slavery paralleled that of William that the cause was liberty and not Calvinism. Motley certainly was quick to identify himself with Lincoln's view in letters to the London *Times* and formal pamphlet work. (Privately, he was among the earliest diplomats to urge emancipation.) His friends were on the threshold of power, and his austerity was not proof against the temptation to follow countless others in pursuit of patronage under the new administration. The secession of the South involved the departure of countless Southerners from the office-hunting ground. But Motley's gentle hope in his letter to Moses Grinnell of November 2, 1860 (he had even got off the mark before the election itself), "that the new government might be willing to give a literary man, who has always been a most earnest Republican, ever since that party was organized, the post of minister at the court at the Hague" (quoted in Barry J. Carman and Reinhard J. Luthin, *Lincoln and the Patronage* [New York, 1943], p. 4 n.), was foredoomed. James Shepherd Pike, who had done the state (or rather the party) some service in Maine, fully ensured that they would know it. He was disappointed in his turn in his hopes for Brussels—Henry S. Sanford had diplomatic experience, which was more than could be said for Pike (or Motley)—and so The Hague became his consolation prize. Ironically, Pike had openly preached northern recourse to disunion after the assault of Preston Brooks on Charles Sumner, and he cited Sumner in favor of his

Belgian claim. Motley, having returned to the United States dis-
heartened, found some hope when the Austrians rejected Congressman
Anson Burlingame (who had to be compensated with China). This
time Sumner came to the rescue, and Lincoln, grinning at the greed of
Massachusetts, obliged. Motley wrote his wife on June 20, 1861, that
Lincoln seemed "sincere and honest . . . and steady"; he was struck
by one remark "about the military plans in progress" when Lincoln
"observed, not meaning anything like an epigram, 'Scott will not let
us outsiders know anything of his plans.'" It would appear that Motley
could be as immune as Sumner to the President's glint of humor. The
interest of the point for him reflected a quality often present in his
writing—that distrust and even dislike of the civilian for the military.
It was not that he feared General Winfield Scott, then more or less
at the end of his tether, would be putting himself above the civil
power, but he clearly noted the implication that he considered himself
superior to it. Again, this view would be later reflected in his view
of Maurice; but it was also exhibited in the distaste for military heroes
that constantly shines through Motley's narratives, whether the object
of disapproval be Egmont, or Don John of Austria, or Maurice. In
part, this derived from his awareness of what military heroes such as
Jackson could do to his own heroes, such as Adams; in part, it stemmed
from their potential prowess as demagogues; in part, it derived from
the very strong tradition in Massachusetts of opposition to standing
armies and, more recently, the powerful crusade against war in general
in which Sumner had been particularly prominent. With the advent
of the war Motley, like Sumner, had perforce to put all the old anti-
militarism behind them, but his picking up of Lincoln's remark about
Scott shows its closeness to the surface.

Motley's place as servant of the Lincoln administration meant a
rapid and secret burial for his former disunionism. His historical
writing reflected it. The emphasis would become more and more the
importance of the preservation of union. It became more urgent when
a quarrel with Lincoln's successor, Andrew Johnson, resulted in his
dismissal from Vienna. Johnson, at war with Republicanism at large
and especially with Phillips and Sumner, had little time for dreaming
up charges against Motley, but the quarrel had arisen from gossip
about Motley's allegedly Anglophile social pretentiousness. Johnson
had taken an early opportunity to charge Phillips and Sumner with
enmity to the Union—indeed, adverse comment of Motley on Johnson,
peddled to the President, which caused their rupture, had probably
originated in that attack on his friends. Motley had been harsh enough
about English policy toward the Netherlands in the earlier volumes
of *The History of the United Netherlands* which appeared in 1860,
but the gossip about Anglophilia offered him strong incentive to lose

nothing of that harshness in his later work. The blistering remarks in
John of Barneveld about James I's academic pedantry dictating his
meddling in Dutch theological bickering, no doubt owed something
to the need for self-defense, for by the time of that work's appearance,
1874, Motley had also fallen foul of the Grant administration and
the Anglophile charge had been renewed. In fact, Motley as minister
to London in 1869 had given offense principally by his support of the
highly anti-British attitude over the *Alabama* dispute as noisily expressed by Senator Sumner, to whose industry on his behalf Motley
owed his new position. But any stick was enough with which to beat
him once his dismissal became a matter of public controversy. Even
on Motley's death it was too early for frankness as to his past, at least
for the protective Curtis and Holmes; his enemy Hamilton Fish,
Grant's Secretary of State, had loyal minions ready to impugn the
illustrious minister (who had in fact been driven from office in an
administration campaign to humiliate Sumner). Fish's protégé J. C.
Bancroft Davis was in the field against Motley's memory, and so also
was Adam Badeau, Grant's devoted amanuensis, who as secretary to
the London legation had done much to poison the atmosphere
against Motley and leave him so sensitive to the plotting against
Oldenbarneveldt.

But Motley himself had effectively reversed the crypto-disunionism
of the *Dutch Republic* in the first volumes that appeared from his pen
after the Civil War, the third and fourth installments of his *United
Netherlands*, carrying the story from 1590. Barely into his narrative,
he took a rare stance on the significance of geography in the destiny
of the Dutch Republic, arguing that its commitment to human liberty
led it to economic triumph over enormous natural disadvantages on
land. He then addressed his fellow countrymen: "What a lesson to our
transatlantic commonwealth, whom bountiful nature had blessed at
her birth beyond all the nations of history and seemed to speed upon
an unlimited career of freedom and peaceful prosperity, should she
be capable at the first alarm on her track to throw away her inestimable
advantages! If all history is not a mockery and a fable, she may be sure
that the nation which deliberately carves itself in pieces and substitutes
artificial boundaries for the natural and historic ones, condemns
herself either to extinction, or to the lower life of political in-
significance and petty warfare, with the certain loss of life and national
independence at last. Better a terrible struggle, better the sacrifice of
prosperity and happiness for years, than the eternal setting of that
great popular hope, the United American Republic."

Yet however much autobiographical rewriting Motley, in common
with so many other Americans, might find necessary, he was not
prepared to dishonor the generous anger of the book which had won

him his reputation. "I speak in this digression only of the relations of physical nature to liberty and nationality, making no allusion to the equally stringent moral laws which no people can violate and yet remain in health and vigour." It was worthy of him. He was outspoken by nature, generous in instant wrath; and he had a hatred of back-sliding. In some respects, indeed, his denunciations of repudiations of past loyalties and actions as expressed in his history—there is a hard word for Grotius' moment of wavering under the threat of death in a chapter otherwise written with the utmost affection for him at the end of *John of Barneveld*—were something of self-flagellation for such evasions and concealments as his circumstances had forced him to make. Motley was not a perpetual judge, and he tried not to be a hypocritical one: his description of the results of intoxication in the ranks of the "sea-beggars" in the early chapters of the *Dutch Republic* are less to be read as the sniffs of a Puritan than as the understanding of the former student in Germany who knew what to be drunk meant and what weight was to be put on its consequences. Above all, he retained his generosity of emotion, never better expressed than in his love for Oldenbarneveldt. "Rarely, in all his writings," wrote the historian of the early Stuarts, Samuel Rawson Gardiner, in the *Academy* February 21, 1874), "has Mr. Motley's personality come out so distinctly. We feel him eager, if it were possible, to break out through the distance of time and to stretch out his hand to stay the progress of the mischief." There is a strange echo of that passion in his repudiation of its converse when speaking to the young Cabot Lodge, recorded by the latter many years later in his "Some Early Memories" published in *Scribner's* for June 1913: "I cannot bear moonlight on the snow. I hate it. It is so cold, so cruel, so unfeeling." Lodge could never forget the vehemence of him.

After he died his friends wrote several bad poems in his memory, among them William Wetmore Story; but Story caught something of reality in the lines

> with a half excess
> As of one running in great eagerness,
> And leaning forward out beyond the poise
> Of coward prudence

That was Motley all right, even in his refusal to observe the cautions which avowed partisans brought into the historical writing of his day. Inevitably he paid the penalty for it. In certain respects his excesses led to the defeat of what he believed. The new scientific generation of American historians shared many of his racial and religious attitudes, and expressed them in a much more insidious form, but the nakedness of his bias left him a target for any neophyte anxious to display his pedantic powers. It did not, outside of the Netherlands, result in any worthwhile contribution to the revision of his historical scholarship, until Geyl's major work was translated by Bindoff and others. It did have serious effects on history for the masses as his generation had written it. The new generation wrote for their own profession. Motley had cheapened the grand manner by his vehemence, and in so doing had brought it into disrepute. Curiously enough, he may have had a salutary effect on Catholic scholarship. He forced it to answer questions as to its commitment to liberty, and his Protestant crusading made more astute Catholics realize that they did their cause no good in blanket defenses of ostensible Catholic champions who were in fact as political as their enemies. Acton is an obvious figure reflecting this tendency. In the next century the increase in racial tension brought with it extreme ethno-religious defensiveness in scholarship. The rabid indictments of all Protestant regimes by Hilaire Belloc invited imitation by American Catholics embittered at the widespread anti-Catholic sentiment of the 1920's, and such writers as W. T. Walsh essayed defenses of Philip II which were all too reminiscent of Motley at his worst. Indeed Motley, read or unread, bears responsibility for the renewal of anti-Catholicism in the public domain, and the readiness to imagine the fires of the Inquisition were about to be rekindled on the White House lawn owed something to his violence echoed in sermons in the Bible Belt. More directly, the involvement of the United States in a contemptible war against Spain, a war bitterly opposed by some of the intellectuals in politics with whom Motley shared most in common, derived from the common stock of anti-Spanish prejudice established by his fulminations. A distinction has to be made here with the cooler prose of the historian of the Inquisition, Henry Charles Lea, whose dislike of the institution was as great as Motley's, but who was much more careful to guard against arousing modern Protestant intolerance.

But Motley retains certain calls on our respect. His cosmopolitanism may have been unfashionable, but it remained an example. His self-training in archival work, and the punishing lengths to which he took it, remains even more instructive, especially since his attempts to deepen and strengthen his historical activity followed a premature success which might have led a lesser man to continue churning out popular material with little effort. In fact, it would probably have been impossible for him to have maintained the pitch of urgency of the *Dutch Republic*, born as it was of the anger, fear, and doubt of a crisis situation. His very excesses stimulated wise and judicious response, notably from Fruin, which may have provided an impetus for Dutch historical scholarship to increase its already spectacular gains. His straddling across the way undoubtedly moved much of the urgency of Geyl, Renier, Bindoff, and their associates in the next century, and if Motley failed in his attempts to deparochialize the English-speaking historiographical world, Geyl proved far more successful. Geyl's recognition came later in America than in Britain, but after World War II, his methods and preoccupations became famous. Ved Mehta in *The New Yorker* singled him out alone of European historians as a force impossible to ignore if Americans were to understand *British* historiographical preoccupations. It would be an amusing paradox to be able to quote Pirenne in the context of Dutch historiography and imply that if there had been no Motley, there would have been no Geyl, as he had said of Mohammed and Charlemagne. Of course, this is not true; Geyl's main preoccupation lay with revising the accepted conventions in Dutch historiography, not in disposing of the extremism of an American vulgarizer of far less repute in the Netherlands. But Motley did supply him with an incentive to bring professional Dutch historiography so firmly to the attention of the English-speaking world.

I would leave you with one final thought. Some four years after Motley's death, in the winter of 1881–82, a Scottish doctor of twenty-two was serving morosely on board ship off the African coast when the newly appointed American minister to Liberia came on board. The minister was black, and was old; old enough to have been born in slavery, to have escaped from it, and to have won a position second only to Frederick Douglass among black abolitionists. Henry Highland Garnet had in fact only a few more weeks to live, and the beginning of their conversation may have been medical and fairly grim. But to the book-starved Scot, the opportunity of talking to a literate American about the historical writing from the country he had never seen, was too good to be missed. Garnet had read Motley, and so had the doctor, and eagerly they discussed his work as they sat on deck while the ship moved on. Little by little they moved from historians to history. The Scot had been born a Catholic, had left his faith, and had been fascinated by the commitment to liberty in the writing of some of its most famous opponents, such as Macaulay and Motley. The transition of the conversation from books to personal experience may well have derived directly from discussion of Motley's passionate advocacy of freedom, and from there it would have been natural to talk of the deeper meaning of freedom which only a former slave can know. "This negro gentleman did me good," wrote the Scot many years later, "for a man's brain is an organ for the formation of his own thoughts and also for the digestion of other people's and it needs fresh fodder." He said no more of the fodder, beyond the fact that they had spoken of slavery, but the results are clear enough. In 1884 the Scot won his first great literary success, a short story called "J. Hababuk Jephson's Statement," which among other things told of the abominations practiced under slavery. Ten years after their meeting he had become famous across the North Atlantic for his short stories of Sherlock Holmes and Dr. Watson, two of which turned on the history of American blacks, "The Yellow Face" being a defense of interracial marriage and "The Five Orange Pips" an attack on the Ku Klux Klan. Certainly Conan Doyle's work acquired new depth and significance from those conversations with Garnet; and that is but one story of the many which might be told of the unknown harvest which many may have reaped by reading and talking of John Lothrop Motley, his saga of the Netherlands, and his identification of its history with the cause of liberty. For whatever his faults, he tried so far as he could to extend human freedom. I think the text on which to leave him, bearing in mind that he thought his country should be synonymous with liberty, is that from the climax of his greatest work:

The statesman then came forward and said in a loud, firm voice to the people:

"Men, do not believe that I am a traitor to the country. I have ever acted uprightly and loyally as a good patriot, and as such I shall die."

"This, Here, and Soon"

Johan Huizinga's *Esquisse* of American Culture[1]

· ❧ ·

MICHAEL KAMMEN

I

To offer yet another essay on Johan Huizinga may understandably seem superfluous. Several fine articles about him have appeared in the United States, even more in Europe, and a great many in his native land. Huizinga has hardly been neglected since his death in 1945. His books remain in print. Indeed, most of them have been translated into various languages, which befits one of the masters of modern historical thought. In the familiar portrait (made in 1936 by H. H. Kamerlingh-Onnes), we see the scholar in his study, notice the inquisitive but calmly reflective face, long and upward-curving lines at the outer edges of his eyes, a short neck, rounded shoulders, and the humped upper back of a desk-bound man, age sixty-five, who had spent so much of his life reading and writing.[2]

Our sense of Huizinga's temperament is equally familiar, for it has been sketched often: anti-Freudian and anti-Marxian because both of those value systems were anti-Christian in their implications, and because Huizinga's mind was too subtle to be trapped by any mode of determinism. Then there is the conservative Huizinga: the man of delicate aesthetic sensibility, the harsh critic of technology (so mechanistic in its social implications) and of mass culture. At a conference held in 1972, at Groningen, to celebrate the one hundredth anniversary of Huizinga's birth, E. H. Gombrich remarked upon his plea for renunciation. The stoic historian "wanted to persuade his contemporaries to exercise restraint, to practise austerity and to seek the simple life."[3]

Huizinga has been criticized for romanticizing the past, for anthropomorphizing culture, for elitism, for a lack of conceptual rigor, and for undue pessimism about the human conditions and its prospects.

The only aspect of the customary characterization of him that has been softened in recent years is the view (initially emphasized by Pieter Geyl and Jan Romein) that Huizinga was indifferent to political realities. As Robert Anchor wrote in 1978, however, Huizinga "plausibly viewed politics as *symptomatic rather than causative*," and "sought to diagnose the disease of which the myths of national and racial superiority, and the new justifications for violence, cruelty, and war were the most conspicuous signs. Such statements, indeed, were not neutral. The Nazis deemed them dangerous enough to detain Huizinga during the occupation in the out-of-the-way town of De Steeg."[4]

Despite familiar criticisms, Huizinga retains our respect. *The Waning of the Middle Ages* (1919) continues to be widely read; it is still regularly assigned as a required text at American universities.[5] When Huizinga's two books on the United States were published together in English translation (1972), that volume, entitled *America: A Dutch Historian's Vision, from Afar and Near*, enjoyed considerable success in various sorts of college courses in the United States.[6] Above all, *Homo Ludens* (1938), which was not translated into English until 1950, is frequently cited by scholars and popular writers alike. In *The Complete Book of Running*, for example, a best-selling manual for joggers published in 1977, Jim Fixx announces that "any decently thorough inquiry into the meaning of sport will eventually bring us to the source of much present-day thinking on the matter: Johan Huizinga's profound *Homo Ludens: A Study of the Play Element in Culture*" (p. 20). If, in fact, *Homo Ludens* has become Huizinga's best-known book, that may well be symptomatic of a remarkable increase in leisure during the past generation, and of our attention to leisure as a many-faceted cultural phenomenon. Surely, much has changed since 1931 when Supreme Court Justice Oliver Wendell Holmes wrote that "one dreams of leisure but as the old farmer said, when he saw the hippopotamus, I don't believe there's no such critter."[7]

Although much has now been said about Huizinga and his views, no one (to the best of my knowledge) has yet undertaken a discrete examination of his changing perceptions of American culture—a story, or relationship, that essentially took place during the quarter century between 1916 and 1941. There are several reasons why I am glad to attempt such an assessment. First, because I must admit not merely my professional admiration for Huizinga, especially the wonderful range of his interests and reading,[8] but even a certain empathy for many of his cultural criticisms and predilections, however unfashionable they may be. Second, because Huizinga had the courage to generalize: about Dutch civilization, about the factors that had shaped the American national character, and, ultimately, about the destiny of humankind and its evolving culture. Wallace Notestein, a distinguished historian from the United States who was nearly Huizinga's contemporary, wrote to a friend in 1933 that "we should all write more about History in its general aspects. Are we all thinking enough about that?"[9] Huizinga most certainly was, especially during that dark decade of the 1930's.

A third reason for looking at Huizinga's changing perceptions of American culture is that they are indicative, in microcosm, of the contrapuntal quality of Dutch-American cultural relations: on again, off again, alternately apathetic and enthusiastic. Between the 1860's and 1953 a frieze of frescoes was painted in the Rotunda of the Capitol in Washington, D.C. The frieze depicts many important aspects of American history, including the contributions of Columbus, Cortez, Pizarro, De Soto, Pocahontas, William Penn, and many others. Yet the role of the Dutch in the New World is strangely neglected. Nevertheless, American art and iconography obviously owe a substantial debt to the Netherlands. We can see it in the Hudson River School, and particularly in a major historical painting that was offered for sale in 1980: Robert Weir's large canvas called "The Landing of Henry Hudson," done in 1838. One finds evidence of confusion during the early 1930's about Dutch colonial settlements and traditions in America. But by 1937 a Netherlands Pioneer and Historical Foundation had been established, and a few years later the Library of Congress housed a Netherlands Studies Unit. In 1974 Paul O'Dwyer, president of New York's City Council, insisted that the official date for the founding of New York be changed from 1664, the time of England's conquest, to 1625, when Dutch colonists began to arrive. O'Dwyer introduced a bill in the City Council to alter the date on both the city's flag and its official seal. When interviewed, O'Dwyer explained that his initiative "was an effort to set history straight and to recognize the city's Dutch heritage on the 700th anniversary of the founding of the city of Amsterdam."[10]

Fourth, and perhaps most important, I believe that an examination of Huizinga's sketches of the United States will enhance our understanding of him as a writer in at least two, paradoxically contradictory ways. On the one hand, I find that his comparatively unfamiliar books on the United States (first published in 1918 and 1927) explicitly anticipate the major themes of his better-known books, especially *In the Shadow of Tomorrow* (1936) and *Homo Ludens* (1938). But on the other hand, I also find that Huizinga seems to have compartmentalized his studies of America and of Europe, with the result that emphases and insights that inform his work on the New World are often strangely missing from his writings on the Old, and vice versa. Curious? To be sure; but historians in general, even the very

Johan Huizinga, by H. H. Kamerlingh-Onnes, 1936

best, are neither consistent nor lacking in elements of the non-rational. A close look at Huizinga on America can teach us something fresh about the complexities and curiosities of the historian's craft.

II

In about 1915 or 1916, Huizinga became interested in American history. He began to read those materials available to him in Holland, and in 1917–18 offered a general course at the University of Leiden on the history of the United States. Explaining that "we know too little about America," he published four long essays in 1918, and then two years later revised them as a book. Geyl rendered the title of this study as *Man and the Crowd in America*. Professor Herbert H. Rowen of Rutgers, whose fine translation has made the work accessible to those of us unable to read Dutch, calls it *Man and the Masses in America*.[11]

Call it what you will, the volume is interesting and important for many reasons. For example, it reversed the popular and *politique* image that Dutch and American history were remarkably similar. On January 18, 1912, Horace White, a prominent newspaperman and Republican politician, spoke at the annual dinner of the Holland Society of New York (held at the Waldorf-Astoria). In response to the toast "The Netherlands and the United States," White remarked that "the Netherlands and the United States have much in common, both in history and purpose. Each wrested independence from a powerful empire after a protracted struggle; each forged in the fires of that struggle a chain of inseparable parts; each in her time became a refuge for the oppressed, and the home of freedom, tolerance and good will. From her trials, and as the outcome of her heroism, each country reared a great man—soldier, statesman, ruler—William the Silent, and George Washington."[12]

Huizinga was much too shrewd, as well as too knowledgeable, to follow that route of reductivism. In comparing the American Revolution with the French and "the controversy over the Dutch Patriots" (of the 1770's and 1780's), he found it "at once apparent that the American Revolution was more conservative than either of these others. There was no towering political and social structure to be overthrown, as in France." Not only did Huizinga repeatedly anticipate the provocative thesis of Louis Hartz's *The Liberal Tradition in America* (1955), but by comparing English, Dutch, and French colonies in the New World he also anticipated Hartz's pioneering volume, *The Founding of New Societies: Studies in the History of the United States, Latin America, South Africa, Canada and Australia* (1964).[13]

Huizinga is equally fascinating in his treatment of democracy in

America. Repeated references to Tocqueville and Bryce indicate his thorough familiarity with their classic inquiries. But much had changed in the United States since Bryce published *The American Commonwealth* in 1889. Consequently Huizinga's observations are suitably fresh and acute. He emphasized the decline of democracy in American life, and was attracted to the Turner thesis because it helped him to explain the demise of "the old individualist pioneer democracy." Huizinga believed that Americans achieved efficiency at the expense of democracy; that powerful economic forces worked against egalitarianism; that governmental institutions were becoming less democratic in their actual operations; and that workers were not adequately represented on juries.[14]

He was ahead of his time, moreover, in commenting that "conservatism and democracy are not contradictory" in the United States. "Bourgeois democracy has an old and strong tradition in America . . . and when we see institutional processes such as initiative and referendum work in a conservative way, we have, from the American point of view, absolutely no right to call the result undemocratic for that reason." Huizinga believed that America's self-proclaimed mission had long been "to give the world the model of a wise, mighty, and prosperous democracy." He argued that American society had been "too thoroughly commercialized" and that "too many individuals are involved in keeping the machinery of production in operation, for a revolutionary doctrine to be able to get much of a grip there." He accurately regarded Woodrow Wilson as a conservative democrat.[15]

The compatibility of contradictory tendencies in American culture fascinated Huizinga. He repeatedly mentions the dominance of practical-idealism (see pp. 166, 176), and collective-individualism (see pp. 50, 165, and 173). As he concluded his lengthy first essay, "the twin concepts of Individualism and Association are felt as a contradiction in American history much less than one would expect on the basis of European history."[16] Although he echoed Tocqueville on the inevitability of conformism in the United States, he nonetheless found that individualism had been able to coexist, and even flourish, alongside the powerful pressures to conform. "While conservative piety and obedient imitation nourished traits of tame conventionality, the living and individual element of the national character grew in the struggle with nature."[17]

Again and again I am impressed by Huizinga's ability, despite limited library resources for Americana, and without having been to the United States (yet), to anticipate the shrewdest insights and inquiries of subsequent observers and scholars. His analysis of public opinion, and especially its changing role in politics, predated Walter Lippmann's now classic book *Public Opinion* (1922).[18] Huizinga startles me by wondering, "How did the Yankee grow out of the seventeenth-century Puritan of New England?"—a question that Richard Bushman first began to answer, for one colony, in 1967.[19] Huizinga follows with a fascinating speculation that "notwithstanding what happened in Europe, the Enlightenment in America did not combat faith or at least make it impotent but only pushed it a little to one side." He then adds, in consequence, that the United States avoided "the great struggle of revenge against the Enlightenment."[20] Scholars have yet to develop the implications of that insight, or even test it as a hypothesis. Huizinga was equally shrewd in pointing out that "naïve ancestor worship" was "characteristic of America."[21] His acuity here is all the more impressive because the phenomenon in its most blatant form was of recent vintage (c. 1885–1915) and had not been discussed in works available to Huizinga. Finally, I am struck by Huizinga's recognition that great constitutional issues in the United States had a way of developing from relatively trivial quarrels, or what Huizinga would call "only a paltry affair."[22]

Did his American muse ever nod? Of course it did, though one often cannot tell whether the cause was insufficient information, misleading material, or sheer miscalculation. A few examples may suffice. When he wrote of the early colonists that "little or nothing is brought over of whatever is bound up with the history and legends of the mother country," had he not read Edward Eggleston's *The Transit of Civilization from England to America in the Seventeenth Century* (1900)?[23] Huizinga mistakenly regarded Jefferson as a shrewd and aggressive political organizer.[24] He seems to have misunderstood the nature and significance of Andrew Jackson's political career, failing to realize that Jackson himself was a frontier nabob and nascent capitalist.[25] I also believe that Huizinga seriously underestimated slavery as a social issue, and excessively emphasized tariff protectionism as a major precipitant of secession and Civil War.[26]

I am rather inclined to doubt whether "secrecy, violence, and corruption" were any more characteristic of political action groups in the United States than of their European counterparts. Similarly, Huizinga seems needlessly cynical in generalizing about the self-seeking proclivities of American politicians. Consequently he missed the intense degree of ideological commitment in Thaddeus Stevens and reduced that passionate man's motives in the Reconstruction era to little more than "unscrupulous party policy." Nor did Huizinga understand that the Ku Klux Klan enjoyed episodic bursts of intimidating power long past 1870.[27] And finally, to terminate this recital of shortcomings in the historical essays of 1918–20, Huizinga's assertions about American literary culture are often capricious. He could be quite canny about individual authors: especially Emerson, Thoreau, and Hawthorne. He shrewdly redressed the historians' neglect of Walt Whitman. (Indeed, Huizinga's strong empathy for Whitman is one of the most engaging and surprising aspects of his book.) Nevertheless, Huizinga overlooked the imaginative implications of what Perry Miller labeled Nature's Nation (according to Huizinga, "The great and true spirit of America does not reveal itself in romanticism of any kind"), and was fairly wide of the mark in declaring that "the imaginative element in American literature is primarily defined by dependence on Europe and the European past."[28]

Far more interesting, though, is this twofold question: from whom did Huizinga learn his American history, and how did the addition of that "string to his bow" affect his overall performance as a virtuoso? The answer to the latter question is as curious as the response to the former is obvious. Charles A. Beard and Frederick Jackson Turner were his major mentors. Turner's essays on the frontier and his "Social Forces in American History" are cited quite frequently. As Huizinga wrote to Turner in 1919, "the notions I borrowed from your 'Significance of the Frontier' of 1893 have helped me more than most of my other reading to form a clear understanding of the main substance of American history."[29] Beard's *Economic Interpretation of the Constitution* (1913), his *Economic Origins of Jeffersonian Democracy* (1915), and a textbook called *Contemporary American History, 1877–1913* (1914) were equally important. Huizinga cited Beard more than any other historian, adopted his view of the Constitution as (in Huizinga's words) an "agreement of covetous speculators," and followed Beard's emphasis on the determinative role of economic forces in shaping American imperialism at the close of the nineteenth century. To paraphrase Samuel Eliot Morison, whose early work Huizinga also read, he literally viewed American history "through a Beard."[30]

Yet it does not seem to have affected Huizinga's work in European history—there's the great mystery. He wrote at the very beginning of *Man and the Masses in America* that he wished to use "the facts of American history" as a means of testing the "schematic forms through which we are accustomed to understand history" (p. 7). In his interesting letter to Turner, Huizinga declared that "it has been a great surprise to me to see how much we Europeans could learn from American history, not only as to the subject itself, but also with regard to historical interpretation in general."[31] Nevertheless, the same Johan Huizinga who ascribed such importance to economic factors in his book about America—at times he almost sounds like an economic determinist—has an altogether different tone in *The Waning of the Middle Ages*, a book on which he worked at the very same time, and published in 1919. As Pieter Geyl and S. Muller Fzn. have noted, Huizinga's treatment of French-Burgundian culture in the fifteenth century is characterized by "systematic neglect of economic and political factors."[32]

What is one to conclude? Did Huizinga fail to do what he told Frederick Jackson Turner he would do: namely, expand his mode of historical interpretation? Did Huizinga take off one set of eyeglasses and put on another when he shifted back and forth from the Old World to the New? Yes, I suspect that he did, and for two reasons. First, because writing about the United States was not exactly writing *history* for Huizinga. Despite his insistence that his analysis would be that of a cultural historian (pp. 3–5), his approach more nearly approximated that of serious, high journalism: the analyst of contemporary affairs, the author of *In the Shadow of Tomorrow* (1936) and related essays. I find it very significant that Huizinga did not care for early American history, despite the fact that the Dutch had been important participants in that story and that the colonial period corresponded chronologically with a phase that he cared about very much in his own country's history. One of Huizinga's finest and longest essays is called "Dutch Civilisation in the Seventeenth Century." He dismissed the comparable period in American history, however, because he found it uninteresting and aesthetically unattractive.

> The history of North America before the War of Independence shows all the features proper to colonial history in general; viz., a certain lack of unity, a certain disparity, a certain rusticity. . . . The general reader . . . will not be struck by particular beauty of line or color in the story of the thirteen separate colonies.[33]

The second reason, in my opinion, is that Huizinga seems to have believed in what we now call "American exceptionalism." If civilization in the United States was profoundly different, then an interpretive schema appropriate to the Western Hemisphere might easily be unsuitable elsewhere. Here is a pertinent passage from *Man and the Masses in America:*

> At bottom, every political and cultural question in America is an economic one. On America's virgin soil, which is free of old, strongly rooted social growths, economic factors work with a freedom and directness unknown in European history. Political passions in America are deliberately directed to economic questions, and these are not subordinated to a system of intellectual convictions which become for the man who believes them the content of his culture. (p. 9)

E. H. Gombrich got to the heart of the matter in 1972 when he observed that Huizinga was attracted by the challenge of describing a culture which "could not be encompassed" by the traditional forms applied to European history.[34] Huizinga may well have been misguided in believing that an economic interpretation was suitable for the United States but not for Europe. Many historians have assumed, after all, that the New World was colonized *when it was* precisely because new economic forces had been unleashed in Europe. Be that as it may, Huizinga seems to have believed otherwise. Hence his apparent proclivity for compartmentalization. Hence extraordinary differences in texture and tone between *Man and the Masses in America* (1918–20) and *The Waning of the Middle Ages* (1919). Huizinga would have said to his critics that different eras and contexts present divergent historical problems. Every *problematique* deserves its very own mode, or system, of explanation.

III

During the years from 1920 until 1926, when Huizinga made his only visit to the United States, cultural relations between the two nations intensified in very positive ways. A primary reason seems to have been the abundance of historical anniversaries to commemorate. In 1920 committees were formed in Holland and the United States to plan the tercentenary, beginning August 29, 1921, of the Pilgrims' departure from Holland and their subsequent arrival at Plymouth. In 1923, a Huguenot-Walloon New Netherland Commission came into existence; and the following May a Huguenot-Walloon Tercentenary was celebrated on Staten Island. Meanwhile a professorial chair of Dutch history, ideals, and literature was established at Columbia University; organizations called the Netherland-America Affiliation were created at New York City and The Hague; in 1923 Edward Bok began to publish a series of volumes called "Great Hollanders" (Huizinga's *Erasmus* appeared in that series in 1924); and a Summer School for American Students opened at the University of Leiden in 1924. That same year Victor Hugo Paltsits, chief of the Manuscript Division at the New York Public Library, prepared a paper for the American Antiquarian Society, "The Founding of New Amsterdam in 1626." In 1925 he presented a revised version to the New York Genealogical and Biographical Society; and one year later various exhibitions and publications, popular as well as scholarly, marked the 300th birthday of New Amsterdam (which to many people really meant the genesis of New York as a whole).[35]

A number of the key individuals involved in these activities were either friends of Johan Huizinga or, at the very least, professional colleagues: Dr. Daniel Plooij, archivist and officer of the Leiden Pilgrim Society; Dr. Cornelis van Vollenhoven, professor of international and colonial law at the University of Leiden; Dr. Albert Eekhof, professor of church history at Leiden; and Dr. Adriaan J. Barnouw, Queen Wilhelmina Exchange Professor at Columbia. Nevertheless, Huizinga seems to have had little interest in the historical hoopla that culminated in 1926,[36] and his visit should be described as sociological and cultural rather than historical in orientation. It resulted in a slender book, *Life and Thought in America*, published in 1927.[37]

One immediately notices a radical shift in Huizinga's tone. In 1918, writing the preface to *Man and the Masses in America*, he explained that he found himself "stimulated and fascinated as seldom ever before. . . . Something of America's spiritual élan is transmitted to anyone who takes the trouble to understand the spirit of the country." Eight years later Huizinga found the United States to be a spiritual wasteland. The strongest leitmotif of his critique is summed up in an epithet that he repeated throughout the 1927 book: "This, Here, and Soon." It meant that the United States had become a "transitive" rather than a "transcendental" society, a culture that prized communication as a powerful means of influence, and one in which the American "builds himself a better abode in imagination, he creates a world that recognizes him."[38] In 1918 he had casually noticed the "perpetual tension in America between a passionate idealism and an unrestrainable energy directed to material things." By 1926, however, this gap between altruistic ethos and sordid reality had become a dark obsession in Huizinga's mind. He found a stark contrast between "the attitude of the nation in general and the tone of its literature."[39]

In 1918 he had called attention to efficiency: "what the American wants more than anything else." He returned to this point frequently, and concluded that "in the American mind efficiency and democracy are closely related concepts. The endeavor to democratize the idea of God goes hand in hand with pragmatism, and both arise out of the spirit of 'This, Here, and Soon.'" By 1927 Huizinga's tone had become considerably more shrill. He linked the ugly trends of conformity and standardization to the American penchant for efficiency. He condemned the American passion for "saving time," conserving human energy and not wasting opportunities.[40] "The notion that there could exist anything like over-organization does not torment them." The American expectation that technology and "technological organization" could solve any problem disturbed him deeply.[41]

Progress had become a pejorative concept for Huizinga. He selected as an epigram for the first page of Chapter 1 the observation by William James that "progress is a terrible thing" (even more ironic than Huizinga recognized?), and played variations on that theme throughout the book: that Americans had discarded faith because science had replaced religion, and that "the new materialism" had caused a "spiritual emptiness" in the United States.[42] There is a sense in which our intellectuals have only recently begun to catch up with Huizinga: during the later 1970's, for example, the American Academy of Arts and Sciences, supported by the Rockefeller Foundation, undertook a major, multidisciplinary project "on the transformation of the idea of progress."[43]

In Huizinga's own time, however, a kindred spirit in the United States, Carl L. Becker, took a somewhat different view. In a slim volume called *Progress and Power*, comprising three lectures presented at Stanford in 1935, Becker opened with a point similar to Huizinga's: "Standing within the deep shadow of the Great War, it is difficult to recover the nineteenth-century faith either in the fact or the doctrine of progress." But Becker unfurled, as an open question, the great issue on which Huizinga had already passed judgment: "May we still, in whatever different fashion, believe in the progress of mankind?" Although his answer cannot be labeled as entirely positive, Becker remained more hopeful than Huizinga. Becker began with the assumption "that the multiplication of implements of power has at every stage in human history been as essential to the development of intelligence as the development of intelligence has been essential to the multiplication of implements of power." He concluded that machines are not inevitably beyond man's moral and social control. "The machines, not being on the side of the angels, remain impassive in the presence of indignation, wishful thinking, and the moral imperative, but respond without prejudice or comment or ethical reservation to relevant and accurate knowledge impersonally applied."[44] This was the major difference between Becker and Huizinga on the problem of progress.

Huizinga felt concerned about contemporary American scholarship because in the books that he read "one repeatedly meets a tone of mocking disdain for all faith." Carl Becker, whom he does not mention, would have been a prime example; but Huizinga does deride the "utterly naïve evolutionism" of James Harvey Robinson's *The Mind in the Making: The Relation of Intelligence to Social Reform* (1921), disliked Harry Elmer Barnes's *The New History and the Social Studies* (1925), and expressed particular distate for current work in social psychology. What Huizinga had admired in Ralph Waldo Emerson, "the sense of the direct and constant presence of mystery in and behind everything," seemed to have disappeared in modern America.[45]

The litany of Huizinga's laments would scarcely provide a lift for sagging spirits. It worried him that "the ideal of education is in fact a religion."[46] The democratization of culture could only augment the "mediocrity which permeates American life." He sneered at the "overwhelming success" of his countryman Hendrik Willem van Loon, educated at Cornell and Harvard, who had chosen to remain in the United

States as a popularizer of Dutch, American, and world history. "His unpretentious scribblings, which the least-educated man can understand, meet the minimum commitment which a public of millions has left over for knowledge."[47] It troubled Huizinga that "America's mind is fundamentally antihistorical"; that "America, with its all-pervasive sense of the future, worships the young"; and that "movie romanticism" was merely the most banal manifestation of "hero-worship" in the United States.[48]

Huizinga seems to have encountered too many arrogant and nationalistic individuals during his 1926 tour, even among academics and intellectuals, who should have been, by definition, candid social critics. He considered American society "an extroverted culture," and regarded the press as an especially egregious example of all that was wrong in the United States. He disliked the "selective emphasis" of our newspapers, their unwillingness to moralize about the news, the banality of their political views, the vulgarity of their advertising, and their "trashiness" in general.[49]

One is obliged to respect Huizinga's honesty and intensity of feeling in *Life and Thought in America*, even if one does not concur in all of his judgments.[50] But the book is interesting and important as more than just another critique. It helps to illuminate the genesis of his well-known cultural pessimism of the 1930's and 1940's. *America* adds chronological precision and a certain causal impetus to our understanding of Huizinga's subsequent trajectory as a cultural critic. *In the Shadow of Tomorrow* (1936) does not mention the United States very often; but when it does, Huizinga simply compresses and reiterates what he had written so stridently a decade earlier. Once again he quotes William James's remark that "progress is a terrible thing" (p. 56). More to the point, just as Tocqueville had viewed democracy in America as a harbinger of Europe's destiny, so Huizinga confronted in the United States his anxieties about the potential degradation of a fading European culture that in many respects he idealized.[51]

> Behind the democratic ideal rises up at once the reality of mechanization. . . . The mechanistic conception of social life, with its exclusion of morality and exhortation, seems to leave almost no means for intervention. If we are all just the nearly helpless followers of fashions, manners, and habits defined by our group, the poor slaves of our personal habits, which together determine our character . . . is there any way to bring about *change*, to change and to improve all that which *must* be changed? (pp. 281–82)

> The European traveler finds it almost impossible to concentrate when he is in a big American city. The telephone becomes a curse. The variety of

personal assistance and technical devices causes as much diversion of attention and loss of time as it saves work. (p. 252)

The general leveling of culture also affects love life. Just as intellectual
enjoyment becomes available for everyone in a thousand ways, and hence
loses the quality of something conquered, something which represents
success and to which one pays worship, so there also arises a form of
sexual satisfaction which signifies the dissolution of old forms of civilization. (pp. 262–63)

Note well, however, that Huizinga made very few criticisms of
the United States in 1927 that he did not subsequently make of the
Netherlands in 1934–35 or of Europe generally in 1935–36. As he wrote
in the foreword to *Life and Thought in America*: "Modern civilization
is on trial in America in a simpler way than among us. Will Europe
be next?"[52] In "The Spirit of the Netherlands," Huizinga's testy description of bourgeois life in Holland sounds remarkably like that in
the United States. His "feeling of living in a world that hovers on the
brink of annihilation," his laments about "mankind's astonishing
cultural decline" and "the grim idols of technocracy and over-
organisation" provide a coda to the 1927 book on America as well as
an overture to *In the Shadow of Tomorrow*.[53]

In that profoundly pessimistic and controversial book, the word
"puerilism" is so pejorative yet important that Huizinga devotes an
entire chapter to it. Early in the chapter he hammers this devastating
judgment: "The country where a national puerilism could be studied
most thoroughly in all its aspects, from the innocent and even attractive to the criminal, is the United States." But then he blinks and
softens the blow by adding that "one should be careful to approach it
with an open mind. For America *is* younger and more youthful than
Europe. Much that here would deserve to be qualified as childish is
there merely naïve, and the truly naïve guards against any reproach of
puerilism. Besides, the American himself is no longer blind to the
excesses of his youthfulness. Did he not give himself Babbitt?"[54]

Despite his harsh strictures upon American civilization in 1927;
and perhaps, as Huizinga had predicted, precisely because Western
Europe all too swiftly caught up with the United States, he could not
terminate his interest in 1927 or 1936, any more than he could have
in 1920. As he explained to Frederick Jackson Turner in 1919, "I
hope to revert to American history sometime more for when you have
once been captivated by its enormous problems and its stirring tone,
it will not let you go the rest of your scholarly life."[55] In the academic
year 1940–41, Huizinga selected as one of the principal subjects for his
lectures at Leiden the history of the United States, "a topic which ap-

peals to me again and again."[56] His perception of America at that time appears in a communication presented on January 15, 1941, at the Netherlands Academy of Sciences (Section of Letters). This *esquisse* (referred to in note 33 above) is as bizarre as it is fascinating. It adds a curious "postscript" to the impressions he formulated in 1917–18 and 1926–27.

More than ever, Huizinga in 1941 reminds one of Henry Adams: a similar disdain for the vulgarity of modern culture; a similar affection for the medieval age of faith (Huizinga and Adams both idealized twelfth-century France); and a similar bewilderment at technological complexity. How could one possibly hope to make any sense of it? Huizinga found American history from 1776 until 1865 attractive because its wholeness seemed comprehensible, "its general idea is available to all." The period had "a distinct form" because "its public life [was] conducted by an *élite*. The masses still remain in the background." Despite the conservative pitch of that last statement, Huizinga's criteria seem to have been more aesthetic than ideological. He preferred the period after 1789 because "the historical lines are relatively simple. The persons acting are of a marked type, and the conditions and the conflicts are easy to grasp. In short, the history of those years shows shape and color."[57]

Huizinga's notion of the historian as artist—hence his need for materials of high drama—almost seems to overbalance his sensitivity to human suffering. The American Civil War attracted him as a writer because "only a crisis which breaks the political unity itself can bring again to the fore the *story* quality of history." By contrast, in the period after the Civil War "the history of the United States not only loses dramatic pathos, but is also robbed of comprehensible and striking form. The general reader at least will find it more or less confused, perplexing, and without unity." I cannot tell whether this echo of Henry Adams is intentional or accidental; but Huizinga is explicit about his assessment of the central problem for historiography in 1941. Once again, as in 1926, he looked to the United States as much for its illustrative value as for its intrinsic substance.

> As I speak of the gradual loss of form inherent in the material of modern history, particularly in the history of the United States since the Civil War, I should like to make it clear that I find this increasing shapelessness due not to an optical illusion nor to a deficiency in the forces or fashions of historical imagination, but to a change in the components of history itself.[58]

It irked Huizinga that "history has had to change its record of personal happenings to one of collective phenomena." Had he never read Gibbon's *Decline and Fall of the Roman Empire*, or Burckhardt's *The Civilization of the Renaissance in Italy*? Of course he had; but he went on to add that "in a history dominated by the economic factor—as American history undoubtedly is, far more so than European—the human element recedes into the background."[59] Huizinga's incomprehension of the prime reality in American social history since 1870, the massive and heterogeneous migration from Europe, reinforced his idealization of the individual free to shape his own destiny as well as that of his society.

> Several decades of increasing shapelessness in American history can be explained by the fact that a political unit covering the main part of a whole continent loses, by its very homogeneity, the most fertile of all themes for history: the conflict between independent powers, be they peaceful rivals or hostile opponents. Furthermore, the ever-increasing preponderance in such a continent-commonwealth of economic forces is likely to obscure the human being as an actor in history.[60]

Huizinga concluded this *esquisse* with an observation that distresses me because I believe it to be doubly perverse. It pained him that "the modern world is becoming more and more accustomed to thinking in numbers. America has hitherto been more addicted to this, perhaps, than Europe. . . . Only the number counts, only the number expresses thought." Huizinga here seems truly the intellectual prisoner of a certain type of anti-Americanism. We need look no farther than Matthew Arnold's *Civilization in the United States*, where he observed that "the great scale of things in America powerfully impresses Mr. [John] Bright's imagination always; he loves to count the prodigious number of acres of land there, the prodigious number of bushels of wheat raised," etc.[61] Americans did not invent the quantitative imagination, nor do we enjoy any monopoly over it.

Huizinga ended with a dismal prognosis for history as a discipline. "This shift in the mode of thinking is full of great dangers for civilization, and for that civilizing product of the mind called history. Once *numbers* reign supreme in our society, there will be no story left to tell, no images for history to evoke."[62] The application of quantitative methods to historical investigation has resulted in some dreary and even wrongheaded scholarship, to be sure. But Huizinga was unduly pessimistic about the inevitability of such consequences; for some of the finest works of American scholarship since 1969 have depended heavily upon "numbers," but without any loss of "story" or of "images to evoke." They do not always tell a story, or evoke images, that Huizinga would have found attractive. Yet they surely qualify as innovative, influential, and highly significant works of history.[63]

IV

Like Johan Huizinga, Matthew Arnold wrote essays about American civilization both before *and* after he had visited the United States. Unlike Huizinga, however, Arnold's treatment became more favorable after his initial lecture tour during the winter of 1883–84. He envied the United States its innocence of those impossible problems that seemed to plague England: aristocratic domination of a rigid class structure, an excess of religious dissent, and the Irish question. More positively, he felt that American institutions, being new, were well suited to American needs. After returning to England, Arnold observed that "to write a book about America, on the strength of having made merely such a tour there as mine was, and with no fuller equipment of preparatory studies and of local observations than I possess, would seem to me an impertinence."[64]

One could be tempted to confront Huizinga's ghost with that modest concession, were it not for the fact that he *had* done his "homework," so to speak. Few foreign visitors have made more thorough "preparatory studies" than teaching a university course and doing extensive historical reading about American culture. Huizinga's negativism from 1926 until his death resulted from a special situation: the United States was not merely another country, an exotic culture to be examined. It represented the accelerating thrust of the present as well as an ominous portent for the future. Because Huizinga cared so strongly about the preservation of culture as he had known it, what seemed to be taking place across the Atlantic served as a distressing signal of impending catastrophe.

It is worth noting at least a brief comparison between Huizinga and James Bryce, for their temperaments were as similar as their motives for writing about the United States. In 1882 Bryce decided to follow in Tocqueville's footsteps "to try to give my countrymen some juster views than they have about the United States." He added that he often felt "vexed here at the want of comprehension of the true state of things in America."[65] As a Scottish Calvinist, Bryce's moralistic temperament prevented him from investigating the seamier aspects of American life. He could not, for example, comprehend the coarse pleasures of the working class in the United States. *Unlike* Huizinga, however, Bryce was intensely interested in governmental institutions and the political process. Like so many Britons of his generation, he admired the American Constitution as a remarkably stabilizing keel for our ship of state.

Huizinga has frequently been compared with Marc Bloch, because both were seminal historians who responded very differently to the challenge of Fascism: one with militant activism, the other with quiet resignation. Because they differed so radically—in temperament as well as religious background—and because Bloch was fourteen years younger, I find it somewhat more instructive to compare Huizinga (1872–1945) with four historians who were his exact contemporaries.

Elie Halévy (1871–1937), whose ancestry was Calvinist *and* Jewish, shared Huizinga's austerity and disciplined commitment to scholarship. Like Huizinga, he drifted into history as a calling (Halévy from philosophy and sociology). Like Huizinga, who had ulterior motives, intellectually speaking, for studying the United States, Halévy explored modern British history as a laboratory for understanding liberalism and democracy. He believed that elites had an obligation to elevate republican public opinion, and saw a tension within democratic socialism between a desire to liberate the individual and the overwhelming impulse to organize and regulate him. After passionate involvement in the Dreyfus affair, Halévy withdrew from active participation in public life. In 1900 he wrote two sentences that Huizinga himself might well have written: "A man disposed to fulfil his civic duties, but resolved to keep intact the greatest part of his time for the accomplishment of tasks properly intellectual, must rigorously limit the practical part of his existence. I ignore the Dreyfus affair, I ignore politics." Like Huizinga, also, he was more of a Europeanist than a nationalist, and wished to preserve all that was best in European culture. Following World War I, Halévy fell into a mood of "moral disgust," and devoted the last decade of his life to investigations of contemporary history, particularly the meaning of progress in a democratic society. As a historian Halévy always rejected economic determinism. He regarded Communism and Fascism as equally tyrannical— a view that shocked many of his friends—because he dreaded any form of statism or organized, hierarchical oppression. Huizinga shared that perspective.[66]

Halvdan Koht (1873–1965), the Norwegian historian, decided to visit the United States in 1908–9 because "in America one could study the history of the future." He had very mixed reactions to what he saw. Although delighted by "the unconquerable spirit of progress" that he encountered throughout the country, he also perceived many "imperfections," especially the degree to which Americans seemed bound by social conventions, "outward forms," such as the stigma ascribed to women who smoked.

At Columbia University, however, he came under the influence of James T. Shotwell, William A. Dunning, and especially Edwin R. A. Seligman, whose *Economic Interpretation of History* (1907) impressed him greatly. In 1909 he met Frederick Jackson Turner and John R.

Commons, and then felt eager to introduce the study of American history in Norway. He did so immediately, in 1909–10 at Kristiania (Oslo); and very soon the subject even became a requirement for the degree in history. Koht prepared a section on American culture for an eight-volume history of world culture (1912). In 1920, the same year that Huizinga's *Man and the Masses in America* was published in revised form, Koht brought out (in Norwegian) *The American Nation: Its Origins and Its Rise*. Unlike Huizinga, however, Koht emphasized class conflict, carried the economic emphasis from his American contacts to his work on Norwegian history, and became very active in public affairs.[67]

Arthur O. Lovejoy (1873–1962) shared Huizinga's personal austerity and passion for the history of ideas. Lovejoy differed significantly, however, in preferring to trace ideas through time, in a linear fashion, whereas Huizinga loved to sketch, as a still life, the picture of a civilization at a pivotal moment in time. Lovejoy differed also in his political activism. He worked vigorously as a pamphleteer during both world wars, was a passionate defender of civil liberties, and perceived early in the 1930's that Nazi Germany posed a grave threat to the security of Europe and the United States. He spoke out repeatedly in opposition to Hitler, and after 1939 Lovejoy pushed vigorously for increased American aid to the Allies.[68]

Among this quartet of distinguished contemporaries, however, the most interesting comparison can be made with Carl L. Becker (1873–1945). Like Huizinga, Becker was more of an essayist than a narrative historian rooted in archival research. They shared an interest in significant eras of transition, and both liked to challenge the conventional wisdom of historical periodization. In 1920, just when Huizinga published his revised and expanded work on American history, Becker brought out *Our Great Experiment in Democracy: A History of the United States*, which was also influenced by Turner and Beard. In 1924 Becker made his only trip to Europe, a visit as superficial as Huizinga's to the United States seems to have been in 1926. Becker did the obligatory things, felt quite homesick, and wrote to his wife from Paris that "my foreign travel has come too late to be of any great benefit."[69]

During their final decade (1936–45), however, these two men, who were temperamentally so similar, followed divergent intellectual paths. Although Becker was in many respects socially conservative, he was less apprehensive about the development of technology and social organization (or regimentation) as inevitably oppressive evils. During the later 1930's his faith in democracy was rejuvenated, and he explicitly rejected the counsel of despair that was so much in the air among intellectuals of the day.

Thomas Hart Benton, "Wreck of the Ole '97"—lithograph in the New Britain Museum of American Art (William Brooks Fund), New Britain, Connecticut, U.S.A.

We still hold, therefore, to the belief that man can, by deliberate intention and rational direction, shape the world of social relations to humane ends. We hold to it, if not from assured conviction, then from necessity, seeing no alternative except cynicism or despair.[70]

While Becker was secure in Ithaca, New York, writing *How New Will the Better World Be? A Discussion of Post-War Reconstruction* (1944), Huizinga was under Nazi surveillance at De Steeg, near Arnhem on the Rhine, writing *The World in Ruins: A Consideration of the Chances for Restoring Our Civilization* (1945). It seems fair to say that their divergent circumstances help to explain their relative positions of pessimism and optimism. It may be equally fair to suggest, however, that their divergence can be dated back to the years 1936–39, when Becker recovered from the profound disillusionment with Wilsonian idealism that he underwent after World War I, whereas Huizinga's despair only deepened.

Ultimately, of course, Huizinga's apprehension was not so much political as it was cultural. Therefore defeating Fascism could not provide a sufficient solution to the malaise, indeed crisis, that he perceived in contemporary civilization. Although Huizinga felt disaffected from American culture, his visual sensitivity would have caused him to appreciate a painting done by Thomas Hart Benton in 1943. Entitled "Wreck of the Ole '97," it depicts the crash in 1903 of a fast mail train, No. 97 of the Southern Railway. The train leaped from its tracks while speeding down a steep grade, and plunged into a ravine. Benton's picture suggests that a broken track rather than a reckless engineer was the cause of that catastrophe.[71] His interpretation of the story indicates Benton's belief that man's fate was being determined by a mechanized (and flawed) world, rather than his own will and actions. The tale of No. 97's fatal crash became the theme of a well-known ballad which sold more than a million records in 1939. To Johan Huizinga, who appreciated allegory as much as iconography, the ballad, the mass culture that paid for it, the painting and its lithographic copies for consumers, all would have seemed suitably symptomatic of a culture *and a world* too much in the clutches of "This, Here, and Soon."

NOTES

1 I had intended to use "Huizinga's Vision of American Culture" as my subtitle; but then I saw that in writing about the nature of "historical understanding" Huizinga explicitly rejected the phrase "historical vision." In view of his particular sensitivity to matters of iconography and vision, it would have been cavalier, if not utterly mindless, to employ

a word-concept that seemed to him so inappropriate. Cf. "The Task of Cultural History," in Johan Huizinga, *Men and Ideas: History, the Middle Ages, the Renaissance* (New York, 1959), p. 53.

2   For the portrait, see C. T. van Valkenburg, *J. Huizinga: Zijn Leven en Zijn Persoonlijkheid* (Amsterdam, 1946), plate facing p. 7; or Johan Huizinga, *Geschichte und Kultur: Gesammelte Aufsätze*, trans. and ed. Kurt Köster (Stuttgart, 1954), facing the title page.

3   Gombrich, "Huizinga's *Homo ludens*," in W. R. H. Koops et al., eds., *Johan Huizinga, 1872–1972* . . . (The Hague, 1973), pp. 144, 153.

4   Anchor, "History and Play: Johan Huizinga and His Critics," *History and Theory*, XVII (1978), 85–86; R. L. Colie, "Johan Huizinga and the Task of Cultural History," *American Historical Review*, LXIX (April 1964), 618–19, 629; and Pieter Geyl, "Huizinga as Accuser of His Age," *History and Theory*, II (1963), 231–62. The italics are Professor Anchor's.

5   F. W. N. Hugenholtz, "The Fame of a Masterwork," in Koops, ed., *Johan Huizinga, 1872–1972*, pp. 91–103; Reuel Denney, "Feast of Strangers: Varieties of Sociable Experience in America," in Herbert J. Gans et al., eds., *On the Making of Americans: Essays in Honor of David Riesman* (Philadelphia, 1979), pp. 254, 268, where he appears as John Huizinga.

6   Letters to the author from John M. Gates, November 2, 1981; Charles F. Howlett, November 12, 1981; Jeff LaLande, November 24, 1981.

7   Holmes to Mrs. Charles Warren, March 22, 1931, Warren Papers, box 2, Manuscript Division, Library of Congress, Washington, D.C. For an important example of the impact of *Homo Ludens*, see Allen Guttmann, *From Ritual to Record: The Nature of Modern Sports* (New York, 1978), pp. 4, 6–7, 13–14, 80.

8   In 1936 Lewis Stiles Gannett, who wrote a regular column called "Books and Things" for the New York *Herald Tribune*, asked Huizinga what he was currently reading for pleasure. Huizinga replied with four titles: Gilbert Murray, *Then and Now: The Changes of the Last Fifty Years* (1935); Sir R. W. Livingstone, *Greek Ideals and Modern Life* (1935); Fernando del Pino, *La Gran Decisión* (1936); and Paul Hazard, *La Crise de la conscience européenne 1680–1715* (1935), 3 volumes. Six months earlier he had been reading George Sarton's massive *Introduction to the History of Science* (1927–31), 3 volumes at that time. See Huizinga to Sarton, April 9, 1936, and Huizinga to Gannett, October 1 and 20, 1936, Houghton Library, Harvard University, Cambridge, Mass. Huizinga had already written *In the Shadow of Tomorrow* before he read Murray and Livingstone. I am inclined to believe that Huizinga independently arrived at his pessimism about the present and the future, and therefore was more disposed to select books that eulogized earlier times and nobler cultures.

9   Notestein to August C. Krey, April 14, 1933, Krey Papers, folder 173, University of Minnesota Archives, Minneapolis.

10   Victor H. Paltsits to A. J. F. van Laer, October 20, 1927, Paltsits Papers, New-York Historical Society; Alfred Bagby, Jr., to Lyon G. Tyler, March

2, 1932, Tyler Papers, group V, box 7, Swem Library, College of William and Mary, Williamsburg, Va.; New York *Times*, June 27, 1974.

11 All quotations and citations will be to Herbert H. Rowen, trans. and ed., *America: A Dutch Historian's Vision, from Afar and Near* (New York, 1972). The first volume was noticed sympathetically in *The American Historical Review*, XXV (April and July 1920), 558–59, 742. For Geyl's warm praise of Huizinga's early essays on America, see Geyl, "Accuser of His Age," pp. 245–46. For Colie's translations of the titles of Huizinga's two books on the United States, see "Huizinga and the Task of Cultural History," pp. 612–13.

12 Horace White, "Gifts of Two Nations to Civilization," *Speeches and Writings* (Syracuse, 1932), p. 237.

13 Huizinga, *America*, pp. 8, 17, 18, 31.

14 *Ibid.*, pp. 142–43, 147, 149, 151. See James Bryce to Max Farrand, October 6 and December 3, 1919, and February 20, 1920, Farrand Papers, Henry E. Huntington Library, San Marino, Calif. On October 6, Bryce told Farrand that "there were currents of American opinion & phases of constitutional development which have been changing so much during recent years that I may not fully understand them . . ."

15 Huizinga, *America*, pp. 150, 157–59, 161. In fairness to Huizinga, who is frequently accused of elitism, it should be noted that in 1926 he remarked: "Modern culture must be democratic if it is to be at all." "The Task of Cultural History," p. 50.

16 Huizinga, *America*, pp. 32–33, 57, 60, 173, 229. Huizinga did note similarities between the impulse to "join" in Europe and in the United States, but then relied upon a simplistic explanation that ever since the 1890's Europe had been "much more strongly Americanized than we ordinarily realize" (p. 33). E. J. Hobsbawm's current work on the extraordinary expansion of the middle class at that time is more persuasive. Hobsbawm views "joining" as a pan-Atlantic symptom, and as a means of validating one's membership in the middle class. Huizinga's close attention to "joining" anticipates the seminal essay by Arthur M. Schlesinger, Sr., "Biography of a Nation of Joiners," *American Historical Review*, L (October 1944), 1–25.

17 Huizinga, *America*, pp. 165, 172, 208. The quotation is from p. 177.

18 *Ibid.*, pp. 137, 156, 159–60. Huizinga was acutely sensitive to nuances of language, anticipating Raymond Williams' *Keywords: A Vocabulary of Culture and Society* (New York, 1976). He observed, for example, that "individualism" did not have the same connotations in the American context that it had in Europe (p. 31), and that the word "service" had undergone a process of degradation, with the result that it meant different things to different people (pp. 310–11). See also *America*, pp. 266–68, 275, and Huizinga, "The Spirit of the Netherlands" (1935) in *Dutch Civilisation in the Seventeenth Century and Other Essays* (New York, 1968), pp. 110–12, 127.

19 Huizinga, *America*, p. 178. See Bushman, *From Puritan to Yankee: Character and the Social Order in Connecticut, 1690–1765* (Cambridge, Mass., 1967).

20   Huizinga, *America*, pp. 179–80, 200.

21   *Ibid.*, p. 193.

22   *Ibid.*, p. 19.

23   *Ibid.*, p. 174. Cf. David Grayson Allen, *In English Ways: The Movement of Societies and the Transferal of English Local Law and Custom to Massachusetts Bay in the Seventeenth Century* (Chapel Hill, N.C., 1980); T. H. Breen, *Puritans and Adventurers: Change and Persistence in Early America* (New York, 1980).

24   Huizinga, *America*, p. 50. Cf. Joseph Charles, *The Origins of the American Party System* (New York, 1961), pp. 80–90; and Noble E. Cunningham, Jr., *The Jeffersonian Republicans: The Formation of Party Organization, 1789–1801* (Chapel Hill, N.C., 1957).

25   Huizinga, *America*, pp. 28, 30–31. Our understanding of Jackson has been reshaped by the work of Robert V. Remini, Charles G. Sellers, Richard Hofstadter, Michael P. Rogin, and Thomas P. Abernethy.

26   Huizinga, *America*, pp. 9, 11.

27   *Ibid.*, pp. 49, 137, 47.

28   *Ibid.*, pp. 193, 195, 218–19, 223. I find it odd that Huizinga seems not to have read the four classic volumes by Moses Coit Tyler, *A History of American Literature, 1607–1765* (2 vols.; New York, 1878) and *The Literary History of the American Revolution, 1763–1783* (2 vols.; New York, 1897).

29   Huizinga to Turner, March 10, 1919, Turner Papers, Henry E. Huntington Library, San Marino, Calif.

30   See Huizinga, *America*, pp. 5, 9, 21, 57 n., 124, 134. In addition to printed sources and yearbooks, Huizinga also relied upon John Bach McMaster, Albert Bushnell Hart, Woodrow Wilson, James Ford Rhodes, Andrew C. McLaughlin, Frederick L. Paxson, Arthur M. Schlesinger, Sr., and Walter Hines Page. Among the major American writers, he seems to have read extensively in Emerson, Thoreau, Hawthorne, Whitman, and Henry and William James. Huizinga's *America* often seems strongest when he does not have "authorities" like Turner and Beard to guide him. For those topics where there were "experts," Huizinga was likely to become derivative. In their absence he was much more inclined to be shrewdly speculative and comparative. Understandable, perhaps, but unfortunate nonetheless.

31   Huizinga to Turner, cited in note 29 above.

32   Geyl, "Huizinga as Accuser of His Age," pp. 244–45.

33   Huizinga, "History Changing Form," *Journal of the History of Ideas*, IV (April 1943), 219.

34   Gombrich, "Huizinga's *Homo ludens*," p. 141. It should be noted, however, that one finds clear-cut previews of *Homo Ludens* in *Man and the Masses in America*. See, e.g., pp. 53–54 of the latter.

35   See Arthur Lord to D. Plooij, November 29, 1920, Lord Papers, Pilgrim Society, Plymouth, Mass.; J. Franklin Jameson to Worthington C. Ford, March 8, 1920, Jameson Papers, box 84, Library of Congress, Washington, D.C.; Victor H. Paltsits to Jameson, September 16, 1925, *ibid.*, box 117; Jameson to Victor H. Paltsits, February 2, 1920, Paltsits Papers,

New-York Historical Society. On December 21, 1922, Albert Eekhof sent Paltsits a postcard message from Leiden: "I can not forget you. This afternoon I have sent to you 'registered' a real Dutch Calendar. Every week a picture of Holland. It is a token of friendship and high appreciation for all what [*sic*] you have done for me in so many ways." Paltsits Papers, N.-Y.H.S.

36 See Huizinga, *America*, p. 20, for the only reference in his two books to Holland as an inspiration for American independence.

37 For extracts from the journal that Huizinga kept during his four-month trip, see Leonhard Huizinga, *Herinneringen aan Mijn Vader (Remembering My Father)* (The Hague, 1963), pp. 120–51. I am deeply grateful to Professor J. W. Schulte Nordholt of Leiden for calling this book to my attention, and to Eduard van de Bilt for supplying me with a content analysis. Huizinga's visit to the United States (with a diverse group of Europeans) was facilitated by the Laura Spelman Rockefeller Memorial Fund. Although he enjoyed seeing a few historical sites, such as Mount Vernon, Independence Hall, and the Lincoln Memorial, most of his time was given over to prearranged contacts with professors of law, economics, and business (which did not please him) and to observing political institutions in action, such as the Supreme Court and Congress (which impressed him even less). Nevertheless, Leonhard Huizinga felt that his father's trip to the United States was one of the pivotal events of his life, and that JH gained considerably in self-confidence as a consequence of it.

38 Huizinga, *America*, pp. 283, 314–15.

39 *Ibid.*, pp. 166, 255–56. Cf. James Bryce to Max Farrand, February 20, 1920, Farrand Papers, Huntington Library: "On the whole the changes in America seem to me more beneficial than those I have seen here. I certainly feel a hopefulness about the U.S. which I cannot feel about any people in Europe. . . ."

40 Compare Huizinga, *America*, pp. 94–96, 139, 142–43, 199, with pp. 237, 251, 297.

41 *Ibid.*, pp. 296, 301, 307. For anticipations of these criticisms in 1918, however, see pp. 111, 117, 181.

42 *Ibid.*, pp. 231, 234, 305, 310, 317, 321, 325.

43 See Gabriel A. Almond, Marvin Chodorow, and Roy Harvey Pearce, "Progress and Its Discontents," *Bulletin of the American Academy of Arts and Sciences*, XXXV (December 1981), pp. 4–23.

44 Becker, *Progress and Power* (New York, 1949), pp. xlii, 7, 9, 107. The last quotation appears on p. 111.

45 Huizinga, *America*, pp. 246, 282, 310, 317, 320, 325; Huizinga, "The Task of Cultural History," p. 33. Huizinga repeatedly used as his illustration from social psychology a book by H. A. Overstreet, *Influencing Human Behavior* (1925).

46 This phase, that "education had become the religion of the United States," was very much in the air by the mid-1920's. When President James R. Angell of Yale University used it in a public lecture given at Chicago in 1924, Max Farrand (who previously had taught at Yale, but

in 1924 was an administrator with the Commonwealth Fund) claimed that Angell had picked it up from him. Farrand to Henry L. Greer, October 6, 1924, Farrand Papers, Huntington Library.

47 Huizinga, *America*, pp. 181, 239, 245, 251, 281, 308. In 1924 van Loon was deeply hurt by Huizinga's tart review in *De Gids* of *The Story of Mankind*. As van Loon wrote, with customary self-pity, to a former teacher: "Now that some of my books have been translated into most modern languages, I usually find some sort of welcome in the countries through which I pass. But Holland takes it as almost a personal offense that I should, in some measure, have succeeded after I bade it farewell. I act upon the excellent burghers as a red rag before a steer." Quoted in Gerard Willem van Loon, *The Story of Hendrik Willem van Loon* (Philadelphia, 1972), pp. 151–52.

48 Huizinga, *America*, pp. 205–6, 251, 260–62, 319. See also Huizinga to Turner, March 10, 1919, Turner Papers, Huntington Library. Many in the United States, especially social and political conservatives, shared Huizinga's apprehension about the tendencies of American culture. See, e.g., Morton Keller, *In Defense of Yesterday: James M. Beck and the Politics of Conservatism, 1861–1936* (New York, 1958), pp. 153–56, 158, 160, 197–98; Ralph Adams Cram, *Convictions and Controversies* (Boston, 1937).

49 Huizinga, *America*, pp. 232, 238, 242, 244, 246, 247, 252–53, 265. On p. 265 Huizinga simultaneously seems to echo Walter Lippmann's *Public Opinion* (1922) and *The Phantom Public* (1925) and to anticipate some of the well-known views of Marshall McLuhan.

50 He is responsible for occasional factual errors, especially on p. 295 where he presents incorrect dates for the founding of Harvard (it should be 1636) and the College of William and Mary (it should be 1693).

51 Huizinga, *America*, p. 316.

52 *Ibid.*, pp. 178, 230, 242–43, 314. On p. 305 he quips: "not all Americans think, any more than Europeans."

53 "The Spirit of the Netherlands" (1935) in Huizinga, *Dutch Civilisation in the Seventeenth Century and Other Essays*, pp. 113, 118–19, 122, 136. On p. 128 he defines "conservative" quite positively, "in the worthy sense of wishing to preserve what is good and refusing to kow-tow to the fashion of the day."

54 *In the Shadow of Tomorrow* (New York, 1936), pp. 172–73.

55 Huizinga to Turner, March 10, 1919, Turner Papers, Huntington Library.

56 Huizinga to Hendrik Willem van Loon, October 11, 1940, van Loon Papers, box 13, Department of Manuscripts and University Archives, Cornell University, Ithaca, N.Y. I do not know how or when Huizinga and van Loon commenced a cordial relationship. It is clear that van Loon offered during the summer of 1940 to arrange for Huizinga to come to the United States. Huizinga replied from Leiden on August 15, 1940, that "my place remains here: in my country and in my office, whatever the following times may bring." *Ibid.* I am indebted to Joke

Kardux and Eduard van de Bilt for translations of these two letters from Dutch to English.

57 Gombrich, "Huizinga's *Homo ludens*," p. 148; Huizinga, "History Changing Form," pp. 219, 220.

58 *Ibid.*, pp. 219, 221. Cf. Max Farrand's slim interpretive volume written primarily for Europeans, *The Development of the United States from Colonies to a World Power* (1918), and Farrand's observation to Theodore Roosevelt that "the merit of the book probably lies in having the very definite purpose to explain the great change which came over the United States about 1890. . . ." (August 15, 1918, Farrand Papers, Huntington Library.) Farrand had sought to impose form where Huizinga would find only formlessness.

59 Huizinga, "History Changing Form," p. 222. Huizinga also sounds oddly like a scholar unfamiliar with Henri Pirenne's *Medieval Cities: Their Origins and the Revival of Trade* (1925) and Pirenne's *Economic and Social History of Medieval Europe* (1933). In fact, he had known Pirenne well since 1908—when Huizinga taught at Groningen and Pirenne at Ghent—and greatly admired his work. See Bryce Lyon, *Henri Pirenne: A Biographical and Intellectual Study* (Ghent, 1974), pp. 185–86, 203, 337, 364, 384.

60 Huizinga, "History Changing Form," p. 223.

61 *Ibid.*, p. 223; Arnold, *Civilization in the United States: First and Last Impressions of America* (Boston, 1888), pp. 82–83.

62 Huizinga, "History Changing Form," p. 223.

63 See, e.g., Sheldon Hackney, *Populism to Progressivism in Alabama* (Princeton, 1969); Leonard L. Richards, *"Gentlemen of Property and Standing": Anti-Abolition Mobs in Jacksonian America* (New York, 1970); Joan W. Scott, *The Glassworkers of Carmaux: French Craftsmen and Political Action in a Nineteenth-Century City* (Cambridge, Mass., 1974); Herbert G. Gutman, *The Black Family in Slavery and Freedom, 1750–1925* (New York, 1976); Douglas S. Greenberg, *Crime and Law Enforcement in the Colony of New York, 1691–1776* (Ithaca, N.Y., 1976); Stuart M. Blumin, *The Urban Threshold: Growth and Change in a Nineteenth-Century American Community* (Chicago, 1976); and Alan Dawley, *Class and Community: The Industrial Revolution in Lynn* (Cambridge, Mass., 1976), to mention just a few.

64 Arnold, *Civilization in the United States*, pp. 111, 118–19, 122, 125–27, 136, 152. It should be added that Arnold's *third* essay about the United States (written in 1887–88, shortly before his death) was much less favorable than his second. Arnold's eldest daughter, by the way, had married an American and settled in the United States. See *ibid.*, pp. 173–79, 181, 188–90.

65 Bryce to Mrs. Sarah Whitman, December 14, 1882, quoted in Edmund Ions, *James Bryce and American Democracy, 1870–1922* (London, 1968), pp. 120–21, 127–28. In 1883 Bryce taught a graduate seminar on Tocqueville and American history at Johns Hopkins University. *Ibid.*, pp. 101, 118–20. Bryce, "The Predictions of Hamilton and de Tocqueville," *Johns*

Hopkins University Studies in Historical and Political Science, 5th ser., Vol. IX (Baltimore, 1887). See also the Bryce letters cited in note 14 above.

66   See Myrna Chase, *Elie Halévy: An Intellectual Biography* (New York, 1980), esp. pp. 32, 38–39, 46, 172–73, 175–76, 181, 183–85, 189, 209, 211, 214, 220. Cf. Kurt Köster, ed., *Geschichte und Kultur: Gesammelte Aufsätze* (Stuttgart, 1954), a collection of miscellaneous writings by Huizinga, pp. ix–xl, for an essay on "Huizinga the Historian" that stresses his fear of nationalism and his sympathy for the idea of a unified Europe.

67   Koht, *Education of an Historian* (Oslo, 1951; New York, 1957), pp. 164, 169, 176, 182, 196–97, 202, 205. In February 1910 he gave a lecture before the Academy of Sciences at Oslo on the American Revolution. Printed in English as "Genesis of American Independence," it was his first publication concerning the history of the United States. In 1910 he also published *Money Power and Labor in America*, and in 1949 *The American Spirit in Europe: A Survey of Transatlantic Influences*.

68   Daniel J. Wilson, *Arthur O. Lovejoy and the Quest for Intelligibility* (Chapel Hill, N.C., 1980), pp. 186, 195–200.

69   See Michael Kammen, ed., *"What Is the Good of History?" Selected Letters of Carl L. Becker, 1900–1945* (Ithaca, N.Y., 1973), pp. 94, 97. Just when Huizinga first presented *In the Shadow of Tomorrow* as an address at Brussels in 1935, Becker lectured at Stanford on the difficulty, standing "in the shadow of the Great War," of achieving a judicious perspective on mankind's history and destiny. Becker, *Progress and Power* (1936: New York, 1949), p. 19.

70   Becker, *New Liberties for Old* (New Haven, Conn., 1941), p. 94; Becker, *Modern Democracy* (New Haven, Conn., 1941).

71   The lithograph is reproduced here by courtesy of the New Britain Museum of American Art (William Brooks Fund), New Britain, Conn. The original painting, oil and tempera on canvas, is owned by Marilyn Goodman of Great Neck, N.Y.

American Travelers in Holland Through Two Centuries

· ✦✦✦ ·

HERBERT H. ROWEN

Travelers have been coming to Holland from the United States since long before KLM carried them to Schiphol in jumbo jets, hundreds at a time, to explore a bit of Amsterdam and then journey on to other lands. Most were tourists, but some were people with business in the Netherlands—merchants and managers, diplomats, of course, and students, artists, and scholars. Some deeply admired what they saw, some held their noses, literally or figuratively, and most suffered some baffledom and boredom. Only a very few among them left a record of their impressions in print, but their number is still big enough so that we can venture to take what they wrote as characteristic of what the others, less literate and less articulate, felt and thought.[1]

Few, very few of these accounts have inherent literary merit. Herman Melville left only sketchy notes[2] and Henry Wadsworth Longfellow had a tortured stay, during which his letters discuss only professional matters and finally the death of his wife after miscarriage.[3] But we do have the letters of William Cullen Bryant, original not in what they say but in their prose style, precise but not precious.[4] Most of the visitors were just tourists, who went dutifully where the guidebooks told them to go. They were seldom adventurous. They are of interest to us not for the unexpected insight, the fresh understanding, the intense personalism and personality of a Huizinga in America, but for what they reveal about the travelers themselves as well as about Holland.

Let us not fool ourselves, however. The triteness of phrase that we meet so often in these accounts comes not just out of commitment to the obvious but also from recourse to guidebooks. Until the mid-nineteenth century these were the handbooks for travelers put out by John Murray of London; then they became the ubiquitous Baedekers. Yet we may assume that the tourists who set down reports of their trips, when they drew upon the guidebooks, had not been struck by any inappropriateness in the descriptions they copied out and adapted, usually without credit.

Actually, after 1865, the ordinary American picture of Holland was shaped most strongly not by formal guidebooks but by a book for boys and girls written by a woman who had never been to the country and would not go there for many years afterward. I speak, obviously, of *Hans Brinker, or, The Silver Skates*, by Mary Mapes Dodge. It is a work at once artful and artless. It combines virtually every element of the common picture of Holland—at least every element proper for a child's knowledge—with a simple, heartrending, melodramatic tale with a happy ending. Everything is neatly arranged, every piece of information given a place in the plot. But the human vision is simple in the extreme, and the plot depends upon coincidences so incredible one does not know whether to weep or smile. It all works, however: character, situation, and information are all made memorable, and the book continues to be republished down to our own day, when the real Holland has changed so immensely from that which Mrs. Dodge first saw in her imagination.[5] It was also common for the visitors from America after mid-century to have read the histories of John Lothrop Motley. On occasion, drawing upon the knowledge of the Dutch past acquired from Motley or lesser works, they would comment upon the historical significance of a place or a building.

These tourists from beyond the ocean were invariably well-to-do. Their European journeys lasted from three or four months to two or even three years, and they would usually spend two to three weeks in Holland. They came mainly from the states of the eastern seaboard, although voyagers from Indiana and even from distant Utah, still a territory, recorded their experiences. They were all white, virtually all Protestant—and some emphatically so. All were educated, although not all to college level, and a few had classical culture at their fingertips. A fair number had Dutch ancestors, but none, to my knowledge, knew any Dutch except a scholar or two. Even those who knew German found the "Dutch dialect," as they called it, a puzzle. Until the twentieth century, those who possessed French found it was spoken mainly by the "higher classes," but when popular education went beyond the ABC's during the second half of the nineteenth century, travelers began to meet daughters of tongue-tied shopkeepers with a command of school-taught French. A few visitors stayed long enough to pick up a few phrases of Dutch, a very few learned it well enough to read fluently and easily and speak understandably. The others, in an epoch before group travel with tour guides had been invented, were dependent upon those who spoke English or another shared language, and upon hired guides.

Over the two centuries we find a common picture of Holland.[6] It was, to use the inspired pun of one traveler in a way he did not intend, as platitudinous as the Dutch landscape itself: monotonous, repetitive, without surprise. It was overwhelmingly an external picture, of things seen and not what lay behind them. These Americans were visitors in quest of the "quaint" and the "picturesque"—by which they meant as different as possible from what they were familiar with, but without discomfort to either flesh or spirit. They were seldom interested in things political, social, economic, or intellectual.

Flatness—the long landscapes under the high skies—was, unremarkably, the first thing the visitors noted. Then came the canals, the dikes, and the windmills. They were surprised to find fields separated not by fences, as at home, but by drainage ditches. They noted how thickly populated by cows the fields were, and if they ventured to visit farmsteads, how well cared for the cows were. In the towns they at once saw, again, the canals that served as streets, and too often they smelled the odors that came up from the slow, stagnant waters. They were not much taken with the old houses, especially those that leaned far out over the streets, and they wondered whether it was the fault of bad workmanship or the result of building upon piles in swampland not drained wholly dry. As good Protestants, they visited the churches. But, with the exception of dogmatically precise Presbyterians, they were shocked to see buildings stripped of all interior decoration, with clear glass in the Gothic windows. These Dutch Calvinist churches were not "picturesque," like the Catholic churches they liked in Italy and France, Austria and the Rhineland. They did not see the beauty that we find in de Witte and Sanredam: theirs was an age that would have been bewildered by Mondrian and Rietveld.

The tourists had little real contact with ordinary folk. Not that this mattered much to them. They were persons of substance who had not crossed three thousand miles of water to see poor people—unless, of course, they wore quaint local costumes, clattered about in *klompen*, and were inoffensive. American onlookers generally found the *kermissen* unpretty affairs: the people enjoying themselves in their own way were too vulgar for them. And they liked children if they were pretty and well-mannered, not if they were inquisitive and boisterous, and least of all if they were demanding beggars. The Americans found in general that the Dutch had the characteristics they expected—a passion for cleanliness of home and street that most admired, but a few found fanatical; and a passion for smoking, especially in public, that all abhorred (at least all who mentioned it). It was generally remarked, too, that the people were hard-working, phlegmatic, and sober (a few disagreed, observing intemperance: but these may have been prohibitionists for whom a single beer or gin was one too much).

This picture of the Dutch people was not so much untrue as too limited. And that it had to be when both lack of time and lack of a common language inhibited knowledge. But, more than that, there was not really much interest in the people except as a touristic sight.

The towns visited were almost all very much alike. For those who came across the North Sea or from Belgium, the first city they saw was usually Rotterdam. For those who descended the Rhine, it was Nijmegen or more usually Arnhem. These went on to Utrecht and Amsterdam, and then came south, reversing the route taken by those who landed at Rotterdam. The typical tourist, however, went from Rotterdam up to Delft and then to The Hague. Next came Leiden and Haarlem, Amsterdam and perhaps Broek and Zaandam, even Volendam and Marken. On the way back some went to Utrecht en route to Germany; it was seldom that any went up to Leeuwarden and Groningen, in the north, or down to Flushing and Middelburg, in the south. And that was all. Ventures into other places were so unusual that they are worthy of individual notice, not only for the descriptions and comments but also for the reasons which took the tourists off the well-trod trails.

For those who came to Rotterdam from Antwerp by water, a dull voyage through a bleak countryside all the way to an ugly Moerdijk was followed first by typically Dutch polderland and then by the teeming port—the two faces of Holland, agricultural and commercial. They saw the old city as it existed until May 10, 1940, and they were enchanted by the *Boompjes*, the wharfside street lined with trees. After the railroads were built in the middle of the nineteenth century, travelers from the south took "the cars," entering Rotterdam much as they do today, riding on a high embankment from which they looked *down* upon the city. To look *down* at pasture and town from canal and from railway was a genuinely new experience. In Rotterdam what the visitors found most surprising was the network of canals crisscrossing the city that enabled ships to dock at the doors of warehouses many blocks inland. Sightseeing was limited: the statue of Erasmus, much admired (but how much read?); and the church of St. Lawrence (which these Protestants invariably called a "cathedral," like all other big churches). Some climbed to the bell tower—the Eurotower of its day—to view the far-stretching countryside.

From Rotterdam our friends went, by canalboat and later by train, to Delft. On the way their impression of the Dutch countryside, gained between Moerdijk and Rotterdam, was confirmed and consolidated. It was more of the same, to be sure, but they continued to be charmed, and it was not until they had gone farther north that they would begin to yearn for the variety of hills and mountains. In Delft they saw only a sleepy little town where the age of Dutch grandeur lingered, little changed from the sixteenth and seventeenth centuries because modernity had passed it by. They looked in at the Prinsenhof, displayed their knowledge of history when they saw the holes made by Balthasar Gérard's bullets, and sighed at the fate of heroic William the Silent. They noticed that the canals in Delft did not smell, or at least they remembered that they didn't when they encountered the evil-smelling *grachten* of other towns. But they stayed in Delft only for a few hours.

They stayed longer, usually for several days, at The Hague a few miles on. If they called it the "seat of government" and not the "capital," we may be sure that they were consulting their guidebooks sedulously, for what American to this day can conceive of a capital that is *not* the seat of government? They found The Hague very much to their taste. It was "elegant" and "charming"—the words recur constantly, and though we may hear the echo of the guidebooks in these words, they obviously spoke the viewers' admiration. Men of property although all good republicans, these tourists observed the good taste of the homes of diplomats and nobility which clustered about the royal court. They rode out to Huis ten Bosch, were enraptured by its paintings, and thought it quite a nice place for a Queen to live in, not too royal, as it were. One visitor was especially pleased to see in the Queen's apartment, open to tourists while she was away, a triumph of American industrial ingenuity—a Singer sewing machine, with all the signs of being much used.

The visitors took in the obligatory Mauritshuis museum, which they usually called the "national gallery." Some were thankful for its humane dimensions, especially so, no doubt, if they had already trod the interminable if glorious *longueurs* of the Louvre. Two pictures impressed them most of all, Paul Potter's "The Young Bull" and Rembrandt's "Anatomy Lesson." The meticulous naturalism of Potter's brush and the directness of his subject made it a work of art after their own hearts, and they enjoyed too the good-natured jokes they could make about the danger of wearing red while viewing it. They were more strained by the shocking power of Rembrandt's painting, but were as often repelled as fascinated. It was realistic enough to gain their respect, but they wanted art that pleased without shattering their complacency. The other painters they mention are pretty much those we would expect—usually the lesser lights of the Golden Age by our judgment, but occasionally Hals and Steen, never Vermeer until the end of the century and seldom even thereafter. All in all, there is something paradoxical in the attitude of these visitors: they repeat incessantly that seeing "the pictures" was one of the principal reasons why they had come from afar to this little country, yet it is clear that they enjoyed only the simplest kind of art. To be able to say that they had seen the great Dutch paintings seems to have been more important to them than actually to see the canvases for themselves.

None of our travelers who came to The Hague missed seeing Scheveningen. The approach by Scheveningse Weg enraptured them. The long ride across the dunes between the rows of trees, opening up to a view of the sea and the shore, had a dramatic touch they enjoyed. They found Scheveningen itself two utterly disparate communities. The bathing resort was very much of a kind with Atlantic City, although the "bathing machines" trundled up to the very edge of the beach was something they had not seen before. Those with a gift of eye described the extraordinary straightness of shoreline up and down the coast as compared to the curving beaches of New Jersey and Massachusetts. The visitors were intrigued by the sight of fishing smacks that did not come in to moor at wharves but were dragged up on the beaches. Most of the visitors paid an obedient visit to the fishing village a bit to the south. They found it colorful and picturesque, but wished the children had been less insistent beggars. The more thoughtful realized how harsh the poverty of these fisherfolk was, and how striking the contrast therefore between them and the affluent bathers.

After The Hague and Scheveningen, they made the short journey up to Leiden and Haarlem. Their interest in both towns was limited. They knew from Motley or earlier histories a little of their past significance, and looked, more bored than not, upon city scenes that seemed much like what they had already seen. Leiden's industrial past was a closed book to all but a few, and her university, lacking visual impact, drew little attention. Only the rare scholar ventured into the halls and library and called upon the professors. Haarlem was a bit more interesting. The church of St. Bavo was externally impressive, but what held the attention of all visitors was the great organ inside. They listened to the organist play at his public concerts, and some, informed by their guidebooks that he would put on a special show for those who paid for it, got an hour of dazzling effects for thirteen guilders. Most wonderful, they thought, was a musical thunderstorm, and they repeated with amusement the story that it caused the milk in the farms nearby to go sour. They were also amazed at the *vox humana* for its true-to-life quality. There was even less musical sophistication than artistic subtlety among these Americans, for we know that some Americans did come to study art, but none came to study music. From Haarlem the visitors' route went straight on to Amsterdam, although in the decades during and immediately after the drainage of the Haarlemmermeer, some stopped to see the huge pumping stations and the massive dikes.

Amsterdam itself was something of a surprise. They knew that it was the "Venice of the North," but they did not anticipate its dankness and bleakness compared to the Queen of the Adriatic. Unlike The Hague, it was neither elegant nor charming; and it did not possess the vigorous intensity of port life that they had seen in Rotterdam. They had become accustomed by this time to canals in the streets and all the numberless little details that caught sightseers' fancy everywhere in Holland. Amsterdam was the biggest city in the country and yet held the least interest for them. A few visited the navy yards where ships were built for the fleet, but the huge forges and cutting machines were hardly distinctively Dutch. A few visited the charitable institutions of which there were so many, and which drew the tourists' respectful admiration; but again they were not distinctively an Amsterdam feature. There were few monuments to which they were sent by the guidebooks. There was, of course, the royal palace on the Dam square, which was open to the public most of the time; but this huge pile of stone in neoclassical style was not what they had come thousands of miles to see.

There was less picturesqueness in the people on the streets than elsewhere in Holland; they looked more like folks at home than those in the smaller towns where progress had not yet penetrated. Those who ventured into the Jewish quarter noted that the omnipresent fanatical Dutch cleanliness was absent there, and the smells of the canals were compounded by odors from the homes. Wisecracks about hooked noses told the story of prejudice brought over from home, and we really ask much of these tourists if we expect them to have been interested in deeper understanding of such complex issues as poverty, inter-ethnic relations, and immigration.

The culmination of the visit for almost all was a tour of the "picture gallery," or, after its construction, the Rijksmuseum. As was already the case in the Mauritshuis, they trooped mainly to the well-advertised, world-famous pictures, but generally found the work of the Dutch Golden Age rather dull. They were impressed by Rembrandt's "Night Watch," but it was really van der Helst's painting of the civic guard celebrating the conclusion of the Peace of Münster which they thought was the best thing in the museum. By this time we begin to hear rumblings of dissatisfaction with tramping the galleries, and relief about going to see "quaint" places again.

And what could have been quainter than Broek and Zaandam, a few miles to the north across the IJ? Broek was an inhabited dollhouse, fastidiously cleansed but barred to the hurly-burly of ordinary activities. Most of our Americans were charmed, as they now are at Madurodam; but a small number wondered whether this was the charm of life or of inanition. Reactions were much the same at Zaandam, except that there the massed windmills added interest, and one could visit Czar Peter's little house. Those who went on to Marken and Volendam found tourist traps, all the quaintness consolidated and commercialized with a primitive Disneyification.

Returning to Amsterdam, they resumed their journey, which was now nearing an end. A delightful trip down the Vecht, past the luxuriance of summer homes, to Utrecht. A climb perhaps up the free-standing high tower of the cathedral to see far into the distance all about, as some had down at Rotterdam; a glance down at the distinctive canals a floor below street level—and that was all. Upstream to Germany, stopping at Arnhem perhaps, and admiring its relaxed air as a resort town for the wealthy of Amsterdam—so like the resort towns with which the tourists were familiar back home. And then, past Nijmegen, out of the Netherlands.

Thus far we have merged into a single picture the reactions of numerous writers, taking from each what was common to most, and paying little attention to the distinctively individual. Reduced to a few words, it is a picture that is not too complimentary to either side. The Americans for the most part sought the "picturesque" and the "quaint," but not the significant. They did not see that the Dutch nation was slowly moving through the great reorganization of its political, social, and economic life in the nineteenth and twentieth centuries. The Dutch for their part had little concern for these visitors from afar. Some did go out of their way to be courteous and helpful; others, who made their living off foreign gapers, treated Americans as they treated all other tourists, milking them of their money. We find significance only when we move from the run-of-the-mill tourist to those who were unusual in some way, either in their personal qualities of knowledge and penetration or because they came on business or for renewal of family contacts. And then we find unexpected rewards.

Perhaps the liveliest and least inhibited of all the travelers' tales is the very first. Elkanah Watson came to Holland in 1784 when he was only twenty-six years of age, but he was already an accomplished traveler. An apprentice merchant when he had gone to France in 1779, he had been confirmed there in his American patriotism, his republicanism, and his distaste for the ways of old regime Europe.[7] Going to England after the conclusion of peace, he crossed over to Holland in May 1784, "without any view of business" but to "rub myself a little bright among the Mynheers and Mavrouws." Admitting "total ignorance" of the country and the people, he had hunted the bookstores of London for "some good description of that artificial country," but was astounded to find none factual or thoughtful enough for him. The ten letters written while in Holland the next month, and a retrospective one from London on his return, provide the main content of his rare work, *A Tour in Holland in MDCCLXXXIV*, signed simply "By an American."[8] It is the prototype of the accounts that were to follow during the next two centuries, and one of the best. Many of the elements comprising the general picture we have described are already in its pages, and need not be repeated here. But it is worth our while to pick up some of the individual touches.

Watson was intensely curious, with "greedy eyes" not easy to "glut." He was observant and intelligent: the "quiet and hush" he experienced in Amsterdam an hour before midnight he connected with its slackened prosperity and decline of population. He was sharply aware of what we today call "cultural relativism." Seeing fishermen's daughters in Scheveningen not only guarding male bathers' clothes but toweling them dry as they left the water, he was surprised by the girls' "perfect *sang froid*." Then he reflected "how far custom and habit may reconcile us to any thing."[9]

Unlike most of his successors, who were sedately married, he was an unattached bachelor whose animal spirits did not cease to bubble while he was in Holland. He did not mind telling of his roving eye, and perhaps more, to the obvious discomfiture of his son when editing the old man's memoirs. Upon his arrival Watson found the women of the common class to be so ill-favored that their husbands were "in no *great danger* of wearing horns any more than the sheep." He was not unwilling to bestow horns, apparently, upon husbands of more genteel womenfolk. He reports several flirtations, at least one of which may have gone beyond words and smiles. He was a member of a party of revelers, including a "lovely Miss P——" from America, that followed up a nighttime stroll through the "best streets" of Amsterdam with a visit to the most notorious "spillhouse," or licensed brothel, in the city, to be amused by the sight of sex on sale. Five minutes' view of it was all he could stomach: the "devoted wretches"—a most curious term for harlots—made him think of a slaughterhouse "where calves and sheep are hung up for the highest bidder."[10]

His aesthetic senses were strong. Visiting Huis ten Bosch with John Adams, he found the paintings in the main salon "a luxurious feast for the eyes," since, he said, he had been "born with a painter's soul." Music, too, held him in its spell. We may wonder what the good burghers of Rotterdam thought when they saw this stranger stop in the middle of the street to listen to the ringing of the church chimes. Music was briefly triumphant over religious and ethnic prejudice. Chancing into an Amsterdam synagogue during Saturday services, he was fascinated by the "angelick shrill" of a boy soprano and the magnificent voice of an elderly basso. But the communicants themselves looked like "shabby theives [*sic*] and pickpockets."[11]

During his month's stay, he observed the rising conflict between Orangists and Patriots. His sympathies were, of course, on the side of those who had been friends of America, not England, but his comments reflect both his ingrained republicanism and the explanations of the political situation given him by Adams and John Luzac, the scholarly editor of the *Gazette de Leyde*.[12] It is not these judgments, however, which make Elkanah Watson's *Tour in Holland* a memorable work, but its freshness, its candor, and its undaunted intelligence.

During the next quarter century American tourism in the Netherlands, barely begun, came to a virtual halt. Aaron Burr, in exile after his acquittal on charges of treason, made two trips to Holland in 1811, hoping to convert his holdings in the Holland Land Company into ready cash. His letters are commonplace in their observations, and deserve our attention only because we have a propensity to take more seriously the ordinary words of important people than the more penetrating perceptions of ordinary people.[13]

The end of the Napoleonic wars brought a new flood of American tourists to Europe. It was still a "serious affair," however, not "an every day occurrence," as one visitor to Holland recalled forty years later her journey as a twenty-year-old.[14] Only three years after the conclusion of peace, a professor of chemistry and physics at "New-York Institution," John Griscom by name, crossed the Atlantic to discover what the "unabated spirit of enterprize" was achieving in Europe. It is an unusually insightful report that Griscom gives us; he was obviously no dryasdust academic but well informed about economic and social life. The Netherlands did better in his account of social and intellectual matters than in economic. He observed a people still wealthy despite the damage inflicted by the recent wars, and with general industriousness. Yet there was substantial poverty, alleviated by charitable institutions that practiced "the principles of true and genuine charity" better than anywhere else he had been: by this he meant finding a just balance between excessive indulgence and "too great a destitution." As a scientist, he was pleased to discover a "taste for science" and "diffusion of learning" far more general than he had expected in so commercial a society. At Haarlem he went to see the Teylerian Museum, whose importance for the history of science he noted. As a teacher, he was pleased by the extent of public support of education, remarking that Dutch schools used the system of monitor teaching by older pupils long before it was introduced in England.[15]

Griscom was followed a few years later by a visitor who called himself "The Practical Tourist," because his concern was "pursuing scientific investigations, for the purpose of promoting useful results." Zachariah Allen noted both economic strength and weakness in his trip through Holland in 1825. If Leiden was once "what Manchester now is," it had become a "monument" to the "fluctuating destiny" of an industrial and commercial city. And in Amsterdam he was surprised to find not a single collection of building materials for house construction during his rambles on the streets. In flooded North Holland after a fierce storm, he saw great suffering and the great efforts of the people to alleviate it. He was impressed by the immense labors of reclamation, with English steam engines in use as well as the traditional windmills. He had similarly mixed feelings about the Dutch political scene. The electoral system was insufficiently democratic, and the King had no "very definite" limitations upon his powers. Yet William I himself was "quite a republican" in manners, and his levees were very like those of an American President (this was the age of Monroe and Quincy Adams, not yet of Jackson).[16]

Not surprisingly, it was a diplomat who displayed a close interest in and understanding of political developments quite lacking in ordinary tourists. Alexander Hill Everett, the secretary of the American embassy in The Hague in these years between the creation of the kingdom of the United Netherlands and the Belgian breakaway, published in 1822 a general survey of European conditions, although without putting his name on the title page. He saw and regretted the "cordial hatred" between the Dutch and the Belgians. On the surface, he saw no rational explanation for such "malignant feelings" between peoples of "nearly the same . . . origin and language." But, delving deeper, he discerned the conflicting interests of Belgian industry and agriculture and Dutch trade. Therefore, he anticipated that "the downfall of this ill cemented fabric would probably be the first result of a new convulsion in Europe." He foresaw even worse. Despite his admiration for the Dutch constitution and people, it was "a decayed and decaying nation," economically, intellectually, and, not least, demographically. He feared a time would come when there would be too few Dutch to maintain their country against the inroads of the sea.[17]

The man who more than any other embodies the spiritual relationship of America and Holland, John Lothrop Motley, was not captured by his Dutch interest until he was well along in life. Returning from his post as secretary of the American legation in St. Petersburg in 1842, he had thought of spending a few weeks in the Netherlands, but was easily satisfied with a trip to Belgium. He made his first trip in 1851 and found the country "stronger and more wonderful" than he had expected. It was the polder character of the country that caught his imagination, although the terms in which he described it were quite traditional, if a bit more florid than most tourists could manage. He came back in 1853, already engaged in archival research for his first history. He got to know The Hague very well, finding it in winter "the prettiest town in Europe." On this trip he avoided making more than casual acquaintances, although these were of the highest circles. On his return in 1858, however, he found himself a celebrity and compelled even to be a guest of Queen Sophia. His depiction of a dinner at the Queen's is unique among travelers' tales, and the primary interest of his letters from this time on for our study lies not in the portrait of the country, but in his social life. His acquaintance with the Queen, as we know, ripened into warm friendship, and she placed the Kleine Loo, at The Hague, at his disposal during a working visit in 1871. He then moved to the house on the Kneuterdijk from which Jan de Witt had ridden to his death almost two centuries before. He traveled a bit, notably to Friesland and Groningen, but felt old age coming upon him. (He was not yet sixty years old.) Leaving in 1872, he returned in 1876 to stay with the Queen as her personal guest at Huis ten Bosch, then her summer residence. Both were dead a year later.[18] This relationship of royal person and commoner did both them and their countries genuine honor.

Visitors who brought with them some special body of knowledge and interests were among those whose pictures of Holland are still the most informative and perceptive. This was the case with George E. Waring, Jr., a Connecticut Yankee who, I think, would have won Mark Twain's respect for his competence and lack of pretentiousness. His book, *A Farmer's Vacation*, is a collection of letters written during a visit to Denmark, the Netherlands, France, and the Channel Islands in 1875, and originally published in *Scribner's Monthly*. Waring was mainly interested in European farming at its best, although he did some sightseeing on the way; his curiosity was directed by a sharp intelligence, a knowledge of his chosen field of activity, and an openness to new ideas. He was humorously critical of the "proper feeling of superiority" with which he, like other Americans, came to the country, ready to accept the "oddities and provincialisms" of a people who did not have the advantage of being born American. It was a feeling chastened as soon as he entered the country and "entirely and forever laid" by the time he left, some weeks later, to go to France.

Waring entered the Netherlands as no ordinary tourist did, and indeed still does not do, "by its back door," that is, from East Friesland in Germany into Groningen. Groningers today may complain that their province is a neglected, distant corner of their country, but what Waring found was a land of wealth, with "a most skilful and industrious people" tilling soil of "unequalled richness," thanks to what he called "the transforming hand of the Dutch Wizard of Drainage." There was none of the all too visible neglect and backwardness he had just seen in East Friesland. At first glance, the country he viewed on the train from Nieuwe Schans to Groningen was like that of the American western prairie: a "broad windy stretch of flat country, without much wood, and lying open to the gales," and with some of the "same bleak, unhomelike air." But these were prairies cultivated with the care of suburban market gardens.

He found the Dutch cities quite different from what the guide-books had led him to expect. Groningen was a city nowhere near as strange as it had been painted, indeed with an air very much like that of Philadelphia, with just enough "novelty and quaintness" to add spice. Leeuwarden was "the cleanest large town" he had seen anywhere. Amsterdam too, against the testimony of the guidebooks, was anything but "the Venice of the North," rather a quite workaday city. His main interest was not in seeing the sights most tourists thronged to, but such things as the street life of early morning as the city began its work and the interior arrangements of a wind-powered flour mill, far more "ingenious and practical" than he had connected with the idea of a Dutch windmill.

He devoted a whole chapter to the Dutch art of drainage, to which in praise he gave the Dutch name of *"Droogmakerij."* Everyone knew about Dutch skill in drainage works, but "their knowledge is of that sort which gives an impression rather fanciful than real." He described the work and the problems of the *waterstaat*, or hydraulic administration as he called it: the respect paid to its authority even during political crises on the one hand; the conflicts over the proper level of water between poldermasters and drainage organizations on the other. He examined the great Haarlemmermeer polder in detail, admiring both the stupendous engineering works and the *polderjongens*, or earthwork builders, who might not be the best of men "viewed from the moral stand-point," but deserve "praise and respect" for their vigor, industry, and courage.

Noting that his examination of Dutch farming itself had been too cursory to have direct practical utility for adaptation to American conditions, he still felt it would pay more sustained and careful study. He understood, as very few of his fellow visitors had, that the loss of Holland's trading supremacy had been made up for by an astounding growth of agriculture.[19]

I come now to the culminating figure in my account of Americans in Holland. What John Adams was to American diplomats in the Netherlands, William Elliot Griffis was to American travelers, the one without peer. He was entitled to the vanity implicit in the title of his book, *The American in Holland*, published in 1899, for no American in the nineteenth and even the first quarter of the twentieth century had a richer knowledge and understanding of the Netherlands and none conveyed his vision more extensively and more effectively to his fellow countrymen. I take special pride in his accomplishment, be-cause Griffis was a graduate of Rutgers College, where I have had the honor to be a member of the faculty for the past eighteen years. This college, which from very small beginnings has become the state university of New Jersey, was the first and is still the most eminent institution of higher education founded by Dutchmen in America. Griffis came to Rutgers in 1865, just past his twenty-second birthday (the Civil War had occupied the normal years of college attendance). Born in the city of Philadelphia not far to the south of New Brunswick, he was attracted to Rutgers by its Dutch heritage, not because he himself had any Dutch ancestry, but because he was curious about the people who had been among the first settlers in Pennsylvania and its neighboring states to the north. Most of the eighty-one students at Rutgers in 1865 were Dutch-descended, and the friends he formed introduced him to the lives of their families at homes in upper New Jersey and New York, which still bore a strong Dutch imprint. Motley's work became some of his favorite reading. Upon graduation, he went to the Netherlands in September 1869, at the end of a summer tour of Europe with his sister. It was the first of eleven trips, the last in 1926, two years before his death.[20]

On his return to the United States after the first trip, he was recruited to teach in Japan, which had just entered its Meiji period, and during a stay of three and a half years from 1870 to 1874 he helped to shape the modern educational system of Japan, and it is this accomplishment which makes him not merely an observer and commentator, but a historical figure in his own right.[21]

When Griffis next came to Holland, it was almost twenty-two years after his first visit, and he had become a respected clergyman, first Dutch Reformed and then Congregationalist, with an increasingly rationalist bent. He made four additional trips before he wrote *The American in Holland*. The picture of the Netherlands he paints in this book is a composite of his experience and judgments during these first five journeys. During these trips, Griffis visited all eleven of the provinces and many towns and villages. Some were places of veritable pilgrimage because of their historical associations with the United States in its colonial period. Amsterdam called up "cradle memories" of the founders of New England and New Netherland. He went to Leiden to chat with the liberal Calvinist theologian Professor Abraham Kuenen, as he had in Amsterdam with the sternly Calvinist political leader and founder of the Free University, Dr. Abraham Kuyper. Haarlem and nearby Bloemendaal drew him because of memories of visits to their Manhattan namesakes, Harlem and Bloomingdale. In Haarlem he observed that the design of its Meat House, built with red brick and white marble in alternating stripes, was followed by the architects of many recent New York churches, in a style the populace called "zebra" or "beefsteak." He saw quickly, too, the correspondence between the internal design of the church at Beverwijk and that of early Dutch churches in America. In Franeker and Leeuwarden, he learned how much the Frisians in the 1780's had contributed to Dutch recognition of American independence.[22]

He made a "sentimental journey" to Harlingen, because one of his best friends at Rutgers came from Harlingen, New Jersey (which is just three miles north of my own home). He also saw men making what was anything but a "sentimental journey." These were troops of German farm laborers, the tragic *"Hollandgängers,"* crossing the frontier from East Friesland to work in the fields during the hay and barley harvest, using snaths of ancient design, not modern scythes. Griffis also observed the use of the rich clay of the *terpen,* or ancient mounds, to make the sandy soils for miles around fertile. Like Waring two decades earlier, he saw how "unremitting toil" had rescued the countryside of Groningen from swampland, saving it from "the dragon of malaria and the ghosts of sterility."[23]

In Groningen, Griffis admired not only the "charm" of St. Martin's church after its restoration in 1895, but also a "splendid" new Roman Catholic church. "Most of the elegant new church buildings in the Netherlands," he remarked, "belong to the Roman form of the faith. It is unfortunate, as it is unchristian, that the various sectarians boycott one another, each helping his own." This is the first clear reflection of *verzuiling*—the encompassing organization of Dutch society and politics according to religious-ideological affiliation—that I have found in the travel accounts of American visitors.

I do not know whether we should include under the rubric of *verzuiling* the distinctive garb of Catholic priest and Protestant dominie in the Netherlands. Both "dress in the hue of the crow," Griffis observed, but "by their uniform one may know their sect." They were alike, however, in the probable presence of an umbrella in their hands and in the nearly certain presence of a cigar on their lips. As cigar smokers, they were equal. They might differ about theology, church government, and the validity of "orders," but on the contention that tobacco "is not a luxury but a necessity, the Reformed and the irreformable will face the world in unity."

Griffis' moderation toward Catholicism was illustrated during a visit to a professor of English at the Bishop's College in Roermond. His host was joined by his two brothers, who ran a prosperous religious wood-carving establishment and were also fluent in English. He was surprised that the unnamed professor (who has been identified for me by Dr. Gerhard Beekelaar of Nijmegen as H. J. H. Oor) met so easily with a heretic and Protestant. Griffis was interested in learning about the Dutch province of Limburg; they wanted his religious opinions. "The age-old questions, stereotyped before one of us was born," were discussed with good humor and mutual respect, although it was evident that the three brothers had seldom had such a "free frank talk" with a Protestant. They told him in turn what he wanted to know about Limburg.[24]

Describing the royal inauguration of 1898, at which he was both a reporter for American magazines and a guest honored beyond his expectations, he correctly noted the absence of any coronation proper or a specifically religious ceremony of a single denomination. He pinned down the fault of American (and British) journalists who could not tell the difference between Wilhelmina's enthronement and the coronation of the Russian Czar. A national exhibition of women's work on this occasion in The Hague impressed him as showing great progress in the "women's century" that had been, and anticipating even greater in the next. But would our modern feminist be wholly happy with his conclusion—that "although every town and village proves how good a helpmeet for the man the Dutch woman is, there is no Wellesley or Vassar College here yet."[25] Nor would there be! But Dutch universities are wide open to women nowadays, so in that respect his hope has been made good in the spirit if not the letter.

During this visit, war broke out between the United States and Spain. Griffis reported the uncertainty and even the hostility of Dutch opinion toward the United States, but also the influence of the editor of the *Algemeen Handelsblad* of Amsterdam in swinging opinion to the American side. But, before he left, he had an experience for which only the Dutch word *aardig* is adequate. To his surprise, while attending a performance of music-hall entertainment in Rotterdam, a singing demonstration of Dutch-American friendship was given by seven girls equipped with electric lights. It came to a rousing end with the singing of "Columbia, the Gem of the Ocean" and "Wien Nederlandsch Bloed" to thunderous applause.[26]

All in all, Griffis' pre-eminence as an observer and reporter upon the Netherlands cannot be doubted. His admiration is unstinted, but he does not conceal faults. "It is undoubtedly true that there are in Dutch civilization many points of superiority over ours, and we have yet to learn many excellent things from the quiet Hollanders." He was willing to accept criticism for the Dutch, especially when they did it so "wisely" as in Dr. Cohen Stuart's *Door Amerika*. But he would not concede that Americans were behind: to the contrary, theirs was a "nobler progress," because they had not been afraid to profit by what "Holland and mother England had taught."[27]

World War I brought an interruption of tourist travel and the parallel production of travel books. During the interbellum period, when travel resumed more massively than ever, travel books were going out of style. The changed character of travel in the age of the automobile was reflected in books about travel by car. One of the best of these was by a Pittsburgh physician, J. J. Buchanan, and his trip in Holland—part of a general European tour—was notable for his willingness to venture into places not easy to reach in the age of canalboat or that of railways.[28] Of a quite different character is a work by the well-known Dutch-American author Hendrik Willem van Loon. *An Indiscreet Itinerary* is short, chatty, charming, and relatively well informed: van Loon, though not much of a historian, was an excellent journalist, and he knew the Netherlands intimately because it was his first home. In truth, he does not strictly belong to our group of American travelers, except that his book has so much good sense in it that it would be a pity to exclude it.[29]

World War II did not bring a complete halt to American travel in Holland, not at least until American entry. We do have a striking picture of the Netherlands in the immediate aftermath of the German invasion of May 1940. It came from the pen of a diplomatic officer in the United States embassy in Berlin, sent to the Low Countries and France only a month after the German victory in the West. His name was George F. Kennan, and the qualities which were to make him so famed an ambassador and so powerful a historian after the war were already present. His picture of The Hague and Rotterdam in June 1940 is vivid and eloquent. His fear that a permanent German domination of Europe would break the back of the Dutch economy and the Dutch spirit, and that the country would collapse back into swampland, echoed the forebodings of his fellow diplomat Everett a century earlier. But he pondered, too, on what he had seen, and reflected that "if there was anything in this war that made any sense to me at all, it was the resistance that had produced the ruins of Rotterdam."[30]

Almost four years later, a work appeared for a special audience that belongs to our subject even though it was not a book about past travels, but for travelers-to-be. This was the *Civil Affairs Handbook, The Netherlands* prepared by the United States Army for eventual troops in a liberated Holland. The picture of the Netherlands in this book possesses a richness of detail and a command of significance lacking even in the earlier academic handbooks; although its English is quite idiomatic, it was the work of a Dutch scholar, Bertus H. Wabeke, resident in America. Economics, demography, politics, social structure, and social attitudes—all are clearly depicted. It is dense with respect for the Dutch people and their institutions. The spirit of *Hans Brinker*, the cloying traditional interest in the quaint and the picturesque, is totally absent. The six mimeographed volumes may well be one of the best summaries of the Netherlands that had ever been done, and they deserve our admiration not only for the occasion of their preparation, but also for the quality of mind and judgment that pervades them.[31]

In the postwar world, travel increased immensely, but the works in which Americans now gave voice to their vision of Holland changed in character. Sociological understanding rather than the discovery of the cute became the aim.

The two works that reflect this concern are neither of them by professional sociologists. The first, *The Light in Holland*, published in 1970, was actually by a writer who had become binational, British and American, during the war. For Anthony Bailey had been evacuated to the United States when the blitz came to Britain and then returned, finally taking up residence in America and making his career as a novelist and journalist. The formal purpose of Bailey in *The Light in Holland* was to study in the densely crowded society of the Netherlands how the massed billions of the future world might live in the limited space allotted to them by geography. To do this, he went to live for an extended period in Holland, first in Katwijk and then in Amsterdam. His report, as one would expect of a work that originally appeared in the pages of the sleek *New Yorker* magazine, is not at all formal sociology. Bailey did his homework with hard, dry facts, but remembered that "figures and statistics about growth-rates and densities have always to be tempered with impressions and feelings."

The large picture Bailey paints of a quintessentially small country is one of a land where physical privacy is difficult to maintain and is not even sought, where deliberation, responsibility, and self-sacrifice are emphasized, and yet where social privacy must be defended. This is expressed in the system of *verzuiling*, which makes possible the maintenance of harmony in a thickly settled community. The book is full of little touches that delight. In the end, unfortunately, it does not satisfy. The *New Yorker* touch—writing light as meringue, exquisite control, seriousness but not to the point of straining the reader's attention—ultimately makes one unsure just what the picture means. The original theme has been lost: we really do not know whether Holland in the late 1960's was the foreshadowing of the world's future or just the Dutch at the peak moment of their welfare state.[32]

Dutchness, not Dutch exemplification of universality, was very much the subject of a work published only a year later that is prosaic by comparison with Bailey's sprightly style, but conveys an understanding that comes from more than a bit of living, a bit of studying, and a gift of writing. W. Z. Shetter is an academic to the core, the foremost student of the Dutch language in the United States. His knowledge of the Netherlands comes from sustained study, repeated visits, command of the language and the literature, and wide-ranging interests. What he does in *The Pillars of Society* is to combine his understanding of Dutch character as revealed in the language usage of the Dutch with the sociological studies of *verzuiling*, most of all that of the Dutch-American scholar Arend Lijphart. To these he brings as well his own experiences and his own conclusions. He emphasizes on the one hand that Dutch society imprints upon its members the necessity for far-reaching tolerance in order to be able to maintain one's own characteristic religious-ideological identity; and on the other that the Dutch are far more alike than *verzuiling* might make one think, and most of all so in the intense formalism of their social life.[33]

At the end of our journey through memory, we find that we are also at the end of an epoch. The need to travel by imagination, through the books of those who have actually been there, has diminished almost to the vanishing point. The modern traveler sees with his own eyes, although how well he sees, as always, depends upon the richness of the mind behind the eyes. Americans, I suspect, will come less and less to Holland to look for the quaint and the picturesque, and if they do, a changing Holland will provide less and less of it to them. That is the future, however, and historians can only tell the story of the past. But that story hints that in the future as in the past there will be an affinity of affection between the two peoples.

NOTES

1 For this paper I have examined well over a hundred travel accounts. Many told of itineraries that went directly from England to France, and then on to Italy, Germany, and the Levant, and these serve merely to remind us that the Low Countries, and especially the northern part, the Netherlands in formal language that everyone called Holland, were backwaters of tourist interest. I have found nearly half a hundred, however, in which the journey extended up to Amsterdam, and less than half a dozen that were devoted to Holland alone, or to Holland and Belgium together. To these I have added several volumes of general correspondence which are not travel books as such, although many travelers' accounts were in fact merely reprinted letters to individuals or newspapers.

2 Herman Melville, *Journal of a Visit to Europe and the Levant, October 11, 1856–May 6, 1857*, ed. Howard C. Horsford (Princeton, N.J., 1955).

3 [Henry Wadsworth Longfellow], *The Letters of Henry Wadsworth Longfellow*, Vol. I: *1814–1836* (Cambridge, Mass., 1966), pp. 521–31.

4 William Cullen Bryant, *Letters of a Traveller; or, Notes of Things Seen in Europe and America* (2nd ed.; New York, 1850), pp. 226–33.

5 Mary Mapes Dodge, *Hans Brinker, or, The Silver Skates*, intro. by May Lamberton Becker (reprint ed.; Cleveland and New York, 1946).

6   This picture being drawn from all the works studied rather than con-
    structed from them one by one, the reader is referred once and for all
    to the bibliography at the end of the paper.

7   [Elkanah Watson], *Men and Times of the Revolution; or, Memoirs of
    Elkanah Watson, including Journals of Travels in Europe and America,
    from 1777 to 1831, with His Correspondence with Public Men and
    Reminiscences and Incidents of the Revolution,* ed. Winslow C. Watson
    (New York, 1856), pp. 17–18, 75, 100.

8   [Elkanah Watson], *A Tour in Holland in MDCCLXXXIV.* By an
    American (Worcester, Mass., 1790), pp. 194–230.

9   *Ibid.,* pp. 30, 40, 76, 105.

10 *Ibid.,* pp. 20, 26, 56–60, 130–32, 137–38.

11 *Ibid.,* pp. 43, 78–79, 116–19.

12 *Ibid.,* pp. 88–89, 103.

13 [Aaron Burr], *The Private Journals of Aaron Burr, during his residence
    of four years in Europe; with Selections from his correspondence,* ed.
    Matthew L. Davis (2 vols.; New York, 1858), II, 58, 67–68, 164–88, 222–32.

14 M.G., *Here and There: A Miscellany*; for private circulation (Dresden,
    1869).

15 John Griscom, *A Year in Europe. Comprising a Journal of Observations
    in England, Scotland, Ireland, France, Switzerland, the North of Italy,
    and Holland. In 1818 and 1819* (2 vols.; New York, 1823), II, 135–85.

16 Zachariah Allen, *The Practical Tourist, or Sketches of the State of the
    Useful Arts, and of Society, Scenery, &c. &c. in Great-Britain, France and
    Holland* (2 vols.; Providence, R.I., 1832), I, 202–3, 211–12, 217–25, 237.

17 [Alexander Hill Everett], *Europe: or a General Survey of the Present
    Situation of the Principal Powers; with Conjectures on their prospects.*
    By a Citizen of the United States (Boston, 1822), pp. 16, 240–45.

18 [John Lothrop Motley]. *The Correspondence of John Lothrop Motley,
    D.C.L.,* ed. George William Curtis (2 vols.; New York, 1889), II, 95, 106,
    122, 125–27, 158–59, 210–14, 301–26, 331–37, 350, 354, 391–93.

19 George E. Waring, Jr., *A Farmer's Vacation. Reprinted (with Additions)
    from Scribner's Monthly* (Boston, 1876), pp. 13–121.

20 William Elliot Griffis, *The American in Holland: Sentimental Rambles
    in the Eleven Provinces of the Netherlands* (Boston and New York, 1899),
    pp. 356–70.

21 Edward R. Beauchamp, *An American Teacher in Early Meiji Japan*
    (Honolulu, 1976).

22 Griffis, *The American in Holland,* pp. 22–75, 86–87.

23 *Ibid.,* pp. 98, 101, 107.

24 *Ibid.,* pp. 111–12, 164–65, 260–62.

25 *Ibid.,* pp. 377–78, 381–82.

26 *Ibid.,* pp. 373–75.

27 *Ibid.,* pp. 199–200.

28 J. J. Buchanan, *Take Your Own Car Abroad and Find Your Own
    Europe: A Book on Modern Independent Motor Car Travel* (Pitts-
    burgh, 1930), pp. 243–67.

29 Hendrik Willem van Loon, *An Indiscreet Itinerary, or How the Un-*

conventional Traveler Should See Holland, by One who Was Actually Born There and Whose Name Is (New York, 1933).
30 George F. Kennan, *Memoirs, 1925–1950* (Boston, 1967), pp. 124–27.
31 Headquarters, [U.S.] Army Service Forces, *Civil Affairs Handbook, The Netherlands. Section 1, Geographical and Social Background.* 5, April 1944. Army Service Forces Manual, M-357-1.
32 Anthony Bailey, *The Light in Holland* (New York, 1970).
33 William Z. Shetter, *The Pillars of Society: Six Centuries of Civilization in the Netherlands* (The Hague, 1971).

WORKS CONSULTED

Addresses Made at the Annual Meetings of the Netherlands Society of Philadelphia. Bellevue-Stratford Hotel, 1913 to 1930. [Philadelphia, c. 1930]
ABRAHAMSON, S. S. *Holland and Our Friends the Dutch.* Amsterdam, c. 1910.
ALLEN, Grant. *The European Tour.* New York, 1899.
[ALLEN, Richard L.] *Last Letters of Richard L. Allen.* New York, 1871.
ALLEN, Zachariah, *The Practical Tourist, or Sketches of the State of the Useful Arts, and of Society, Scenery, &c. &c. in Great-Britain, France and Holland.* 2 vols.; Providence, R.I., 1832.
ALLEN, Harrie Trowbridge. *Travels in Europe and the East: During the Years 1858–1859 and 1863–1864.* Printed for private circulation. New Haven, 1879.
ARMSTRONG, Frank. *Travels in European Countries.* Terre Haute, Ind., 1893.
BAILEY, Anthony. *The Light in Holland.* New York, 1970.
BELLOWS, Henry W. *The Old World in Its New Face: Impressions of Europe in 1867–1868.* 2 vols.; New York, 1869.
BENEDICT, Erastus C. *A Run through Europe.* New York, 1860.
BENEDICT, E. L. *Stories of Persons and Places in Europe.* New York and London, 1887.
[BRANDEIS, Louis D.] *Letters of Louis D. Brandeis.* Ed. Melvin I. Urofsky and David W. Levy. Vol. I. Albany, N.Y., 1971.
BRYANT, William Cullen. *Letters of a Traveller; or, Notes of Things Seen in Europe and America.* 2nd ed.; New York, 1850.
BUCHANAN, J. J. *Take Your Own Car Abroad and Find Your Own Europe: A Book of Modern Independent Motor Car Travel.* Pittsburgh, 1930.
BUCKHAM, George. *Notes from the Journal of a Tourist.* 2 vols.; New York, 1890.
[BURR, Aaron.] *The Private Journals of Aaron Burr, during his residence of four years in Europe; with Selections from his correspondence.* Ed. Matthew L. Davis. 2 vols.; New York, 1858.
BUSCH, Noel F. *Lost Continent?* New York, 1945.
CHILD, Theodore. *Summer Holidays: Travelling Notes in Europe.* New York, 1889.
COLMAN, Henry. *European Life and Manners; in Familiar Letters to Friends.* 2 vols.; Boston, 1849.

COWIE, Donald. *Holland: The Land and the People.* South Brunswick, N.J., and New York, 1974.

[CROWNINSHIELD, Clara.] *The Diary of Clara Crowninshield: A European Tour with Longfellow, 1835–1836.* Ed. Andrew Hilen. Seattle, 1956.

DAY, Henry. *A Lawyer Abroad: What to See and How to See.* New York, 1874.

DODGE, Robert. *Diary, Sketches and Reviews, during an European Tour, in the Year 1847.* New York, 1850.

DODGE, Mary Mapes. *Hans Brinker, or, The Silver Skates.* Intro. by May Lamberton Becker. Reprint ed.; Cleveland and New York, 1946.

DUDLEY, Lucy Bronson. *"A Writer's Inkhorn."* New York, 1910.

DULLES, Foster Rhea. *Americans Abroad: Two Centuries of European Travel.* Ann Arbor, Mich., 1964.

DURBIN, John P. *Observations in Europe, Principally in France and Great Britain.* 2 vols.; New York, 1844.

EDWARDS, George Wharton. *Holland of To-day.* New York, 1909.

[EVERETT, Alexander Hill.] *Europe: or a General Survey of the Present Situation of the Principal Powers; with Conjectures on their prospects.* By a Citizen of the United States. Boston, 1822.

FALKNER, W. C. *Rapid Ramblings in Europe: What I Saw at London, Paris, Genoa, . . . Wiesbaden, Amsterdam, Rotterdam, The Hague, and on the Alps and Rhine.* Philadelphia, 1884.

FIELD, Henry M. *From the Lakes of Killarney to the Golden Horn.* 4th ed.; New York, 1877.

———. *Summer Pictures: From Copenhagen to Venice.* New York, 1859.

FISK, Wilbur. *Travels in Europe; viz., in England, Ireland, Scotland, France, Italy, Switzerland, Germany, and the Netherlands.* 6th ed.; New York, 1843.

FORNEY, John W. *Letters from Europe.* Philadelphia, 1867.

G., M. *Here and There: A Miscellany.* For private circulation. Dresden, 1869.

GRIFFIS, William Elliot. *The American in Holland: Sentimental Rambles in the Eleven Provinces of the Netherlands.* Boston and New York, 1899.

———. *Brave Little Holland and What She Taught Us.* Boston and New York, 1894.

GRISCOM, John. *A Year in Europe: Comprising a Journal of Observations in England, Scotland, Ireland, France, Switzerland, the North of Italy, and Holland. In 1818 and 1819.* 2 vols.; New York, 1823.

HALL, Mrs. Herman J. *Two Travelers in Europe: A Unique Story told by One of Them, What They Saw and How They Lived while Traveling among the Half-Civilized Peoples of Morocco, the Peasants of Italy and France, as well as the Educated Classes of Spain, Greece, and Other Countries.* Springfield, Mass., 1898.

HOLDEN, S. J. *A Summer Jaunt through the Old World: A Record of an Excursion made to and through Europe, by the Tourjée Educational Party of 1878.* Boston, 1879.

HOWELL, Charles Fish. *Around the Clock in Europe: A Travel-Sequence.* New York, 1912.

HUBBELL, Orrin Z. *A University Tramp*. Elkhart, Ind., 1889.

KENNAN, George F. *Memoirs, 1925–1950*. Boston, 1967.

KING, Horatio. *Sketches of Travel, or Twelve Months in Europe*. Washington, D.C., 1878.

KIRKLAND, [Caroline Matilda]. *Holidays Abroad; or Europe from the West*. New York, 1849.

[LILIENTHAL, David E.] *The Journals of David E. Lilienthal*. Vol. IV. New York, 1969.

[LONGFELLOW, Henry Wadsworth.] *The Letters of Henry Wadsworth Longfellow*. Vol. I: *1814–1836*. Ed. Andrew Hilen. Cambridge, Mass., 1966.

LOON, Hendrik Willem van. *An Indiscreet Itinerary, or How the Unconventional Traveler Should See Holland, by One who Was Actually Born There and Whose Name Is*. New York, 1933.

MACGAVOCK, Randal W. *A Tennessean Abroad or Letters from Europe, Africa, and Asia*. New York, 1854.

MARTIN, Edward Sandford. *Abroad with Jane*. Privately printed, 1918.

MELVILLE, Herman. *Journal of a Visit to Europe and the Levant, October 11, 1856–May 6, 1857*. Ed. Howard C. Horsford. Princeton, N.J., 1955.

MITCHELL, Donald Grant [pseud. Ik. Marvel]. *Fresh Gleanings: or, A New Sheaf from the Old Fields of Continental Europe*. New York, 1851.

MONTGOMERY, James Eglinton. *Our Admiral's Flag Abroad. The Cruise of Admiral D. G. Farragut, commanding the European Squadron in 1867–68, in the Flag-Ship Franklin*. New York, 1869.

MOORE, Walter W. *A Year in Europe*. 3rd ed.; Richmond, Va., 1905.

[MOTLEY, John Lothrop.] *The Correspondence of John Lothrop Motley, D.C.L.* Ed. George William Curtis. 2 vols.; New York, 1889.

OSBORNE, Albert B. *Finding the Worth-While in Europe*. New York, 1913.

POE, Charles Hamilton. *A Southerner in Europe, Being Chiefly Some Old World Lessons for New World Needs as Set Forth in Fourteen Letters of Foreign Travel*. 3rd ed.; Raleigh, N.C., 1910.

[ROOSEVELT, Theodore.] *The Letters of Theodore Roosevelt*. Ed. Elting E. Morison. Vol. VII. Cambridge, Mass., 1954.

SCHOONMAKER, Frank. *Come with Me through Belgium and Holland*. New York, 1928.

SHETTER, William Z. *The Pillars of Society: Six Centuries of Civilization in the Netherlands*. The Hague, 1971.

SINGLETON, Esther. *A Guide to Great Cities for Young Travelers and Others: Northwestern Europe*. New York, 1910.

[SMITH, George A., et al.] *Correspondence of Palestine Tourists; comprising a Series of Letters of George A. Smith, Lorenzo Snow, Paul A. Schettler, and Eliza R. Snow, of Utah. Most Written while Traveling in Europe, Asia, and Africa. In the years 1872 and 1873*. Salt Lake City, 1875.

SMITH, H. Lyle [pseud. A. Piller, Doctor]. *Mary and I Go to Europe. An Unbiased Account (E. & O.E.) of a Little Journey in the World during the Months of June, July and August, 1896*. Hudson, N.Y., 1898.

SMITH, F[rancis] Hopkinson. *Well-Worn Roads of Spain, Holland, and Italy: Traveled by a Painter in Search of the Picturesque*. Boston and New York, 1887.

STAVER, Mary Wiley. *Fifty Years After: A School Girl Abroad Fifty Years Ago.* Bethlehem, Pa., 1899.

STEVENSON, Burton E. *The Spell of Holland: The Story of a Pilgrimage to the Land of Dykes and Windmills.* Boston, 1911.

TERHUNE, William L. *My Friend, the Captain: or, Two Yankees in Europe. A Descriptive Story of a Tour of Europe.* New York, 1898.

THWING, Edward P. *Outdoor Life in Europe, or Sketches of Seven Summers Abroad.* New York, 1888.

TOPLIFF, Samuel. *Topliff's Travels: Letters from Abroad in the Years 1828 and 1829.* Ed. Ethel Stanwood Bolton. Boston, 1906.

TOUSEY, Sinclair. *Papers from over the Water: A Series of Letters from Europe.* New York, 1869.

[UNITED States Army] Headquarters, Army Service Forces, *Civil Affairs Handbook, The Netherlands. Section 1, Geographical and Social Background.* 5 April 1944. Army Service Forces Manual, M-357-1.

[UTRECHT, University of.] *Jaarboek der Rijksuniversiteit te Utrecht, 1908–1909.* Utrecht, 1909.

WALLER, Mary E. *Through the Gates of the Netherlands.* Boston, 1914.

WARING, George E., Jr. *A Farmer's Vacation. Reprinted (with Additions) from Scribner's Monthly.* Boston, 1876.

[Watson, Elkanah.] *Men and Times of the Revolution; or, Memoirs of Elkanah Watson, including Journals of Travels in Europe and America, from 1777 to 1831, with His Correspondence with Public Men and Reminiscences and Incidents of the Revolution.* Ed. Winslow C. Watson. New York, 1856.

———, *A Tour in Holland in MDCCLXXXIV.* By an American. Worcester, Mass., 1790.

[WOODS, Matthew.] *Rambles of a Physician: or, a Midsummer Dream.* 2 vols.; Philadelphia, 1889.

Dutch Travelers in the United States

A Tale of Energy and Ambivalence

· ҼᵴҲᵴⱺ ·

J. W. SCHULTE NORDHOLT

T HE title of this paper indicates, more accurately than I had initially expected, what it really is about. It is about travelers that we are talking, not about tourists. Let me try to define the difference between the two. The purpose of the tourist is to escape from reality, to find peace in some dreamlike landscape, some Shangri-La. The traveler, on the other hand, is on a voyage of discovery; it is not a dream he is looking for, but a new reality. The tourist wants to comprehend his world, encompass it, store it somewhere, preferably in his camera. The traveler is overwhelmed; he sees only a part, his quest never ends. The tourist wants to recognize, the traveler to discover. The tourist sails on a lake, the traveler on the ocean. The tourist looks for the past, the traveler for the future.

Forgive me for starting with such bold generalizations. The tentative conclusion that I want to draw from them, with excuses to my dear friend Professor Herbert Rowen, is that American travelers in Holland were mostly tourists, but that Dutch tourists in the United States were travelers. In America there was something to be discovered. It was a country with an aureole of mystery, a mythological margin. A country without limits and without history, a gigantic shape in time and space. It had something unreal, and it was at the same time of current interest. It might be far away beyond the horizon, yet it was, in the belief of most visitors, the land of the future. What happened in America was bound to happen later on in Europe, in Holland.

That is why travelers were more involved in America than in any

(TOP) A Pioneer Cabin

(BOTTOM) The St. Nicholas Hotel in New York—
from W. T. Gevers Deynoot, *Aanteekeningen op eene reis door
de Vereenigde Staten van Noord Amerika en Canada*
(*Notes made on a journey through the United States
of North America and Canada*)
(*The Hague, 1860*)

other country. But it also meant that they had a certain awkwardness toward it. For the judgment about a country so limitless fell always short of reality, certainly when made by people coming from a small, well-organized, and conveniently arranged country like Holland.

The realization of that shortcoming was often present. Several travelers confessed it. One of the most perceptive, the Amsterdam editor Charles Boissevain, wrote in 1882: "From a trim, neat and tidy, immaculately clean, well-polished little country . . . where everything dovetails into everything, like pieces of a jigsaw puzzle . . . we find ourselves transported to a country where people think in terms of miles rather than inches." A professor of theology, H. Bouwman, warned: "It is so easy to be superficial, biased or unfair when you have to pass judgment on a country so vast as America. The United States is not a country like Western European countries, but a continent almost as big as Europe." America, adds a modern observer, is the name of a country, or better of fifty countries, together the United States of America . . . America is an immoderately huge chunk of land."[1]

But this feeling of impotence toward the colossus of the New World never prevented the visitors from writing a book about their experiences and passing many judgments. In the nineteenth and till far into the twentieth century there was hardly a Dutch visitor to the United States who did not, when he returned, publish a travel book on the true America, and to that happy arrogance we owe great gratitude. For it enables us to understand a bit more of what our ancestors felt toward the United States.

There were, of course, several approaches possible. Besides the travelers there were the diplomats who sent their reports to The Hague. They would be worth studying, but their interests in America were in general much more limited to their diplomatic business and to the narrow world of the capital in which they lived.[2] There were also the many, many immigrants, whose letters home are of the greatest interest, but whose concern for America was very different from that of the travelers, since they were more involved and had less distance from what they saw.[3] Here, in this paper, I must limit myself to the travelers. There were many of them and they have never been studied. While there are many good books on French and British visitors, nothing has as yet been done on the Dutch, who, after all, wrote in their own peculiar language.[4]

It is true that the Dutch came a bit late. There are very few Dutch travelers before the Civil War, and among these few there are only two of real significance, one at the very beginning, who was probably the most perceptive of all, Gijsbert Karel van Hogendorp, whom I am inclined to call the Dutch Tocqueville.[5] And one at the very end of this period, the interesting Willem Theodoor Gevers Deynoot, who came to America in 1859 and saw slavery still in action.[6] But the great stream started only after 1865, when the Netherlands experienced a kind of economic renaissance and became interested in the rest of the world again. Many now came, from all fields of life, among them some of the best and most important men and women of Holland. There were authors and journalists like Charles Boissevain, C. J. Wynaendts Francken, and R. P. J. Tutein Nolthenius, statesmen like Abraham Kuyper, theologians like Martinus Cohen Stuart, Petrus Hermannus Hugenholtz, and Hendrik Bouwman, artists like George Hendrik Breitner and Willem Witsen, poets like Albert Verwey and Frederik van Eeden, a great architect like Hendrik Pieter Berlage, a great feminist like Aletta Jacobs, and a great historian like Johan Huizinga.

They really deserve a book. In this essay I can hardly give them what they are entitled to. I have to limit myself, in two ways. First of all, in terms of time. The best travel books were written in the late nineteenth and the early twentieth century, when people evidently still had the time to write well and to read well. That coincidentally is also the period when America, to use a common expression, was coming of age, when it broke through its isolation and became a world power, of interest to the Europeans. So I have decided to set my boundaries there, roughly between the Civil War and World War I. In a way this period may stand as a *pars pro toto*, an exemplary part of an eternal occupation: watching America. It shows an America in full growth, already plagued by many problems which are still around, a different country, yet in essence similar to the United States of today.

I also have to limit myself in terms of materials. I shall use only the books written and published by Dutch travelers. A more complete study would require utilizing other sources, such as letters and newspaper articles, but this is an essay, not a book.

The Dutch travelers were not tourists, as I have said. But of course they did some sightseeing. There were certain tourist attractions which were not to be missed. In the late nineteenth century three of them were really obligatory: Niagara Falls, the slaughterhouses of Chicago, and the polygamous Mormons. There are some chapters on these subjects in almost every travel book. But there was more to America.

To begin with the land itself, almost all the travelers were overwhelmed by the grandeur and beauty of nature in America. Many of them wrote hymns of praise about the prairies and the mountains. But already here the ambivalance so typical of all European judgments on the New World becomes evident; that almost compulsive need to simultaneously say yes and no to the phenomenon of America. Nature might be magnificent, but the way in which the pioneers dealt with it was terrible to behold. It was used and exploited without any respect:

Niagara Falls was completely spoiled by advertising, the magnificent woods were cut down, the animals killed without any compassion. "I always speak with respect for the glorious energy, the optimistic courage, the indomitable willpower of the Americans, but I lose part of my respect for them when I see with what wanton fury and reckless barbarism they ravage and destroy what never can be restored," writes Boissevain in 1880. And Tutein Nolthenius repeats that complaint in 1900: "What a pity that the energy flowing from their industry murders nature so recklessly."[7]

These complaints were made in the years when the Americans themselves began to realize what had happened. The books of George Perkins Marsh had already been published and the first National Park founded. Yet the struggle to save nature had only begun, what the Dutch travelers saw at the end of the century was still common reality. The struggle has never ended.

The deeper question was why. What exactly was the cause of so much recklessness? The travelers were not sociologists, the explanations they gave were not theoretical arguments. Key words were used and continually repeated. There is no word that one encounters so often in the reports as the word "energy." The Dutch, careful, cautious observers, coming from a country where everything was done with much deliberation—how John Adams could complain about that Dutch quality!—were deeply impressed by the pace, the mobility, the agitation of American life. They looked at it with a mixture of praise and criticism, ambivalent as ever. Energy meant wealth and progress, but also destruction and brutality and ugliness. Nature was destroyed and with what was it replaced?

Nowhere was energy so frightfully visible as in the great cities. To arrive in New York was already an overwhelming experience. In the Dutch travel reports of around 1900, one can follow the growth of the skyscrapers almost step by step: ten stories, twenty, thirty! There seemed to be no limit to American enterprise. But New York was not the city which became to the Dutch visitors the symbol of American energy. They felt that New York was not America, as Paris is not France, nor Amsterdam, Holland. The heart of the New World was beating, as many travelers testified, in Chicago. The same city which played such a dominant role in the consciousness of the Americans themselves, the "alabaster city . . . undimmed by human tears" of 1893, made a deep impression on the visitors from Holland. "The man who has not visited Chicago has not seen America," Cohen Stuart wrote. In Chicago everything was bigger and faster and dirtier and uglier than in any other place in America. Chicago, as another observer, also a theologian, remarked, embodied the grandeur and the misery of the New World. It was marvelous and terrible. In 1926 Johan

Huizinga experienced the same ambivalance; writing one day in his diary: "Now I see that Chicago is an impossible city and a disgrace to humanity. I am almost ashamed to sit here in this good hotel." But some days later: "Even detested Chicago has its magnificent aspects and above all . . . magnificent possibilities for the future."[8]

What was so impressive, so awful about the "Queen of the West" was its undiluted, unashamed dedication to material things, its passionate materialism. It was a kind of materialism that the Dutch visitors did not recognize. They certainly were materialists themselves, but in a different way. Chicago's, America's materialism was careless, reckless even. Americans had a passion to make money, but they did not save it. "One thing I do not understand," wrote the priest van den Elsen, "is that while money has such power here, it is squandered as though it has no value at all." Making money, as another Dutchman observed, seemed to be a kind of game, a sport, a foolish passion, like collecting stamps.[9]

Money made all the difference in society. But everything was changing so fast that the Dutch visitors could not use their traditional distinctions of rank and station. And so we come to another essential question that was put by all travelers: was there more real equality in America than in Holland? Van Hogendorp had been struggling with that problem, he had seen a certain distinction between what he described as "gentlemen" and "persons in lower life," but he had also noticed that in daily intercourse there was much more equality than in Holland. And the cause of this was, he believed, to be found in the character of a country which had no historical tradition.[10]

A hundred years later, in a very different America, the same observations were still made. Of course, one must realize that at that time the Dutch still came from a society with a traditional class structure, recognizable even in dress and behavior. In America they saw how fashionable people and workingmen mixed easily on buses and trains, and did not really differ very much in accent and manners. Both were disliked. The American accent was considered very ugly, as compared with real English. Manners in America were a theme in themselves, not often omitted from the reports. Equality, as the Dutch saw it, meant vulgarity. The society was marked by a complete lack of good manners. Shouting, chewing tobacco, spitting, sitting with legs on the table, were common everywhere. "The Americans I have met till now," wrote Gevers Deynoot in 1859, "I found in general rather rude, uncouth, and not very polite in their manners." That complaint was repeated endlessly, the pioneer spirit evidently had great disadvantages.[11]

But that was only true for men. American equality had given women a much better position than was enjoyed by their sisters in the Old World. All travelers agreed on this point. Some found the American ladies "healthy, supple, well-built, less scrawny than the daughters of Albion, less corpulent than the German women," but others thought them too lean and lank, too loud-voiced.[12] But all admired the role of the American woman in society. Men might be behind, but women were ahead! In society and also at home! Of course, much depended on the point of view of the visitor. The Calvinist Kuyper praised the American housewife. The feminist Aletta Jacobs was impressed by the social status and political activities of women; she made many friends among them, like Jane Addams and Carrie Chapman Catt.[13]

Women were a minority which hardly could be called that. But other minorities were not so lucky. To begin with the most important, the poor, what was their fate in the land of equality? They certainly were a minority, living in the darkness, as Bertolt Brecht has called it, and hence not even seen by most travelers. But a few were not put off by American friends and did penetrate into the slums of the great cities. They were bewildered by the existence of so much misery in a country so prosperous. A Dutch navy officer noted in 1883: "Wealth and luxury of unbelievable proportions are to be seen here, but also poverty and misery beyond our imagination." The Reverend Cohen Stuart, who visited the slums of New York ten years earlier, was extremely upset by what he saw, but he still wanted to believe that the malady of poverty was acute, not chronic. A quarter of a century later Tutein Nolthenius observed how chronic misery still was, and he had an excellent guide, "a Dane," he wrote, "who has long since been established in New York and works as a journalist, dedicating himself to the amelioration of public housing." That must have been Jacob Riis, who knew like no other "how the other half lives."[14]

Just as chronic and miserable seemed the situation of another minority, the blacks. That was a problem which Dutch travelers did not have at home, and hence did not know how to judge. On the one hand they were inclined to moral indignation, but on the other hand they shared, especially in the late nineteenth century, all the prejudices of their age. The result was that they were easily influenced by their white American acquaintances. Such was the case with van Hogendorp, whose fascinating remarks on slavery were mostly derived from his long conversations with Thomas Jefferson. But not completely; he also developed his own vision, prophesying that one day the Negroes would be educated and then would participate in American society.[15]

In general, the opinions of the Dutch travelers on the blacks are nothing but an echo of what they had heard in America. So their judgment was rather mild and optimistic during the Reconstruction period, but in later years it developed into the racism current in the late nineteenth century. A very perceptive witness of the situation of the freedmen in the South is again Cohen Stuart. On his travels in

(TOP) A Mississippi Steamboat

(BOTTOM) A Steam Fire Engine in Cincinnati—
from W. T. Gevers Deynoot, *Aanteekeningen op eene reis door
de Vereenigde Staten van Noord Amerika en Canada*
(*Notes made on a journey through the United States
of North America and Canda*)
(*The Hague, 1860*)

1874 he made a special trip to see for himself how the blacks were involved in the operation of democracy. He was bitterly disappointed. When attending a session of the South Carolina legislature he saw the tumult and turbulence in full force. He almost refused to believe what he saw, but he had to, and later on, as he mentions in a footnote, his sad experience was confirmed when he read James Pike's *The Prostrate State*. Nonetheless, he still clung to the belief that all this misery was only the result of the oppression of centuries and not an innate deficiency of the black race.[16]

Ten, twenty years later most authors accepted such a deficiency as a matter of course and believed everything that was told them by American friends. Perhaps someday the blacks could be raised from their backwardness, but that had to be done gradually, it would take many, many years to uplift them. Total equality was a chimera. The writer Henriette S. S. Kuyper, who in 1905 followed in the steps of her father, made a trip to the United States, and wrote a book about it, tells the story of her encounter with Booker T. Washington. With her hostess she attended a meeting in New York where both Mark Twain and Booker T. Washington gave a lecture. She was very impressed by the strong personality of the founder of Tuskegee, but on the way home her white friend explained to her that such a man was, of course, a rare and exceptional case. In all blacks, she asserted, there was something of the animal, and it would take at least a hundred years to civilize them.[17]

Observations on other minorities are of the same kind. Those who visited California found the Chinese lazy and unreliable. The Indians were "a vanishing race." White American civilization placed its stamp on the visitors. A society of such energy could not allow atavisms, weaknesses, remainders of the past. It was, or at least it considered itself, a superior society. All visitors were confronted with the bragging and the chauvinism of the Americans. But the perceptive observer sometimes noticed that there was much insecurity behind the loudness, as if people were overstraining their voices. Gevers Deynoot remarked: "They mostly consider America the first country of the world, in liberty, in progress, and even in knowledge, and yet they cannot get rid of a certain feeling of respect for Europe." Others confirmed this, the "ridiculous chauvinism" was probably an expression of doubt. Yet many visitors were irritated by it: "There is here a spirit of conceit that fancies to be able to do everything, to be far above other nations, and to acknowledge no limits to the realization of the wildest fantasies," Kuyper wrote. That was, he believed, especially the case in the great cities, where American jingoism (Kuyper came in 1898!) was rampant.[18]

In connection with the loudness and gaudiness of American society, we come to another eternal question, posed by all travelers. America might be the country of progress and technical wonders, but did it have any real culture? Where was the art of America, where was that finer civilization that was so characteristic of the Old World? Van Mourik Broekman, a liberal theologian who for a few years (1910–13) worked in the library at Berkeley, showed all the typical European condescension when he wrote: "If I begin to speak of civilization and go on to speak of American civilization, I believe that those acquainted with American life will hardly be able to suppress a smile. . . . For those two words in conjunction grate on each other and give forth a jarring sound. American civilization! The greater the civilization, the less American it will be!"[19]

So much for European conceit! America might be ahead in practical matters, it was still far behind in the essentials of life. It was too energetic to reflect on real values, too much involved in material things to have higher aspirations. It had only a future, no past, and there could be no culture without tradition. Considerations like these were of course very common in nineteenth-century Europe, perhaps they still are. In the famous adage of Louis Agassíz: "Europe thinks, America acts." We cannot repeat here those fascinating but rather theoretical discussions. But we find them reflected often in the books of the travelers.

They were, in general, very much interested in culture. And culture meant for them, as for most people, first of all what was recognizable. So they admired the neo-Gothic and neo-Baroque, St. Patrick's Cathedral on Fifth Avenue and the City Hall of Philadelphia, and many other churches and buildings. But at the end of the century some of them were impressed by new developments. Richardson's Trinity Church was esteemed, but most travelers shrank back from more advanced architecture.[20] The skyscrapers were recognized as an expression of energy, not of beauty. It required a connoisseur, the great Dutch architect Hendrik Pieter Berlage, to give a proper evaluation of the work of architects like Louis Sullivan and Walter B. Griffin, both of whom he met personally, and of Frank Lloyd Wright, whom he admired greatly. Even his standards were European, the skyline of New York reminded him of the towers of San Gimignano in Tuscany. But America's architecture was good because it was rooted in everyday life and no longer determined by religious and aesthetic traditions.[21]

In other forms of art we see the same approach. Most travelers like what is traditional and recognizable, but some appreciate what is new. In literature Longfellow was considered the great giant, and also a kind of tourist attraction. Several travelers visited him in his stately house in Cambridge.[22] Yet even before 1900 some Dutchmen got a taste for Walt Whitman. The first translation of his *Leaves of Grass* appeared in 1891. Whitman expressed what to the Dutch was the most striking aspect of America: its energy. It is fascinating to see how well he was understood and esteemed by a typical European spirit such as Huizinga, who admired him as the mythical representative of the true America.[23]

One of the most curious phenomena of American society was, to the Dutch travelers, the religion that was so ubiquitous. Curious, because it was so different from what they were accustomed to in their own very religious country. Many of the Dutch visitors were clergymen who came to visit their coreligionists in Michigan, Iowa, and Wisconsin. Their books are an interesting source on American religious conditions. They contain reports on services and social activities; sometimes they copy almost complete sermons by popular preachers like Henry Ward Beecher, Thomas de Witt Talmage, Robert Collyer, and the like. It depended, of course, on the personal background of the reporter how positive or negative his judgment was. In general, there was praise for the common sense and straightforwardness of the American religious approach. Dutch travelers were amazed that the preachers did not have a special pulpit voice or language, but talked as they did in daily life. But there was much criticism of the shallowness and superficiality of religious life, the lack of dogmatic depth. Religion, as one observer had it, was not a belief but an act, not a principle but an effect. Sermons, another added, were like butterflies.[24]

Here again there is the typical ambivalance: admiration mixed with mistrust, the new balanced against the old and found wanting.

There is in every traveler to the New World something of the ambivalence so tersely expressed in a line by the Dutch poet Martinus Nijhoff about a man who sees that, in spite of what he fears, it happens as he wants. But what exactly it is that he fears and wants he does not know. That is the problem of all travel books. America is too big to comprehend, and the result is that yes and no always go together. The traveler always looks for a standard of comparison, always tries to find something recognizable. For the Dutch, who had their share in the making of America, this meant in the first place that they were on a quest for historical relationships. The chauvinists among them were rewarded. More than any other nation, Kuyper wrote, the Dutch have contributed to the American society and constitution. The American, Tutein Nolthenius asserted, resembles the Dutch more than anybody else; both nations are democratic melting pots. The Dutch, Knobel believed, are the brothers of the Americans, the British are only their cousins. The stamp of the Netherlands was deeply imprinted in the American character. That was told to Kuyper's daughter by all the friends of Holland she met in the States: William Elliot Griffis, Caroline Atwater Mason, Edward Bok, and especially Hendrik Willem van Loon.[25]

Travelers always found what they were looking for. That is a general truth about America. What Friedrich Schlegel remarked about the longing to visit Greece—namely, that everybody found there what he was looking for, especially himself—is just as true about America. As E. M. Forster wrote: America is like life itself, "you can usually find in it what you look for."[26] Dutch travelers experienced the same. The liberal politician Charles Boissevain applauded the liberal character of America (angrily excluding the tariffs); the Christian Kuyper had great praise for the Christian character of American public life.[27]

But essentially such recognition could not do justice to the complicated reality of America. The United States was neither the liberal nation of Boissevain nor Kuyper's Christian state, but a new, a different reality. And happily the Dutch travelers did not in general remain stuck with their domestic recognitions. Happily there was in them still much of the old spirit of openness and curiosity which had distinguished the discoverers of past centuries. Happily they did not degenerate into tourists.

But all the stronger was their ambivalence toward the New World. The old discussion about the advantages and disadvantages of the past, about the contrast between old and new, experience and innocence, corruption and naïveté, was eagerly carried on in the travel books. America had the future and hence it excelled in everything practical, it was full of energy and force. But because of that it lacked depth, spiritual wealth. The whole country, even the landscape, had, according to Huizinga, "something artless, without consequence, without depth, as if it had one dimension less."[28] The Americans were too mobile to mature. In short, they were children. That was the eternal epithet used by all Europeans. Its roots may go back, I would suggest, to the quasi-scientific theories of Buffon. Since the late eighteenth century it was used by most travelers, from van Hogendorp on.[29]

America was reviled and extolled, in endless ambiguity. It was the country where civilization would be completed. Several travelers repeated the famous myth, classically formulated by Bishop Berkeley, about the westward course of empire. At the same time America was the country that was never finished, a world in being.[30]

It was too big to comprehend with whatever generalization. The final metaphor on America sometimes encountered is that it was like life itself. Everybody could recognize part of it, nobody the whole. It was too vital, too overwhelming.

The Dutch, coming, as was said before, from their small, overorganized country, were perhaps in the best position to recognize that element of vitality in American society. It permeated all their writings. It still does. The interesting fact is that whatever may have changed in our relations with the New World in the past hundred years, that energy is still to us the most essential quality of the United States, for better and for worse. The excellent travel books of the past have now, alas, been replaced by hasty journalistic reports, by telegrams and television reels. But from time to time some perceptive things are still written about America, and they still contain the same bewildered *No* and the same emphatic *Yes*. The same ambivalence is expressed in a very recent interview with the author Inez van Dullemen, who has written some excellent books on her travels in the United States. Allow me to conclude with some of her remarks; they are a condensation of everything I have been trying to say on the subject. The interviewer asked her whether she still had sympathy for America, after all that had happened: Vietnam, Watergate, etc. And then it continues: "She is familiar with this question, and she answers with a kind of apology: 'I am still fond of America. . . . I still want to break a lance for America. There are always counter-movements, counter-currents there. . . . It is a jungle full of dangers, but also full of flowers, with magnificent highlights. Very foolish things can happen—but when I compare the Netherlands to it! Why, it is like a little park, trim and neat, and well cared for, more friendly, and so much more dead.' "[31]

NOTES

1 Charles Boissevain, *Van 't Noorden naar 't Zuiden, Schetsen en Indrukken van de Vereenigde Staten van Noord-Amerika* (2 vols.; Haarlem, 1881–82), II, 111–12; C. J. Wijnaendts Francken, *Door Amerika, Reisschetsen, Indrukken en Studiën* (Haarlem, 1892), pp. 69–70; H. Bouwman, *Amerika, Schetsen en Herinneringen* (Kampen, 1912), pp. 162–63; A. de Swaan, *Amerika in Termijnen. Een Ademloos Verslag uit de USA* (Amsterdam, 1967), p. 9.

2 J. W. Schulte Nordholt, "The Civil War Letters of the Dutch Ambassador," *Journal of the Illinois State Historical Society*, LIV, No. 4 (Winter 1961), 341–73.

3 There are many book on Dutch immigration. The best recent survey of the subject is by Robert P. Swierenga, "Dutch," in S. Thernstrom et al., eds., *Harvard Encyclopedia of American Ethnic Groups* (Cambridge, Mass., 1980), pp. 284–95.

4 On the French there is no general book, but an excellent introduction in the bibliography by F. Monaghan, *French Travellers in the United States 1765–1932* (New York, 1933). On the British the literature is endless; I mention only a recent book which covers the same period as this paper: Richard L. Rapson, *Britons View America, Travel Commentary, 1860–1935* (Seattle and London, 1971), with an excellent bibliography.

5 J. W. Schulte Nordholt, "Gijsbert Karel van Hogendorp in America, 1783–1784," *Acta Historiae Neerlandicae*, X (1978), 117–42.

6 W. T. Gevers Deynoot, *Aanteekeningen op eene Reis door de Vereenigde Staten van Noord Amerika en Canada* (The Hague, 1860); on the author, Lenting, *Levensbericht van Jhr. Mr. Willem Theodoor Gevers Deynoot* (Leiden, 1880).

7 Boissevain, *Schetsen*, I, 77; R. P. J. Tutein Nolthenius, *Nieuwe Wereld, Indrukken en Aanteekeningen tijdens eene Reis door de Vereenigde Staten van Noord-Amerika* (Haarlem, 1900), p. 253; Hendrik P. N. Muller, *Door het Land van Columbus een Reisverhaal* (Haarlem, 1905), p. 141.

8 M. Cohen Stuart, *Zes Maanden in Amerika* (2 vols.; Haarlem, 1875), I, 331; Bouwman, *Amerika*, pp. 74–93; Boissevain, *Schetsen*, II, 7–58; Tutein Nolthenius, *Nieuwe Wereld*, pp. 121–33; A. Oppenheim, *Vijf Weken in Amerika, Indrukken van het Land, zijn Bewoners, zijn Spoorwegen enz.* (Rotterdam, n.d.), p. 58; F. M. Knobel, *Dwars doozhet Land van Roosevelt* (Amsterdam, 1906), p. 28; Leonard Huizinga, *Herinneringen van aan mijn Vader* (The Hague, (1963), pp. 166, 171.

9 G. van den Elsen, *Twintig Brieven uit Amerika* (Helmond, n.d., 1907), p. 15; Cohen Stuart, *Zes Maanden*, I, 143; M. C. Mourik Broekman, *De Yankee in Denken en Doen, Karakterteekening van het Amerikaansche Leven* (Haarlem, 1914), pp. 1–2, R. H. Rijkens, *Licht en Schaduwbeelden uit het Amerikaansche Leven* (The Hague, 1907), pp. 264, 268; Bouwman, *Amerika*, p. 49.

10 *Brieven en Gedenkschriften van Gijsbert Karel van Hogendorp*, ed. F. and H. van Hogendorp (7 vols.; The Hague, 1866–1903), I, 284–85.

11 Gevers Deynoot, *Aanteekeningen*, pp. 65–68, 125; Mourik Broekman, *De Yankee*, pp. 22–23; J. de Brauw, *Herinneringen eener Reize naar Nieuw-York, Gedaan in de Jaren 1831 en 1832* (Leiden, 1833), p. 70; G. Verschuur, *Door Amerika, Reisherinneringen* (Amsterdam, 1877), pp. 93, 98, 102–3.

12 Muller, *Land van Columbus*, pp. 6–7; de Brauw, *Herinneringen*, p. 84.

13 Aletta Jacobs and C. V. Gerritsen, *Brieven uit en over Amerika* (Amsterdam, 1906), pp. 122–27; cf. Aletta Jacobs, *Herinneringen* (Amsterdam, 1924), 243–46 and *passim; Knobel, Land van Roosevelt*, pp. 17–19; Rijkens, *Licht*, pp. 134–36, Wijnaendts Francken, *Door Amerika*, p. 250; W. A. Kok, *Amerika Bekeken door mijne Bril. Beschreven in een paar intieme Brieven* (Rotterdam, 1882), p. 44; Tutein Nolthenius, *Nieuwe Wereld*, p. 191.

14 Kok, *Amerika*, pp. 64–65, Tutein Nolthenius, *Nieuwe Wereld*, p. 45; Mourik Broekman, *De Yankee*, pp. 8–9, 18–21.

15 *Brieven van Hogendorp*, I, 313, 333; Archief van Hogendorp, no. 54-n, in Algemeen Rijksarchief, The Hague.

16 Cohen Stuart, *Zes Maanden*, II, 288–300; cf. on Pike the revealing book by R. F. Durden, *James Shepherd Pike, Republicanism and the American Negro, 1850–1882* (Durham, N.C., 1957).

17 H. S. S. Kuyper, *Een half Jaar in Amerika* (Rotterdam, 1907), pp. 360–

63; Boissevain, *Schetsen*, I, 128–29, II, 225–66; A. Kuyper, *Varia Americana* (Amsterdam and Pretoria, 1899), pp. 9–12; Tutein Nolthenius, *Nieuwe Wereld*, pp. 55–104; Mourik Broekman, *De Yankee*, pp. 57–58; Rijkens, *Licht*, pp. 240–50, Knobel, *Lan van Roosevelt*, pp. 154–55.

18 Gevers Deynoot, *Aanteekeningen*, p. 68; Cohen Stuart, *Zes Maanden*, I, 363; A. Kuyper, *Varia Americana*, pp. 16–17; Boissevain, *Schetsen*, II, 67–76; Wijnaendts Francken, *Door Amerika*, p. 257; Rijkens, *Licht*, pp. 17–23, 30; P. H. Hugenholtz, *Licht en Schaduw, Indrukken van het Godsdienstig Leven in Amerika* (Amsterdam, 1890), pp. 33–34; Bouwman, *Amerika*, pp. 177.

19 Mourik Broekman, *De Yankee*, p. 226.

20 Cohen Stuart, *Zes Maanden*, I, 198–99; Boissevain, *Schetsen*, I, 88, 214–15; A. Kuyper, *Varia Americana*, p. 34; Muller, *Land van Columbus*, pp. 12–13; Tutein Nolthenius, *Nieuwe Wereld*, p. 357.

21 H. P. Berlage, *Amerikaansche Reisherinneringen* (Rotterdam, 1913), *passim*.

22 Cohen Stuart, *Zes Maanden*, II, 230–32; Boissevain, *Schetsen*, I, 216–32; H. S. S. Kuyper, *Een Half Jaar*, pp. 247–57. Longfellow's *Hiawatha* was translated by the great Flemish poet Guido Gezelle, whose translation far surpassed the original.

23 J. Huizinga, *Mensch en Menigte in Amerika, Vier Essays over Moderne Beschavingsgeschiedenis* (3rd ed.; Haarlem, 1928), pp. 185–87, 238–48, cf. the translation by Herbert H. Rowen, *America: A Dutch Historian's Vision, from Afar and Near* (New York, 1972), pp. 169–71, 216–25; Hugenholtz, *Licht en Schaduw*, pp. 197–98; Tutein Nolthenius, *Nieuwe Wereld*, has a motto from Whitman.

24 Boissevain, *Schetsen*, I, 259–62; Wijnaendts Francken, *Door Amerika*, pp. 238–42; Bouwman, *Amerika*, pp. 185–87; Mourik Broekman, *De Yankee*, pp. 280–325; H. S. S. Kuyper, *Een half Jaar*, pp. 184–220; Hugenholtz, *Licht en Schaduw*, pp. 32–34 and *passim*; Rijkens, *Licht*, pp. 114–20.

25 A. Kuyper, *Varia Americana*, pp. 61–62; Tutein Nolthenius, *Nieuwe Wereld*, pp. 415–16; Knobel, *Land van Roosevelt*, pp. 116–17, 125; Bouwman, *Schetsen*, pp. 108–9; H. S. S. Kuyper, *Een half Jaar*, pp. 202–9, 296–304, 335–38, 412.

26 Peter Conrad, *Imagining America* (London, 1980), pp. 4–5.

27 Boissevain, *Schetsen*, II, 67–76; A. Kuyper, *Varia Americana*, p. 22.

28 Leonard Huizinga, *Herinneringen*, p. 134.

29 *Brieven van Hogendorp*, I, 298–99, 287; H. S. S. Kuyper, *Een Half Jaar*, pp. 21, 186; Mourik Broekman, *De Yankee*, pp. 172, 259–63.

30 A. Kuyper, *De Gemeene Gratie* (3 vols.; Amsterdam and Pretoria, 1902–4), II, 664–67; A. Kuyper, *Het Calvinisme, Zes Stone-Lezingen te Princeton* (Amsterdam, n.d.), pp. 25–27; H. S. S. Kuyper, *Een Half Jaar*, pp. 441–42; Berlage, *Reisherinneringen*, p. 48.

31 Agnes Koertz, "Waakzaamheid is de Beste Levenshouding, Inez van Dullemen over haar Ontwikkeling als Schrijfster," *Opzij, Feministisch Maandblad*, December, 1981, pp. 52–54.

Contributors

ERNST HANS VAN DER BEUGEL, born in 1918 in Amsterdam, has a master's degree in economics from Amsterdam University. He served, successively, as secretary to the Dutch cabinet, head of the office of the Marshall Plan and of the OEEC, and director general of economic and military affairs. He was also state secretary for foreign affairs and roving ambassador of the Netherlands government. From 1959 to 1963 he was executive vice-president and president of KLM. In 1965 he received his Ph.D., cum laude, from Leiden University, where he is presently professor of international relations. Professor van der Beugel is also chairman of the International Institute for Stategic Studies in London.

OWEN DUDLEY EDWARDS was educated at Belvedere College and at University College in Dublin. He was a graduate student in history at Johns Hopkins University (1959–1963) while serving as an American correspondent for the *Irish Times*. He has taught in the United States at the University of Oregon, California State University, and the University of South Carolina. He has also taught at the University of Aberdeen and the University of Edinburgh. He is the author of *Burke and Hare, P. G. Wodehouse,* and *The Mind of an Activist: James Connolly,* and co-author of *Celtic Nationalism.*

FRANK FREIDEL is Bullitt Professor of American History at the University of Washington and Charles Warren Professor of American History, emeritus, at Harvard University. He was Harmsworth Professor at Oxford University from 1955 to 1956 and has taught at a number of other institutions. He has twice lectured at the Salzburg Seminar. He is a past president of the Organization of American Historians and is a fellow of the American Academy of Arts and Sciences. He is the author of a number of books, including *Our Country's Presidents* and *America in the Twentieth Century,* and is editor of the *Harvard Guide to American History*. His major work is a multi-volume biography of Franklin D. Roosevelt.

JAMES H. HUTSON received his Ph.D. in history from Yale University in 1964. He is currently executive secretary, Council of Scholars, the Library of Congress. He is the author of *Pennsylvania Politics, 1745–*

1770 (Princeton, 1972) and *John Adams and the Diplomacy of the American Revolution* (Lexington, 1980), which was awarded the Gilbert Chinard Prize for 1981 by the Society for French Historical Studies. His most recent work is *Creativity: A Continuing Inventory of Knowledge* (Washington, D.C., 1981). Dr. Hutson also directs the Historical Publications Office in the Manuscript Division at the Library of Congress.

MICHAEL KAMMEN is Professor of American History and Culture at Cornell University. He received his Ph.D. in history from Harvard University, and is a member of the American Academy of Arts and Sciences, the board of directors of the Social Science Research Council, and the board of trustees of the New York State Historical Association. He is the author of *People of Paradox: An Inquiry Concerning the Origins of American Civilization* (winner of a Pulitzer Prize in 1973), *Colonial New York—A History* (1975), and *A Season of Youth: The American Revolution and the Historical Imagination* (1978), and editor of *The Past Before Us: Contemporary Historical Writing in the United States* (1980).

LAWRENCE S. KAPLAN, who received a Ph.D. from Yale University in 1951, is University Professor of History at Kent State University. He has also served as Fulbright Lecturer at the Universities of Bonn, Louvain, and Nice, as Visiting Research Scholar and Lecturer at the University of London, and as Visiting Professor at the European University Institute at Florence. He is the author of *Jefferson and France* (New Haven, 1967) and *The American Revolution and a "Candid World"* (Kent, Ohio, 1977); editor of *Colonies into Nation: American Diplomacy, 1763–1800* (New York, 1972); and co-author of *Culture and Diplomacy: The American Experience* (New York, 1977).

ROBERT R. PALMER is emeritus professor of history at Yale University. Born in Chicago, he studied at the University of Chicago and at Cornell University. He served on the faculty at Princeton University and has been adjunct professor at the University of Michigan. His main interest has been the French Revolution, and his most important work is *The Age of the Democratic Revolution: A Political History of Europe and America, 1760–1800,* in two volumes (Princeton, 1959, 1964).

JAMES C. RILEY, an associate professor at Indiana University, is the author of *International Government Finance and the Amsterdam Market, 1740–1815* (1980); "The Dutch Economy after 1650: Decline or Growth?" in the *Journal of European Economic History;* and *The Medicine of the Environment in Europe and North America, 1660–*

1800. Professor Riley is working on a study of the money supply in eighteenth-century Europe.

HERBERT H. ROWEN received his doctorate from Columbia University in 1951. He has taught at Brandeis University, the University of Iowa, Elmira College, the University of California, and the University of Wisconsin; at present he is professor of history at Rutgers University. He is a foreign member of the Royal Netherlands Academy of Sciences, Division of Letters. His books include *The Ambassador Prepares for War: The Dutch Embassy of Arnauld de Pomponne (1669–1671)* (1957), *John de Witt: Grand Pensionary of Holland, 1625–1672* (1978), and *The King's State: Proprietary Dynasticism in Early Modern France* (1980). He has translated into English works of John Huizinga, Jan Willem Schulte Nordholt, and Jacques Godechot.

JAN WILLEM SCHULTE NORDHOLT, born 1920 in Zwolle, received his Ph.D. in history from the University of Amsterdam in 1951. Since 1963 he has occupied a chair for American history and culture at Leiden University. He has been a guest professor at Brooklyn College and at the University of Michigan and has published many books on American history in his mother tongue. His special interest in recent years has been the historical relation between the Netherlands and the United States. An English translation of his latest book is being published by the University of North Carolina Press under the title *The Dutch Republic and American Independence.*

ALFRED VAN STADEN, born 1942, studied political science at the University of Amsterdam and wrote his doctorate thesis on the role of the Netherlands in NATO. He is currently professor of international relations at Leiden University. His main areas of interest are Dutch foreign policy, the making of foreign policy in general, and strategic problems and arms control. He is co-author of several books dealing with domestic sources of foreign policy and has written on a variety of international topics. Professor van Staden is a member of the Netherlands Foreign Ministry Advisory Committee on Problems of Disarmament and International Security and Peace. He teaches international relations at the Dutch War College in The Hague.

ROBERT P. SWIERENGA, Ph.D., is professor of history at Kent State University and managing editor of *Social Science History*. A specialist in Dutch emigration and settlement in North America, he was awarded the Fulbright–Hays Silver Opportunity Research Scholarship in the Netherlands and was made a Fellow of the American Council of Learned Societies. He is the author of more than fifty articles and of the following books: *Pioneer and Profits: Land Speculation on the Iowa Frontier* (1968), *Acres for Cents: Delinquent Tax Auctions in Frontier Iowa* (1976), *Quantification in American History: Theory and Research* (1970), and *Beyond the Civil War Synthesis: Political Essays of the Civil War Era* (1975). He is presently preparing a book on Dutch immigration to the United States in the nineteenth century.

JAMES TANIS is Director of Libraries and Rufus Johnson Professor of Religion at Bryn Mawr College. He received a doctor's degree in theology from the University of Utrecht, the Netherlands. His field of specialization is the interplay of Dutch and American ideas in the seventeenth and eighteenth centuries. He is the author of *Dutch Calvinistic Pietism in the Middle Colonies* (The Hague, 1967) and of a number of articles that have appeared in scholarly journals.

HENRI and BARBARA VAN DER ZEE are journalist-writers who live in London. He was born in the Netherlands and in 1955 joined *De Telegraaf*. In 1967 he became its correspondent in London, where he met his future wife, Barbara Griggs, a Fleet Street fashion writer. In partnership, Henri and Barbara van der Zee have written two historical works: *William and Mary,* a biography of the Dutch Stadtholder-King and his English wife; and *A Sweet and Alien Land,* the story of Dutch New York. Both books were published in Britain, the United States, and the Netherlands. Barbara's history of herbal medicine, *Green Pharmacy,* has been published in Britain and the United States, and Henri's documentary study of occupied Holland in the last months of World War II, *The Hunger Winter,* has been published in Britain and the Netherlands.

Index